VIOLENCE RISK
ASSESSMENT AND MANAGEMENT

VIOLENCE RISK
ASSESSMENT AND MANAGEMENT

Christopher D. Webster
Simon Fraser University
University of Toronto, Canada

Stephen J. Hucker
University of Toronto, Canada

John Wiley & Sons, Ltd

Other Wiley Editorial Offices

John Wiley & Sons Inc., 111 River Street, Hoboken, NJ 07030, USA

Jossey-Bass, 989 Market Street, San Francisco, CA 94103-1741, USA

Wiley-VCH Verlag GmbH, Boschstr. 12, D-69469 Weinheim, Germany

John Wiley & Sons Australia Ltd, 42 McDougall Street, Milton, Queensland 4064, Australia

John Wiley & Sons (Asia) Pte Ltd, 2 Clementi Loop #02-01, Jin Xing Distripark, Singapore 129809

John Wiley & Sons Canada Ltd, 6045 Freemont Blvd, Mississauga, ONT, L5R 4J3, Canada

Wiley also publishes its books in a variety of electronic formats. Some content that appears in print may not be
available in electronic books.

Library of Congress Cataloging-in-Publication Data

Webster, Christopher D., 1936–
    Violence risk : assessment and management / Christopher D. Webster,
Stephen J. Hucker.
        p. cm.
    Includes bibliographical references and index.
    ISBN-13: 978-0-470-02749-3 (hbk : alk. paper)
    ISBN-13: 978-0-470-02750-9 (pbk. : alk. paper)
    1. Dangerously mentally ill. 2. Violence. 3. Risk assessment.
I. Hucker, Stephen J. II. Title.
    [DNLM: 1. Violence–psychology. 2. Risk Assessment–methods.
3. Social Behavior Disorders. 4. Forensic Psychiatry–methods.
5. Mentally Ill Persons–psychology. WM 600 W378v 2007]
    RC569.5.V55V5644 2007
    616.85′82–dc22

                                        2006032499

British Library Cataloguing in Publication Data

A catalogue record for this book is available from the British Library

ISBN-13 978-0-470-02749-3 (hbk) 978-0-470-02750-9 (pbk)

Typeset in 10/12pt Times and Helvetica by Thomson Digital
Printed and bound in Great Britain by TJ International. Padstow, Cornwall
This book is printed on acid-free paper responsibly manufactured from sustainable forestry
in which at least two trees are planted for each one used for paper production.

Portly fellow
Light on his feet
A man of the theatre
Educated and dramatic
Cultivated and debonair
Something of an aristocrat
Ironic and mischievous
Commanding presence

A presence Fred uses
In the team he leads
Kindly and thoughtfully
With restrained compassion
When it comes to talking
To benighted people
Entangled with the law
Ferreting out what happened
In some desperate alley
Crowded in against the gang

It will call for a diagnosis
That's what courts look for
In deciding what must be done
But could the Bard also assist?
Or Marlowe or Dostoyevsky?
Sometimes it takes more
Than a police report
To get to the nub of it.

Dr. F.A.S. Jenson
(1924–1994)
Former Clinical Director, Metropolitan Toronto
Forensic Services (METFORS),
Clarke Institute of Psychiatry

CONTENTS

ABOUT THE AUTHORS

Christopher Webster received his Ph.D. in Experimental Psychology from Dalhousie University in 1967. After a few years as a Research Scientist at the then Addiction Research Foundation in Toronto, he moved to the Clarke Institute of Psychiatry and coordinated research and clinical programs for children with severe developmental and conduct problems. In 1975 he was appointed Professor and Director of the School of Child and Youth Care at the University of Victoria. Returning to Toronto after a few years, he was again appointed a Research Scientist at the Clarke Institute and also Professor of Psychiatry, Psychology, and Criminology. It was during this period that he developed an interest in forensic mental health, with emphasis on violence risk assessment and treatment. In 1993, he was appointed Professor and Chair of the Department of Psychology, Simon Fraser University in Burnaby, British Columbia. There he continued to develop his interests in structured professional judgment (SPJ) approaches to risk assessment in collaboration with Kevin Douglas, Stephen Hart, Derek Eaves, Randy Kropp, Deborah Ross, Henrik Belfrage, Rudiger Müller-Isberner, Jim Ogloff, and many others. Returning to Toronto in 1997, he has continued to work with his colleagues in British Columbia, but formed new alliances with Mary-Lou Martin at St. Joseph's Healthcare in Hamilton, Ontario, and Johann Brink and Tonia Nicholls of the Forensic Psychiatric Services Commission of British Columbia. Work on SPJ projects in Toronto over recent years owes much to Leena Augimeri, Chris Koegl, and Hy Bloom. He is a Fellow of the Canadian Psychological Association, the American Psychological Association, and the Royal Society of Canada. At Simon Fraser University he is Professor Emeritus of Psychology, and at the University of Toronto, he is Professor Emeritus of Psychiatry.

Stephen Hucker obtained his medical and psychiatric qualifications in the United Kingdom before completing his forensic psychiatric training at the Clarke Institute of Psychiatry in Toronto. He was Head of the Forensic Programme there from 1982 until 1993 and then spent five years as Professor of Psychiatry, Psychology and Law at Queen's University in Kingston, Ontario. From 1998 until 2005 he was Professor of Psychiatry at McMaster University and Head of Forensic Services at St. Joseph's Healthcare in Hamilton, Ontario.

Over the years Dr. Hucker has conducted research on a number of forensic psychiatric topics, has lectured widely to scientific and professional audiences across North America as well as in Great Britain and Australia and has conducted many administrative reviews of forensic and correctional facilities. He also maintains a busy forensic psychiatric practice and is frequently called upon to provide an opinion to defense lawyers and prosecutors, community agencies and parole boards, and often testifies as an expert witness. In all these circumstances he has gained extensive practical experience in risk assessment and management.

Dr. Hucker has been Professor of Psychiatry at the University of Toronto since 1998 and he resumed his affiliation with the Centre of Addiction and Mental Health in the Law and Mental Health Programme in 2005.

LIST OF CONTRIBUTORS

R. Karl Hanson completed his Ph.D. in clinical psychology from the University of Waterloo (Ontario) in 1986, after which he conducted clinical work with sexual and violent offenders for the Ontario Ministry of Correctional Services and the Clarke Institute of Psychiatry (now Centre for Addiction and Mental Health). Since 1991, he has been a senior research officer with Public Safety and Emergency Preparedness Canada (Ottawa), and adjunct research professor in the psychology department of Carleton University. Most of his research focuses on the assessment and treatment of sexual offenders. Recent projects involve the identification of dynamic risk factors, the empirical evaluation of treatment effectiveness, and methods for improving the community supervision of sexual offenders. He is the principal developer of Static-99, the most widely used risk assessment tool for sexual offenders. Professional distinctions include being a Fellow of the Canadian Psychological Association and the 2002 recipient of the Significant Achievement Award from the Association for the Treatment of Sexual Offenders.

P. Randall Kropp is a clinical and forensic psychologist specializing in the assessment and management of violent offenders. He works for the Forensic Psychiatric Services Commission of British Columbia, Canada, is a research consultant with the British Columbia Institute against Family Violence, and is adjunct professor of psychology at Simon Fraser University. He has conducted numerous workshops for mental health professionals, police officers, and corrections staff in North America, Australia, Asia, Africa, and Europe. This training has focused on risk for violence, psycholegal assessments, and criminal harassment (stalking). He has frequently consulted with provincial, state, and federal government ministries on matters related to violence against women and children, and the assessment and treatment of violent offenders. He has published numerous journal articles, book chapters, and research reports, and he is co-author to several works on risk assessment including the *Manual for the Spousal Assault Risk Assessment Guide*, *Manual for the Sexual Violence Risk – 20*, and the *Risk for Sexual Violence Protocol*.

Mary-Lou Martin is a clinical nurse specialist at St. Joseph's Healthcare Hamilton and is an associate clinical professor at the School of Nursing, McMaster University.

She received a Masters of Science in Nursing and Masters of Education from the University of Toronto. Mary-Lou is a practitioner, consultant, educator, researcher, and leader in the area of mental health/mental illness. Her clinical work includes risk assessment and management with forensic and psychiatric patients. Mary-Lou's past research has focused on aggression, therapeutic relationships, the transitional discharge model, smoking in individuals with schizophrenia, the Sexual Knowledge Interview Scale (SKIS), sexuality health teaching, and primary nursing. A recent project with colleagues included the development of the Short-Term Assessment of Risk and Treatability (START), a structured clinical guide for the assessment of violence to self and others that measures seven risks (risk to others, self-harm, suicide, unauthorized leave, substance use, self-neglect, being victimized). Her current research projects include police mobile crisis services, depression in women with sexual abuse histories, knowledge transfer in practice, and the effects of Tai Chi on individuals with serious and persistent mental illness.

Chapter 11 was written with contributions from Patricia Stefanowska of McMaster University, Ontario, Canada and Randy Starr, a citizen of the United States of America.

FOREWORD

In *Violence Risk: Assessment and Management,* Christopher Webster, Stephen Hucker, and their colleagues provide mental health and correctional professionals with a succinct, to-the-point synopsis of a vast and often disjointed field. Forecasting whether violence is likely to occur, and deciding which actions to take to thwart its occurrence, have always been daunting tasks. Webster and Hucker logically organize and cogently articulate what is known about how best to perform them. Correctly noting that the pessimism about risk assessment and risk management, so prevalent only a generation ago, has largely lifted, they offer clear-headed and clinically relevant advice – enriched by vivid case studies – that will quickly bring the frontline professional up to speed on the agreed-upon, as well as on the contested, premises that guide professional practice in confronting violence risk.

Since Webster and Hucker distill so well the state of the art of violence risk assessment and management, and explain so clearly how the field got to where it is at this stage in its development, let me offer a word on where the field may be going. I predict that when the next edition of this book is written, the authors will have before them considerably more research bearing on four topics.

The first development in violence risk assessment that I anticipate is the running of 'horse races' among the various statistical or quasi-statistical risk assessment tools described in the current edition of this book. One tool will be compared with another tool in its ability to accurately predict violence in a given mental health or correctional population. The field will benefit greatly from this study of the comparative validity of competing risk assessment devices. Which instruments are best at predicting which kinds of violence among which kinds of patients or prisoners is a crucial question, and efforts are already underway to answer it.

Second, I foresee a great deal of 'drilling down' regarding the workings of specific risk factors. Take, for example, major mental illness as a risk factor for violence, variations of which appear on several structured risk assessment instruments. What the practitioner needs to know is: What *specific* symptoms in which *particular* diagnoses indicate an increased risk of violence? A major step in answering this question was taken by Jeffrey Swanson and his colleagues (2006) in the Clinical Antipsychotic Trials of Intervention Effectiveness (CATIE) study among patients diagnosed with schizophrenia at over 50 sites in the United States. They found that 'positive' psychotic symptoms, such as persecutory ideation, increased the risk of serious violence, while 'negative' psychotic symptoms, such as social withdrawal, lowered the risk of serious violence. It was the combination of high positive symptoms and low negative symptoms that was most associated with increased violence.

Third, studies of DNA and gene–environment interactions are transforming many areas of science, and I expect that violence risk will be no exception. Consider the landmark research by Avshalom Caspi and his colleagues (2002). They studied a large sample of children in New Zealand from birth to adulthood to determine why some children who are maltreated grow up to develop antisocial behavior, whereas others do not. The enzyme called monoamine oxidase A (MAOA) was found to dramatically moderate the effect of maltreatment. Maltreated children with a genotype conferring low levels of MAOA expression were much more likely than maltreated children with high levels of MAOA to become antisocial as adults.

Finally, and related to the study of biological aspects of violence just mentioned, I believe that the future will see the rise of a number of medications to treat the substance abuse that so frequently accompanies all forms of crime and violence. For example, the opiate agonist named Naltrexone has been shown to be effective among volunteers in the treatment of heroin addiction and alcoholism. Ongoing research is seeking to determine whether Naltrexone is similarly effective in treating addiction among parolees and probationers. The recent approval of a 30-day injectable 'sustained-release' formulation of the drug might go far in reducing non-adherence, a problem that has seriously hampered the use of this and other potentially violence-reducing medications (O'Brien and Cornish, in press).

These are only speculations about the directions in which the field will move. For the foreseeable future – until its next edition – *Violence Risk: Assessment and Management* will serve handsomely as a guide to evidence-based clinical practice in dealing with individuals who would harm others.

John Monahan
John S. Shannon Distinguished
Professor of Law, University of Virginia

REFERENCES

Caspi, A., et al. (2002). Evidence that the cycle of violence in maltreated children depends on genotype. *Science*, 297, 851–854.

O'Brien, C., & Cornish, J. (in press). Naltrexone for probationers and parolees. *Journal of Substance Abuse Treatment.*

Swanson, J., et al. (2006). A national study of violent behavior in persons with schizophrenia. *Archives of General Psychiatry, 63,* 490–499.

PREFACE

This book deals mainly with decision making in cases where future violence is a possible issue. The emphasis is on how best to conduct violence assessments on behalf of individuals from civil psychiatric hospitals, forensic mental health services, and the criminal justice systems. Little is said about how police officers assess risk for violence in the heat of the moment or how correctional and psychiatric nursing staff deal with immediate crises. Instead, the text focuses on the very difficult question of how best to protect society while avoiding the undue restriction of individuals. The first chapter outlines the operation of Canadian provincial Mental Health Acts (MHAs), Part XX.1 of the *Criminal Code* of Canada (Mental Disorder), and the Correctional and Condition Release Act (CCRA). Although written around these particular acts, it needs to be realized that similar statutes are in place in the United States and many European and Scandinavian countries. Indeed, much Canadian legislation in this area was originally imported from England, and our neighbors to the south.

The aim of the book is to draw together some fairly well-agreed principles that can, and perhaps should, be used in decision making around violence risk. Although these principles may seem reasonable at this time, it needs to be recognized that the risk assessment literature is building very rapidly. The pessimism of 30 years ago has largely dissipated (see Ennis & Litwack, 1974, for example) and been replaced by an idea that, of necessity, mental health workers have to make day-to-day risk decisions and also advise courts and review boards as, with guidance from the law, and with a practical eye as to what resources may or may not be available to the individual, they struggle to help people to make safe adjustments to institutional or community living.

The text aims to provide a readable account of the scientific and professional literature which deals with 'dangerousness,' or, in more modern terms, 'risk assessment' and 'risk management.'[1] We have largely avoided the use of statistics and we have eschewed complicated legal considerations. Although originally intended for mental health and correctional professionals in the several disciplines, the authors hope that it will in fact be of interest to lawyers, bureaucrats, policy makers, police officials, and administrators. Indeed, given the coverage allotted daily in the newspapers to the subject of violence risk assessment and management, the topic, in theory anyway, ought to appeal to a wide readership. Rare is the person who, when pressed, does not have some idea about what ought to be done to or for spousal assaulters, sex offenders, those who exhibit 'road rage,' psychopathic killers, mental patients who assault neighbors while apparently under the influence of delusions, drunk drivers, 'hockey dads,' and the many other types of individuals who seem impelled to act from time to time in ways that are threatening or worrying to family members, relatives, or society at large. When young children use powerful firearms to shoot people to death in the playground, it is not only a select group of professionals who ask: What were the precursors to the tragedy?; Who ought to have noticed that something peculiar was occurring in the children's lives?; To what extent, can such horrific events be forecast?; What kinds of policies need to be instituted in violence-prone places like workplaces and schools?; and How can physical environments be designed to encourage safety and discourage risk of violence? Surviving victims of 'senseless' assaults also ask these kinds of questions over and over. When death and serious physical or psychological injury occur to family members, those remaining find it extremely difficult to find answers that provide anything close to relief.

There is then a very human side to the story unfolded in this book. The 'narrative descriptions,' compressed personal accounts (supplied by the first author and included to mark the start of the various chapters), are meant to anchor the book in terms of clinical and everyday realities. They are also there to remind the reader, if such a prompt is needed, that those who write clinical accounts have personal views of their own. Good clinicians know this and construct their reports and testimony in suitably fair, qualified, and professional ways. But the 'unedited' narratives, as offered here, were written on the basis of actual experience with patients and parolees. They have not been modified into 'respectability,' aside from changing names and some circumstances. Some readers will like these 'raw' phenomenological accounts, others will pass them over.

At a more substantive level the book tries to deal with the emerging realization, one that should perhaps have been obvious from the start, that violence risk in the individual case depends crucially on the way a variable number of factors are in play and interacting at any given time. Moreover, these individual patterns, almost chaotic (Marks-Tarlow, 1993), are themselves being influenced by external circumstances which are difficult to see in the present and predict in the future. This means that, to yield statistically significant effects summarized across large numbers of people, particular factors seen in isolation or even in limited combinations, have to be very powerful to 'show through.' By these statistical exercises it has been 'discovered' in the past quarter century that, as novelists have long told us, prior violence foretells future violence, that severe conduct problems in childhood influence later criminality, and that people who lack conscience are more apt to be violent than those who do not. The difficulty is that these 'capturable,' 'state of the art' results, when purveyed to clinicians and decision makers as the sole available verified scientific information, can limit not broaden the scope of inquiry when applied to the individual case. Researchers have sometimes failed to realize that their studies rest on what they are presently able to measure, that a good deal of hard-to-index information necessarily remains crucial in the forming of opinions about persons under assessment.

A word is needed about the style in which this book is written. Although we have been at pains to include notes in the various chapters for the benefit of some readers, the text is not intended as a full scholarly work. Without going into unnecessary and perhaps exasperating detail, it discusses the kinds of research which has so far been conducted on the topic of interest. It is anchored in everyday life in mental hospitals, forensic units, prisons, and the community. The sub-text of this book could have been expressed something like: 'Creating and refining knowledge in the course of routine professional mental health and correctional work.' Almost as much as the actual topic of risk assessment and management is the question of: How can interdisciplinary research be conducted in such a way that all colleagues in their various professions contribute to the task of inspiring and creating ideal clinical and research practices? The authors knew in advance that this might seem a little ambitious but decided nonetheless to stick with the format in the hope that it might make a slightly more interesting read than might otherwise have been the case.

NOTE

1   We have recently re-published in the form of an edited book many of the original articles which influenced the development of this test (see Bloom & Webster, 2007).

ACKNOWLEDGEMENTS

A previous version of this text was published in 2003 by St. Joseph's Healthcare in Hamilton, Ontario, Canada. In that version we thanked a number of persons for the advice and help they gave. We remain grateful to St. Joseph's, to the National Parole Board of Canada, and to many individual clinicians, researchers, and policy makers.

The original manuscript was entered and formatted by Suzy Konick and Bruce Konick. They undertook the many revisions and, throughout, contributed ideas, suggested substantive changes, made publishing arrangements, and generally kept the project on track. They also entered and shaped the present text.

We are grateful to colleagues at John Wiley & Sons who took up the idea of publishing the text and brought it to fruition in a helpful and timely way. Gillian Leslie deserves particular thanks as do Claire Ruston, Ruth Graham, Nicole Burnett and Tessa Hanford.

W.W. Norton and Company graciously gave permission to cite from *The Perfect Storm* by Sebastian Junger (see page 77). Penguin allowed a quotation from Sir Arthur Conan Doyle's *The Sign of the Four* (see page 15).

The authors thank their wives, Dianne Macfarlane and Gayle Stoness, for their sustained interest in the project and for help in seeing it to completion.

1

LAWS

ROBERT

This is a really tough one
Which keeps me awake at nights
Has this odd compulsion   to touch and run
Which is great unless   you've been groped or worse
Loads of intelligence   here, quite a smart kid
And his family though   constricting tries
Even got a girlfriend whose   smart and presentable
Doubtful if being sent to prison did any good
Even though the reports said he benefited
From sex offender   treatment
Week by week his thinking   gets more odd
And I fear for the girl in the   household
So we admit him to a hospital   where
Contrary to our understanding   he's certified
On account of violence which   is really fear
My stock is dead low with him   and the family
But it's academic anyway be-   cause his parole expired
I now wait for the inevitable   about which I may never learn[1]

'The Law' said that great jurist Jennings, 'walks a respectful distance behind science'.

(Haward, 1981, p. 16)[2]

Perhaps the most important aspect of all violence decision making relates to the pertinent law, be it national, provincial, or state. Statutes, and how they are interpreted by case law, determine how the violence risk assessment should proceed. Because scientific 'certainty' changes almost day to day, the law tends to incorporate the fruits of research with caution. Certainly it retains the power to lay out what kinds of information and evidence should and should not inform decisions in cases where there is at least a suspicion of mental disorder. Some law is quite vague in its wording about 'dangerousness' and violence risk, some is remarkably detailed; some of it is more or less unaffected by contemporary medical and social research findings and observations, some of it has incorporated recent scientific thinking and language. What is important to note, though, is that assessors and decision makers alike are obliged to work within the ambit of the applicable law (as well as their own professional ethical standards). It is the necessary starting point (Webster, Hucker, & Bloom, 2002). The law will also offer some guidance about what kinds of penalties or restrictions may eventually come to be imposed on persons who have been under assessment.

Although this text is not written to promote understanding of the Canadian legal approach to mentally disordered offenders in particular, it is nonetheless instructive to outline this particular approach. The issues which arise will, of course, differ across national borders (e.g., Behnke, Perlin, & Bernstein, 2003). Yet something like the Canadian system can be found in Great Britain, Ireland, Germany, Norway, Sweden, the Netherlands, most states within the US, certain jurisdictions within Australia, and elsewhere (see Blaaw, Hoeve, van Marle & Sheridan, 2002).

Part XX.1 of the *Criminal Code* of Canada, the Mental Disorder provisions, deals mainly with accused persons found Unfit to Stand Trial (UFST)[3] and Not Criminally Responsible by Reason of Mental Disorder (NCRMD).[4] Each province or territory is authorized under the *Code* to establish and staff its own Review Board. The Board conducts annual hearings which must take 'into consideration the need to protect the public from dangerous persons, the mental condition of the accused, the reintegration of the accused into society and the other needs of the accused' (S672.54). A Review Board has three options: to discharge absolutely; to discharge subject to conditions; or to detain in custody at a hospital.[5] It is enjoined to make the disposition 'that is the least onerous and least restrictive to the accused'. Before discharging an accused absolutely the Board must be of the opinion that 'the accused is not a significant threat to the safety of the public'. Snow's (2002) *Criminal Code* cites the case of Owen to make the point that: 'the threat must be 'significant' both in the sense that there must be a real risk of physical or psychological harm occurring to individuals in the community, and in the sense that this potential harm must be serious. A miniscule risk of grave harm will not suffice, nor will a high risk of trivial harm. Further, the conduct or activity creating the harm must be criminal in nature' (Snow's, 20.1–16). Just as the law distinguishes between severity and frequency of actual and threatened acts, so too does the scientific literature. This should become clear in later sections.

In Canada each province and territory has its own Mental Health Act (MHA). Since these Acts vary across provincial and territorial jurisdictions, it is not possible to describe a single legal approach to 'civil' release decision making. For the sake of example, we list here the key elements of the Mental Health Act of Ontario (RSO, 1990, January 11, 2002). Under the Act there are three conditions for involuntary admission to a psychiatric facility. The attending physician must be able to certify that 'the patient is suffering from mental disorder of a nature or quality that likely will result in, (i) serious bodily harm to the patient, (ii) serious bodily harm to another person, or (iii) serious physical impairment of the patient' (s.20,5). Persons are eligible to have their certificates rescinded if these prerequisites are no longer met (s. 41,31).

Persons subject to detention within the federal correctional system in Canada are subject to the Corrections and Conditional Release Act (CCRA; 1992, c.20, March 1998). Part 1 of the Act deals with institutional and community corrections. It specifies rules and regulations which govern the conduct of offenders themselves and the persons appointed to supervise them. Part II of the Act covers conditional release and long-term supervision. It specifies that the purpose of conditional release 'is to contribute to a just, peaceful and safe society by means of decisions on the timing and conditions of release that will best facilitate the rehabilitation of offenders and their reintegration into the community as law-abiding citizens' (s.100). The Act goes on to say that protection of society is the 'paramount consideration', that parole boards must consider all available, relevant information, that they must exchange such pertinent information with other parts of the criminal justice system, that they must 'make the least restrictive determination consistent with the protection of society,' that board members must be trained to carry out their duties, and that offenders must be given access to information and the results of reviews (s.101). For parole to be granted the Board must be of the opinion that 'the offender will not, by reoffending, present an undue risk to society before the expiration according to law of the sentence the offender is serving' (s.102 a) and also that 'the release of the offender will contribute to the protection of society by facilitating the reintegration of the offender into society as a law-abiding citizen' (s.102 b).

Since Part II of the CCRA explicitly states that the Parole Board must consider 'information and assessments provided by correctional authorities, and information obtained from victims and the offender' (s.101 b), it is important to consider how the Act approaches risk assessment under Part I. It requires the Correctional Service of Canada to obtain 'as soon as practicable': (a) information about the offence; (b) personal history information (including social, economic, young offender history and criminal record); (c) court recommendations at sentencing; and (d) information from the victim or other sources.[6] Part II of the CCRA becomes quite specific in its demands. It requires the Board to consider: (1) whether the individual is planning to commit a serious offence against another person before the end of sentence; (2) the number and seriousness of prior offences causing physical or psychological harm; (3) brutal behavior; (4) prior threats of violence; (5) use of weapons; (6) the extent to which the person has difficulty controlling violent or sexual impulses; (7) evidence of 'a substantial degree of indifference on the part of the offender as to the consequences to other persons of the offender's behaviour'; and (8) presence of medical, psychiatric or psychological illness or disorder. Interestingly, the Board is also called upon to take into account 'protective factors'. The Act calls for consideration of the possible availability of 'supervision programs that would offer adequate protection to the public from the risk the offender might otherwise present until the expiration of the offender's sentence according to law' (s.132.1 d).[7] Our point in referring to this Canadian Act is to drive home the notion that mental health professionals, depending on the jurisdiction, and when the law was last revised, can often use the law to clarify for themselves what is actually expected of them. It can also help them select an approach to a risk assessment that is consonant with the law.

As should now be clear from the Canadian example, the Mental Disorder provisions of the *Criminal Code*, the pertinent MHA, and the CCRA prompt different approaches to decision making. In each case, specially constituted review boards make release decisions for civil psychiatric patients, forensic patients,[8] and persons convicted criminally. Although some basic violence risk-assessment principles apply across the Civil Mental Health System (CMHS), the Forensic Mental Health System (FMHS), and the Criminal Justice System (CJS), there can be no doubt that the three settings face issues particular to them. As well, each is supported by a range of social and mental health services which differ in their accessibility. Although perhaps a little artificial, it is helpful to think of there being a fourth setting consisting of the general community, the one in which the wide majority of people, live, work, and conduct their family and social lives. To an extent, the community is regulated by police forces.

Mentally disordered offenders in Canada and elsewhere do not necessarily pick a 'career' (Menzies, 1989) and stick with it. Indeed many are more or less continually 'floating' among the four systems. There tends to be a high degree of interconnection among them. Most complaints, disruptions, or criminal activities of any seriousness are dealt with by police officers. When they attend an incident they have to make a decision as to whether the individual is best routed to the criminal justice or the mental health system. Of course, in many instances, they cannot exercise much discretion. If the incident is highly serious, one involving substantial physical injury, they have no alternative but to lay charges. In the majority of cases they have to make what seems to be the best decision they can at the time. Whether they drive to the police station or the local mental health facility will depend on a wide array of factors such as the attending officers' previous experience with the hospital under similar circumstances, the wishes of friends or relatives at the scene, the individual's known history of mental illness, highly bizarre or unusual conduct before, during, or after the incident, and so on. If the decision is made that the person is best routed to the mental health facility, the person may consent to a voluntary admission, may be certified, or may be released. If certified under provincial or territorial law, the individual will be held on certificates, which may be successively renewed. In due course the person will be decertified by the medical authorities or the certificate allowed to lapse. An appeal against continued detention could be launched. If so, this will be decided by the pertinent provincially or territorially constituted review board. Court appeals may also be possible.

Should the person be dealt with by the courts and there is no apparent issue of mental competence in the present or previously at the time of the incident, he or she will be processed criminally in the usual way. If found guilty and sentenced to a prison term of some length, the possibility of parole will usually arise in due course. It also may well be that once ensconced in the CJS, some persons become evidently mentally disordered and in need of special services. If remanded for mental examination under Part XX.1 of the *Criminal Code*, and if found UFST by the court following psychiatric testimony, the person will come under the jurisdiction of the *Criminal Code* Review Board. Should the person seemingly become 'fit' after a period, he or she will be returned to court where a determination will be made. If found fit, the person will proceed to trial in the usual way. One possibility is that, now fit, a case may be made that the person was NCRMD at the time of committing the alleged offence (i.e., that under section 16 of the *Code* he or she was 'unable to appreciate the nature and quality of the act'). Again, if so found NCRMD, the accused person will revert to the authority of the Review Board and the case will be reviewed annually.[9] Persons retained under the power of the Board are held in provincial mental health facilities or supervised in outpatient programs. As already noted, the Board is compelled to grant an absolute discharge if it is not satisfied that the person poses a 'significant threat'.

It has long been noted that the mental health system does not operate in isolation from the criminal justice system, and vice versa (Menzies, 2002). As the population in the one rises, the other tends to drop (Penrose, 1939). A similar trend has been observed lately with respect to the interconnectedness of civil mental health and forensic psychiatric services. When Bill C-30 passed into law in Canada in 1992 it became somewhat easier to direct persons to the forensic system than had been the case previously. The result has been a rise in number of forensic psychiatric patients (Schneider, 2000) and a drop in number of 'ordinary' civil psychiatric beds (Seto, et al., 2001). This trend, an expansion of the forensic system at the expense of the civil system, is not unique to Canada. It serves to emphasize the point that the nature of violence risk assessment can shift dramatically with legal changes. Such changes can also greatly affect clinical, administrative, and research practices.[10] It also serves as a reminder that a risk assessment conducted for some specific purpose under one set of laws may yield information of little or no relevance in another legal context.[11]

NOTES

1 Robert was free in society but on parole as part of a prison sentence for a sexual assault. Visiting him at home the author of the descriptive narrative becomes alarmed and decides that Robert should be in hospital. After some effort, Robert agrees to a voluntary admission. Yet shortly after he is certified. The narrative provides an example of how a person can commit a crime, receive treatment while in prison, return to society, enter the civil mental health system, and end up back in the community without any kind of restraint or supervision. Robert has been affected by criminal law, correctional policy, and civil law.

2 Haward (1981) discusses the relationship between law and science. He reminds us that lawyers in the early part of the twentieth century 'regarded the new science as coming from decidedly dubious parentage and were suspicious of the statements made by scientists. 'The Law' said that great jurist Jennings, 'walks a respectful distance behind science'. Perhaps this is as it should be; the wisdom of the judicial process has accumulated, slowly and painfully, through every century of human social history. The course of science, on the other hand, is littered with the wrecks and relics of outdated ideas and of theories espoused too soon' (p. 16).

3 A court may declare a person UFST if, *in the present*, he or she is unable to understand the nature of the pending charges and is unable to participate in a defense.

4 The NCRMD defense is reserved for an individual who, *at the time of the offence*, was unable to appreciate the nature and consequences of the act. In some jurisdictions this will include the death penalty. So, in effect, the mental health expert witness is expected to comment on 'fitness to be put to death'.

5 See Schneider, Glancy, Bradford, and Seibenmorgen (2000) who provide a summary of the *Winko* case and its likely effects on release decision making in the context of Part XX.1 of the *Code*.

6 These kinds of information generally supply a kind of legal framework for the HCR-20 and related risk assessment schemes (s.19 CCRA). This is particularly so when factors under section 132 of the CCRA are added. It may be important for assessors, though, to remember that the Act requires that 'correctional policies, programs, and practices respect gender, ethnic, cultural and linguistic differences and be responsive to the special needs of women and aboriginal peoples, as well as to the needs of other groups of offenders with special requirements' (CCRA Principle 4h).

7 It is important to note that violence risk projections under the CCRA are bounded by the reality of having to consider only violent acts which might occur before sentence expiry. These set dates influence risk-assessment procedures. This is different than working within a provincial MHA where it is often necessary and possible to renew a certificate. Similarly, a Review Board constituted under the Mental Disorder provisions of the *Criminal Code* has the power to detain an individual on a year-to-year basis.

8 The *Code* uses the term 'accused person'.

9 In Canada, 'Dangerous and Long-Term Offenders' can be detained indefinitely under section 753 of the *Criminal Code*. Specific guidance concerning the assessment of Dangerous and Long-Term Offenders is given in Eaves, Douglas, Webster, Ogloff, and Hart (2000).

10 It is interesting to note that some individuals can be administered by two systems simultaneously as in 'dual status' offenders who are both criminally convicted and held accountable to the Review Board constituted under the *Criminal Code*. The division between provincial mental health and federal correctional services are not necessarily as cut and dried as might appear. Sometimes persons under Review Board authority are held in federal penitentiaries.

11 An example might be some incidental, and likely unrelated, remarks made about violence potential in the course of a fitness-to-stand-trial examination used several years later in the context of a new criminal proceeding of major magnitude.

2

PHILOSOPHIES

CHRISTINE

Why did she chuck her baby out the window?
To be sure she was blind drunk at the time
But is that all there was to it?
Seems quite odd to her and to us.
The baby's had it
Case of child abuse
If ever there was one
But what can she do now?
And what can we do for her?
She's actually an attractive person
Took a wee bit of a shine to me anyway
And the brain scan's alright
But there's nothing wrong with her psyche
So she'll just have to face the music.[1]

BACKGROUND: THE EMERGENCE OF 'BIG THEORY'

In the mid-1900s there was intense competition among leading social, psychological, and medical scientists each bent on espousing some particular theoretical framework which might offer the 'best' conceptual point of view, the one with the greatest power to explain why people think and behave the way they do. It was assumed that the 'paradigm' (Kuhn, 1962) which eventually proved its right to dominance would have wide applicability to issues in mental health and corrections (and of course, education, work, and many other fields).

Psychoanalysis was represented in this struggle. The richness of some of its main constructs were acknowledged by many and efforts were made to take further advantage of analytic notions through rigorous definition of terms and experimental test of the theory's basic posits. Yet there was a sense that, once stripped down, the core constructs had dissolved into different, less energetic, entities. This left basic psychoanalysis, and most of its variants, open to the charge that the theory was untestable outside the 'unscientific' framework within which it was conceived. Once the cornerstone of the 'medical model' within psychiatry and the allied fields, it has now become a 'sidebar' having been largely replaced by a vigorous emphasis on neuroscience, psychopharmacology, neuropsychiatry, neurophysiology, and associated fields of study and practice (though see Doctor, 2003).

The client-centered phenomenology of Rogers (1959) was another theory popular in the mid-twentieth century. Its view of humankind was perhaps somewhat more positive than that offered by Freud and his adherents. Rather than seeing people propelled by instinctual urges, Rogers and his adherents focused on the idea that persons had within them the seeds for their own self-fulfillment and sound mental health. It was argued that extensive therapy guided by an expert may not be altogether necessary in most cases and that life can be lived forward optimistically even if there has been no full resolution of major conflicts likely to have emerged early in the person's childhood. This position linked well to the existential psychology of its day (Laing, 1969; May, 1969). It is one that stresses the uniqueness of each and every person. It also connects well to the recent formulation of 'life narratives' (McAdams & Pals, 2006). Neither psychoanalysis nor existential phenomenology, though differing sharply in certain fundamental aspects, held anything in common with statistically driven 'conventional behaviorism' so much in vogue in psychology at the time (Hull, 1951).

A large part of the 'conventional behaviorism', founded in the Hullian tradition of carefully controlled experimentation, took the position that a whole worldview could be formed on principles extracted from laboratory research on animals and humans. This approach placed reliance on the use of formally stated postulates, the random assignment of participants to differing experimental groups, and the analysis of results through application of between-group statistics (relying on the averaged scores across participants assigned to the various experimental conditions). Much of this work was grounded in research with animals but there was also strong interest in establishing 'dimensions of person-ality' (e.g. Eysenck, 1952). Classification, of an almost Darwinian approach, was and remains central to this approach. It is a position which stresses the common-ality among humankind. New clinical methods were expected to follow directly from basic research. There was great effort in an allied 'tests and measurement' tradition to create and standardize personality and clinical tests. This tradition continues strong (Blanton & Jaccard, 2006).

Conventional behaviorism allied itself quite easily to a physiological approach and a comparative (cross-species) approach. Here the emphasis was on determining which parts of the brain are responsible for motivations of various sorts, for perceptions, for memory, for how drugs of various kinds affect behavior, and so on. Knowledge of this kind would allow for the addition of fine-grain principles to the broader principles exactable through behavioral experimentation. It also, with its statistical leanings, lent itself to the use of epidemiological methods, which have become so important in many fields, including the study of mental health and violence (e.g., Epidemiological Catchment Area study; Swanson, 1994).

The conventional behaviorism approach differed strong from a so-called 'radical behaviorism' (Keehn & Webster, 1969). This was the line adopted by Skinner and colleagues and is often referred to as 'operant conditioning'. The idea is that researchers should stick to what they can observe and avoid reliance on 'inner explanatory fictions' (e.g. anxiety, depression, personality types). This was and remains very much a *situational* approach concerned with the study of 'contingencies'. Methodologically, proponents of the approach were extremely distrustful of results obtained by statistical averaging, insisting that the discovery of new 'laws' of behavior will arise through analysis of the reward and punishment contingencies as they affect individual persons. This approach also led to the development of its own form of clinical intervention sometimes called 'functional behavioral analysis'. If the task can be broken down into small enough steps behaviors can be built, shaped, chained together, through the provision of 'reinforcement' (of a material kind, or through praise, encouragement, and the like). This is well explained by Spaulding, Sullivan, and Poland (2003, pp. 180–220). Much of the goal is to aid persons to become capable of exerting their own self-control (Skinner, 1953). In recent years, despite Skinner's lack of appetite for 'mind'-related constructs, the term 'cognitive' has become affixed to 'behavior therapy' to yield 'cognitive behavior therapy' (CBT) and is implicated in a current focus on 'dialectical behavior therapy' (DBT; Linehan, 1993; McMain & Courbasson, 2001).

THE RELEVANCE OF 'BIG THEORY' TO CONTEMPORARY ISSUES IN RISK ASSESSMENT AND MANAGEMENT

Why, it might be asked, do the present authors choose to resurrect theories from a half century back or more? There are three reasons. First, although these theories might lack something of their previous wide influence and force, they have by no means died. They may have transformed and developed but they continue to exist and, indeed, to contribute to our understanding of the human condition. Second, contemporary 'dangerousness' and 'risk assessment' literatures easily give the impression of being somewhat atheoretical. As mentioned in the previous chapter, some individuals suffering from a variety of disorders are moved more or less constantly from civil to forensic, from forensic to correctional, from correctional to civil, from civil to community, and so on. This has the effect of obliging practitioners to become highly pragmatic as they work with persons in the context of laws, policies, and changing physical and social settings. Yet in fact the courts, review boards, and other such tribunals tend to be on the lookout precisely for theoretical information as they try to render optimal decisions on behalf of the individual persons for whom they have assumed responsibility or for whom they are considering relinquishing control (Foucault, 1978). Some grounding in theory is, then, essential for mental health practitioners. Third, whether they consciously acknowledge the fact or not, mental health and correctional practitioners work within one or more of the traditions outlined above. It is our contention that mental health practitioners in all the various disciplines need to be attentive to their own personal and professional viewpoints. This is important because these perspectives change gradually as a result of study and clinical experience. As well, individual clinicians should, ideally, be cognizant not only of where their colleagues stand in terms of Weltanschauung but be ever on the lookout for the incorporation of new ideas and outlooks. This becomes especially important when it comes to participating in a multidisciplinary team, a point we reinforce in Chapter 18. A skillful leader can ensure not only that 'all the bases are covered' when it comes to a consideration of possible factors influencing risk (Chapter 9) but in a more general, and perhaps more fundamental way, that the client has been viewed from a variety of philosophical positions.

RECENT THEORETICAL INNOVATIONS

The various positions we have sketched above can be distinguished in many different ways (e.g., by the extent to which they emphasize or eschew formal diagnostic formulations, pharmacological interventions, inductive versus deductive methods for creating knowledge, and so on). One such kind of separation lies in considering how different kinds of theories are held by 'lay' people (which would include, importantly, mental health and correctional clinicians and clients). Molden and Dweck (2006) recently argue that as *well as* searching for 'universal principles of human behavior and information processing' (p. 192) there requires to be considerations of 'another primary goal' which is to 'understand how people give meaning to their experiences and to their relations with the world around them' (p. 192). They are arguing that no matter how important or necessary it may be to isolate universal principles it is as well vital to dwell on 'how real people actually function' (p. 192). These authors remind us that 'by attempting to describe only the average one runs the risk of describing nobody in particular' (p. 192). The argument is that people vary considerably in how they put themselves forward in the world. These theories or styles of self-help determine how information is dealt with and how it affects future action. It comes as no surprise, perhaps, that persons from different cultures are apt to form different 'lay' or 'naive' theories. This would presumably apply not only to culture in a broad sense but also to cultures of research, of psychiatric practice, of nursing practice, of psychological practice, of social work practice, and so on.

Molden and Dweck (2006) suggest that persons form lay theories of two main types: *entity* theory and *incremental* theory. Entity theory has it that basic attributes like personality or intelligence are relatively fixed or 'static'. These attributes are not expected to change or develop much over time. In contrast, incremental theory holds that human attributes are malleable and apt to develop and change over time according to circumstances. Whether or not a client is able to make progress in treatment or therapy probably depends to some extent on the worldview they hold. It makes a difference whether the self-perception is a static or an incremental, dynamic, one. The same may be said of mental health and correctional staff in the various disciplines. It will be one thing if they 'come at it' from a static point of view akin to conventional behaviorism; another if they bring some variation of existentialism or phenomenology or even radical behaviorism (all of which accentuate the idea that positive change can be coached into occurrence). Later in this text, in Chapter 10, we return to the distinction between static (fixed entity) and dynamic (incremental points of view). Our position is that *both* kinds of theory are important and that it is for this reason that structured professional judgment (SPJ) guides have become so vital in contemporary research and practice in the area of violence risk assessment (see Chapter 11). The matter of attaining balance between these positions through the possible creative use of multidisciplinary teams is revisited in Chapter 17. In Chapter 15 we mention that, in contemporary times, the challenge is not so much to isolate the one perspective that will best suit the client but rather to figure out which perspective, or indeed perspectives, are seemingly most appropriate at each particular stage of rehabilitation. What is called for is an 'integrated rehabilitation paradigm' (Spaulding et al., 2003, see especially pp. 16–22).[2]

NOTES

1   Christine has apparently been examined from a number of perspectives. The author of the descriptive narrative notes the idea that she seems capable of relating to other people. We are also told that there does not seem to be anything obviously wrong with her physiologically. That there is 'nothing massively wrong with her psyche' suggests that she has received standard psychological testing and has been examined psychiatrically. It is not hard to imagine that, looking ahead, when Christine 'gains insight' into this tragic event and her role in it, she will need some skillful therapy.

2   These authors provide a compelling account of the possibilities inherent in such a paradigm.

3

PREDICTIONS

'Winwood Reade is good on the subject, said Holmes. He remarks that, while the individual man is an insoluble puzzle, in the aggregate he becomes a mathematical certainty. You can, for example, never foretell what any one man will do, but you can say with precision what an average number will add up to. Individuals vary, but percentages remain constant. So says the statistician. . .'

(Arthur Conan Doyle, *The Sign of Four*, p. 84, Penguin edition, 2001. First published, 1890).[1] By permission.

It is helpful to distinguish two kinds of violence predictions, those made by frontline police, security officers, and staff working in general medical and psychiatric emergency services (Hillard & Zitek, 2004), in contrast to mental health and correctional personnel as they strive to compile prediction pictures on individual clients given the relative luxury of weeks or months in which to complete the assessment (Daniel, 2004).

Although this text concentrates on the latter, more 'reasoned' type of decision making, a good deal has been written in the past about how best to restore calm during rapidly developing and escalating emergencies (e.g., de Becker, 1997, Hillard & Zitek, 2004). Of late, some reviewers have pointed to the importance of studying 'rapid cognition' and of exploring the strengths and limitations of 'intuition' (Winerman, 2005). In a recent publication, we have found it helpful to use the mnemonic THREAT to describe the kinds of emergencies referred to in the preceding paragraph (Webster, Martin, Brink, Nicholls, & Middleton, 2004, pp. 31–32). By this is meant THREATS of HARM that are REAL, ENACTABLE, ACUTE, and TARGETED. Persons on the front line often face challenges in ensuring that their rapidly taken actions are free of biases of various kinds. Also they have to be as certain as possible that their response does not exceed that which is necessary (Webster, 1983–1984). Daniel (2004) notes that '. . . a front-line service provider's observations, the nature and quality of his or her decisions, as well as the accuracy and thoroughness of documentation, are heavily relied upon by both clinicians and forensic experts to address the aspects of the case that are relevant to their areas of decision-making' (p. 388).

When assessments are conducted under settled conditions, it is generally useful to distinguish between four activities: risk attribution; risk prediction; risk assessment; and risk management. Risk *attribution* can be regarded as a kind of 'subclinical' activity (Pfäfflin, 1979). All that is meant by the term is that an aspect of 'dangerousness' is attributed to another person on the basis of characteristics that may be largely if not completely irrelevant (e.g., body size, a previously applied, inaccurate, psychiatric diagnosis, etc.). Such attributions are defensible neither legally nor psychiatrically. An example might be the use of a term like 'sexual acting out' which tends in routine clinical practice to be ascribed more to women than to men and to be in effect a 'moral judgment' (Eisenman, 1987).[2] Another might be facial appearance (Esses & Webster, 1988).

Risk *prediction* is an activity that can be performed clinically or from a research point of view. The various pertinent laws mentioned in Chapter 1 invite the making of predictions by those who advise courts, boards, and other tribunals. But the prediction will always be contained within a surrounding, broader, *assessment* process. Within that process the likely validity of the prediction will ordinarily be subject to close scrutiny,[3] as will the way the evaluation has been completed (i.e., its thoroughness, its adherence to accepted legal and scientific standards, its attendance to ethical and procedural matters, etc.). Risk *management* provides information about how, conceivably, violence risk may be contained. It deals with the kinds of supervision, interventions, and treatments that are apparently required in the particular case in order to minimize violence risk. More is said about this topic in Chapter 15.

Risk prediction can be viewed in two different but not necessarily exclusive ways: according to grouped statistical data and according to the individual case (see Chapter 2). Dealing first with the statistical approach, it has long been hoped that some approach to violence risk assessment might enable clinical and correctional professionals to make convincingly accurate projections of violence risk. To an extent this has proven possible. One of the more compelling demonstrations comes from the correctional sphere in Canada. This entails use of the so-called General Statistical Incidence of Recidivism scale (G-SIR; Nuffield, 1982; Bonta, Harman, Hann, & Cormier, 1996). The scale, which aims to forecast *general* recidivism, is in standard use within the Correctional Service of Canada (CSC) and the National Parole Board (NPB). It contains items relating to the index offense, past offenses, previous imprisonments, etc. Normative data collected over many years on many offenders allow stipulation of the level of probability for failure over a defined number of years.

Another scale is the Violence Risk Appraisal Guide (VRAG; Quinsey, Harris, Rice, & Cormier, 1998, 2006), used in some forensic and correctional settings. This is dealt with in fuller detail in Chapter 7 of this text. Both the G-SIR and the VRAG can yield information that is extremely helpful to assessing violence risk. Yet decision makers, even when in possession of properly gathered and interpreted 'actuarial' information, continue to wonder about its pertinence in the particular instance. While it may possibly be true at the present time that, from a *statistical* vantage point, actuarial scale scores will outperform other kinds of projections, especially over the long term, decision makers could hardly abrogate their responsibility to ensure that the individual's case is being appropriately contextualized.[4] The distinction between 'actuarial' and 'clinical' prediction is dealt with in greater detail in Chapter 10.

Attention can now be turned to contextualizing prediction in the individual case. Jackson's (1997) six facets are helpful in this respect:

- Facet 1 is *risk factors*. These could be selected from historical, demographic, biological, clinical, cultural, situational, or many other domains. In this text we consider some of these without in any way implying that our list is exhaustive (see Chapter 9).
- Facet 2 deals with the *strength of the evidence* for these risk factors. It could be that particular factors seem to measure some important aspect of the individual or circumstances. They might be related to violence or they might predict it. It is also possible that they could explain the violence or even provide a sound causative explanation.
- Facet 3 deals with *which person* or group of persons are being considered as possible perpetrators of violence. Emphasis could be on an individual or on specific types of persons who stand out because they belong to some class of persons (e.g., those who score high on the Hare PCL-R, those who have a history of particular kinds of serious mental illness, those who have previously breached parole or release conditions).
- Facet 4 covers the *legal status* of an act and the circumstances of the person being implicated. It may be relatively easy to predict that an individual will be *accused* of committing a violent act, harder to forecast whether or not that person will actually *commit* the act, and harder still to predict a *conviction* for the offense.
- Facet 5 deals with *type of behavior* being predicted. This could range anywhere from a parole or release condition violation, a property offense, an impulsive action, irresponsible or dangerous behavior, or a violent act.[5]
- Facet 6 deals with the *time period* over which a projection is made.[6] This could be a matter of weeks or months. It could hinge on administrative considerations, such as expiry date of parole. It might be a period in the more or less indefinite future (e.g., a research study to find out which persons discharged absolutely by a Review Board *eventually* recidivate).

As Jackson (1997) points out: 'It is simply suggested that prior to data collection, the element(s) of Facet 6 that are of substantive interest to the research must be clearly specified' (pp. 237–238).[7] We would add that this highly demanding standard holds for clinical practice as well as research studies. The same could be said for Jackson's (1997) remark: 'It is salutary to note that without a clear *a priori* specification of the elements of this facet (or any other facet), it cannot be determined what the predictions derived from the research do in fact predict' (p. 238, original emphasis). Again, we would argue that this statement will hold with respect to scientifically conducted, single-subject, clinical case work. A simplified 'mapping sentence' for violence prediction, following Jackson, is outlined below

> What (1) risk factors _____, (2) predict (3) which person _____, (4) will commit (5) the following particular kind of act _____, (6) within the following specified time period_____.[8]

The mapping sentence forces attention to a key issue raised in Chapter 1; namely the distinction between the potential seriousness of a violent act and the frequency with which it is likely to occur. Although the sentence urges a standard probably largely unrealizable at present, it does help sharpen the prediction, and hence the assessment, tasks. Readers will, of course, recognize that this emphasis on specificity is likely not shared by fortune tellers who, generally, make their living by offering the broadest possible projections (especially ones which can scarcely help but come true – as in 'You will meet a tall handsome stranger').[9,10]

NOTES

1 Conan Doyle reminds us that prediction in the individual case is one thing, prediction based on statistical averaging is another.

2 The description of Pete following is an example of sheer, thoughtless, 'attribution', not a statement that could be defended from a professional point of view. The writer makes no attempt to mask his dislike of Pete. Expressed in narrative form, it is as follows: Of all the odious sods I've seen/This guy takes the cake/ It's not clear why he was sent/Because he's beyond my reach/File says he's a pimp/We talk about his 'work'/Makes no effort to conceal/His attitudes/Toward women/Does not come/A second time/Which is fine/By me.

3 Clinicians who use actuarial violence risk-assessment devices and well-standardized personality scales as part of their routine evaluations must become familiar with being cross-examined in court or before boards about the pertinence of normative data to the case at hand.

4 Some have argued that, given the seemingly poor relative standing of unstructured clinical opinion against actuarial data, it might be best to place main if not total reliance on the latter (Quinsey et al., 2006, p. 197).

5   Although the facet type of analysis may seem ideal, it is worth noting that the law itself may not hold experts to such an exacting standard. By way of example, the CCRA does *not* hold Canadian decision makers to the standard of making highly specific predictions. It says: 'In determining whether an offender is likely to commit an offense causing death or serious harm to another person, a sexual offense involving a child or a serious drug offense, it is not necessary to determine whether the offender is likely to commit any particular offense' (s.129(10)).

6   Since the Review Board hearings for persons held under the Mental Disorder provisions of the *Criminal Code of Canada* are normally held annually, members will largely be attempting to gauge risk for violence under specified conditions over the forthcoming 12 months. This is in contrast to persons being dealt with under the CCRA where the prediction is ultimately bounded by sentence expiry (except in the case of Dangerous Offenders whose sentences are indefinite).

7   Jackson (1997) states that 'a mapping sentence serves the purpose of specifying the logical relationships between and classifying the context of, the basic units of the problem ...' (p. 235).

8   A fuller mapping sentence would read as follows: What (1) risk factors _____ (2) are related to/predict/explain/cause (3) which person_____/type of person will (4) be accused of/commit/be convicted of (5) the following particular kind or kinds of specified acts _____ within (6) the following specified time period _____.

9   Note, too, the chances of prophecy being fulfilled in that the 'expert', through the prediction, gives the client some license to bring the projection to fulfillment.

10   In terms of currently available SPJ assessment guides, readers are referred to the RSVP (2003) by Hart et al. (see Chapter 11). These authors invite assessors to consider a variety of vignettes that might apply to the individual case under evaluation. A similar invitation is extended under the START (2004) by Webster et al. (see Chapter 11).

4

ERRORS

FRED

Big admin bugger up so they want him back inside
Goes to boss and gets a few days off the car wash
Nice obliging Parole Officer drives him out of town
So he can be on ice for a while with his old lady
But they fight and moneyless he wants back home
Officer too is
On the lam
Can't be reached
So Fred robs house
Scores a gun
And a truck
Not bad, eh?
Guns make him feel powerful especially if hungry
So he robs a convenience store just to eat you know
In the course of this little operation he kinda panics
And shoots the proprietor dead which ain't so hot
To top it off he's hit by a car as he escapes
Off to hospital
Then to remand
He's angry
But denies
He feels it
So tells the PO
He hates his father
Just to get rid of him
Stupid stuff
It oughtn't to
Have happened.[1]

[after Dennis E. Bolen, *Stupid Crimes* (1992)]

Error, of course, is a core component of all science and it comes in an assortment of
varieties.

(Faigman & Monahan, 2005, p. 645)

One of the main reasons why the violence risk-assessment literature has developed so rapidly over the past quarter century is that Henry Steadman and Joe Cocozza early showed that clinicians are likely to err in the direction of overpredicting violence. Their 1974 book, *Careers of the Criminally Insane*, was based on a large four-year follow-up study of persons released by order of the US Supreme Court from New York's Dannemora State Hospital for the Criminally Insane. Baxstrom had previously been convicted for an assault but while serving his sentence was transferred to Dannemora. The researchers found that, despite previously having seemingly been thought 'dangerous', very few of their sample in fact acted violently following release into the community.[2] This finding was replicated in the state of Pennsylvania shortly afterward in the Dixon case (Thornberry & Jacoby, 1979). These observations had the effect of galvanizing research into violence prediction, assessment, and management. Certainly, they had a strong influence on John Monahan as he wrote his highly influential 1981 text.

In that book Monahan described the basic 2×2 table which is reproduced in one form or another in most accounts of violence risk prediction. There are two prediction possibilities: low risk, and high risk. Similarly, there are two possibilities at outcome weeks, months, or years later: violence occurred or did not occur. A low-risk prediction without subsequent violence is an ideal outcome. There were no victims and the decision makers were correct. This is called a 'true negative' (TN), meaning that the prediction was negative and it turned out to be true. The other way of being correct is to predict high risk and find that violence did in fact occur subsequently. This makes for a 'true positive' (TP). As a result, there would have been a victim or victims. Of course, this occurs frequently in routine parole and other release decision making. Decision makers may realize that there is high chance of future violence in the particular case, but in the absence of extraordinary measures, the individual will have to be released at sentence expiry.[3] A board is largely powerless to prevent such true positives and its members may take small comfort from the fact that the incident occurred once it lost jurisdiction.

Just as there are two ways of being correct, so, too, are there two ways of making 'wrong' release decisions. The first occurs when a person deemed low risk for future violence, actually goes on to commit such an act. This is the so-called 'false negatives' (FN). The person turned out to be positive for violence. She or he had been incorrectly predicted to be safe. Individual mental health and correctional professionals, like decision-making boards, do not wish to attract false negative error. It is the stuff of which newspaper headlines are made.[4] The second kind of error is called a 'false positive' (FP). Here the prediction for future violence is positive but it turns out to be false. Such decision-making error often yields continued detention of an individual in an institution or a life to be lived in the community under possibly very strict controls. The real 'victim' in such cases turns out to be the particular accused person, inmate, or psychiatric patient.

The 2×2 table, though sometimes oversimplifying matters (Hart, Webster, & Menzies, 1993),[5] helps draw out the very difficult nature of measuring the accuracy of predictions. It is easy to understand how the pressure to avoid false negative error increases the likelihood that there will be a high preponderance of seemingly unnecessary detention and community supervision (FPs). The catch is, of course, that, in the understandable zeal to prevent FNs, some persons are detained for longer and under conditions more secure than necessary. Predictions are not normally tested. Only under extraordinary and very rare instances, like the two American studies mentioned in the opening paragraph of this chapter, are persons considered 'dangerous' released outright.

With the 2×2 table outlined above, it is now convenient to summarize some data from the Baxstrom study. Ninety-eight patients were released from hospital and followed over four years. We see that the bulk of cases were TNs (59 persons considered not violent were nonviolent). In 11 cases, persons predicted to be violent were violent (TPs). Only in three cases did persons behave violently over the four years after have been predicted nonviolent (FNs). Finally, there were 25 cases in which persons classified as potentially violent did not behave so (FPs). Of course, it could be that the reported high proportion of FPs was at least partly due to the fact that not all violence in the community was 'captured' in records.

The 2×2 table also helps drive home the point that it is no easy task to devise prediction instruments sufficiently convincingly accurate that they could take over a larger role in release decision making than at present. Mossman (2000) invites us to assume for the moment that 1 in 100 people will kill. Assume further that a scale or test is 95 % accurate in identifying potential killers and that it were possible to assess 10,000 people. Out of 100 killers, 95 will be accurately identified (TPs). This would be a compelling finding. Yet out of the 9,900 who would not kill, 495 would be incorrectly identified as potential killers (FPs). It goes without saying that no such 95 % accurate test exists at the moment or that such predictive precision can be anticipated anytime soon. And, of course, if and when such devices become available, they will still come with at least some false-positive cost attached.[6]

NOTES

1   Bolen makes the point about a man, here called Fred, that this was a senseless violent crime. On parole, Fred was ordered back to the institution for technical reasons. It is an administrative mistake. There was presumably no actual increase in Fred's inherent violence risk. This unexpected encroachment on his liberty (which even the Parole Officer thinks to be unwarranted) destabilizes Fred with tragic consequences for the proprietor of the store.

2 Of 98 patients released outright only two committed felonies (see pp. 138–139). One was for grand larceny, the other for robbery. Most of the rest of the convictions were for offenses not considered felonious.

3 Members of review boards constituted under the Mental Disorder provisions of the *Criminal Code of Canada* (XX.1) do not normally face this difficulty since detention or community supervision can be ordered indefinitely on a year-to-year basis. Yet there will be some cases where the board is obligated to grant an Absolute Discharge since the 'significant threat' criterion for continued detention or supervision is no longer met (see Schneider et al., 2000). This may be necessary even though the board may have concluded that some further aberrant, antisocial, aggressive, or even violent conduct will likely occur in the future.

4 For example, 'Officer slain: Parole Board feels 'horrible', *The Vancouver Sun*, March 7, 1995. An example of the cost of making a false negative error was recently brought to light in Ontario, Canada. The Ontario Court of Appeal ruled that a psychiatrist was at fault for not detaining a delusional man in hospital involuntarily. Six weeks after his release he killed his own sister. The psychiatrist is now to pay a C$ 172 000 jury award to the family. The *Globe and Mail* noted that 'The case is thought to be the first in which a psychiatrist has been held civilly responsible for a killing committed by a psychotic patient she has released into the community' (Saturday, 21 October 2006, p. A16). The paper also reports that: 'The Ontario Court of Appeal stated firmly that there was *solid evidence* that, but for Dr Stefanin's decision to release Ms Johannes, his 39-year old sister would not have been killed' (p. A16, emphasis added).

5 Hart et al. (1993) define terms like 'sensitivity', 'specificity', 'positive predictive power', and so on.

6 These and other issues are discussed by Kennedy (2001).

5

DISORDERS

Multiple disorders are difficult to diagnose because the symptoms of each disorder are altered by the presence of another disorder. As well, the severity and the course of each disorder appear to be different than when the disorder is present in pure form. Even the response to treatment differs when more than one disorder is present. Unfortunately, the recognition that mental disorders coexist is new, and consequently very little is known about this phenomenon.

(Hodgins & Côté, 1995, p. 17)

Many people suffer from symptoms which could easily be considered as mental disorders. Most of them neither seek nor receive psychiatric attention. Their difficulties may be acute and perhaps be prompted by the expected stresses of living (e.g., deaths of family members, job losses, and so on). Other people manage to cope throughout their lives despite actually quite severe psychiatric symptoms and without benefit of professional attention. When carefully conducted studies have been carried out on large populations in ordinary communities, they consistently turn up levels of disorder much higher than might have been expected (Swanson, Holzer, Ganju, & Jono, 1990).

That such studies can be conducted in the first place requires that there be available accurate descriptions of a wide array of mental disorders. This is accomplished through the use of classification systems based on a consensus of experts and experienced clinicians, such as the World Health Organization's ICD-10 Classification of Mental and Behavioural Disorders (1992) and the American Psychiatric Association's *Diagnostic and Statistical Manual*, Fourth Edition, Textual Revision (DSM-IV-TR; 2000). These systems have evolved gradually over years and are revised periodically on the basis of both the results of newly accumulated scientific findings and the opinions of senior practitioners. In this sense, each edition might be viewed as, though definitive for a time, a 'work in progress'.

Since the diagnostic systems just mentioned take into account all types of mental disorder, and since such disorders tend to be quite common in psychiatric, correctional, and forensic populations, it is not possible to omit such a central topic from a book of this kind. This is especially true as different kinds of mental disorder tend to feature prominently in the various risk-assessment and management devices considered in subsequent chapters.

It would not be realistic to outline here even a fraction of the literally hundreds of disorders listed in the 'official' classifications. Fortunately this is not necessary. Even though mental health professionals in general mental health, forensic, and correctional psychiatry will often have to reach beyond the categories most usually linked to violence potential issues, the majority of cases require consideration of the following general categories: (i) childhood disorders; (ii) schizophrenia and other psychotic disorders; (iii) mood disorders; (iv) substance-related disorders; (v) impulse control disorders; (vi) sexual and gender identity disorders; and (vii) personality disorders. In certain cases, assessors will have to turn attention to categories like delirium, dementia, amnesia and other cognitive disorders, anxiety disorders, and adjustment disorders. And, as has already been pointed out, mental health professionals may have to range into considerations of disorders not often found in the populations of interest to readers of this volume.[1] Although relatively rare, such conditions may nonetheless bear strongly on the case at hand. This applies also to conditions proposed in the DSM-IV-TR for purposes of further study, e.g., premenstrual dysphoric disorder,[2] caffeine withdrawal,[3] or depressive personality.[4]

In the following subsections (A to H) we have used the DSM-IV-TR to provide the basis for our brief descriptions of various disorders, with some mention of differences from the ICD-10. Although much of the strength of the DSM-IV-TR arises from its stipulation of the various criteria, which must be met before a specific diagnosis is applied, a lot more is required of the clinician than mere ability to discern and enumerate particular symptoms. It takes considerable general scientific training and practical clinical experience to be able to elucidate psychiatric symptoms, to gauge their likely effects on behavior and experience, and to monitor their changing patterns over time. One disorder often shades into another and, very often, diagnostic pictures alter as people mature and their environmental circumstances change (Hodgins & Côté, 1995, see opening quote for this chapter). Because of this state of affairs, it is often difficult to demonstrate good agreement among clinicians about precise diagnostic ascriptions.

A final point to be made about diagnoses is that, generally speaking, by themselves they tend not to have much statistical power when it comes to violence prediction. Diagnoses are helpful to the extent that they can be used to summarize a great deal of information, aid in problem conceptualization, and assist in communication. Yet as Blumenthal and Lavender (2000) put it, 'problems arise when psychiatric classification is rigidly adhered to, and when a category is given the characteristics of an object in the real world' (p. 6).[5,6,7]

NOTES

1 It is in fact very difficult to find categories of disorders that have no pertinence to persons within the CJS, the CMHS, and the FMHS. Consider, for example, sleep disorders. Within its ambit comes 'sleepwalking disorder'. It is possible for some sleeping persons to get out of bed, to walk about, even to leave a building. There have been celebrated cases on both sides of the Atlantic where serious offenses have occurred during such states and individuals been acquitted. Thus, in Canada, a man was found not criminally responsible for committing a murder while asleep [*R. v. Parks*, 1992, Lamer, C. J. C., 75 C.C.C. (3d), pp. 287, Court File 22073, Supreme Court of Canada]. Another example might come from the category of adjustment disorders. These are stress related and to meet criteria must occur within three months of onset of the stressor and last no more than six months after the stressor has been relieved. It can be a 'gateway' to other conditions. DSM-IV-TR observes that: 'Adjustment disorders are associated with suicide attempts, excessive substance abuse, and somatic complaints' (p. 680).

2 A proposed essential feature is 'persistent irritability, anger, and increased interpersonal conflicts' (p. 771).

3 One proposed research criterion is 'clinically significant distress or impairment in social, occupational or other important areas of functioning' (p. 765). Conceivably, in some cases such distress may underpin irritability and aggressivity.

4 Although not part of the formal DSM-IV-TR as yet, the research criteria include elements that would seem to have a bearing on possible aggressiveness and violence (e.g., 'is negative, critical, and judgmental towards others', p. 789).

5 Criticisms of psychiatric diagnostic systems are not hard to find. Some have concluded that 'psychiatric nosology is not a true specialist language' (Agnew & Bannister, 1973, p. 73).

6 Kendell and Jablensky (2003) recently put it well when they said: 'it is important to distinguish between the validity and the utility of all diagnostic concepts and of their formal definitions. Otherwise, the term 'valid' will continue to mislead, implying some kind of scientific respectability but actually meaning little more than 'useful.' At present there is little evidence that most contemporary psychiatric diagnoses are valid, because they are still defined by syndromes that have not been demonstrated to have natural boundaries. This does not mean, though, that most psychiatric diagnoses are not useful concepts. In fact, many of them are invaluable. But, because utility often varies with the context, statements about utility must always be related to context, including who is using the diagnosis, in what circumstances, and for what purposes' (p. 11).

7 Tengström et al. (2006) speak further to the point made in Note 6 above. Speaking of their own recent research on the HCR-20 items (Chapter 11), they say 'if the results could be replicated they suggest that only assessments which take account of diagnosis and the behavior being predicted are likely to be *useful* for guiding treatment and for measuring the success of interventions' (p. 51, emphasis added).

STEVE

Young Steve he's just turned twelve years old
There are three of us professional folk
Sitting here in the room with him and his mom
Things are not good
Just right now
Charged with robbery
If you hear his side of it
It was just a bit of pushing a kid
Over a bike, no big deal
But the report
Sounds a different note
Kicks to the head
There's also been lots of trouble
At school with various teachers and staff
Not welcome back at last year's academy
At home wrecks the floor with roller blades
Mom finds all this a mite exasperating
Though dammit she believes in her kid
There ought to be a way of turning him around
Which is why we're here talking together
Steve's kinda bored with all this chatter
We're not the only helpers
Who've given it a go
Tells us he's been taken to
A dozen folks like us
Tough exterior
No one's going
To step on his toes
With his history the academics project a life of violence
Maybe they're right since most studies point that way
Which doesn't mean we don't continue to try
To find just the right angle for him.[1]

(A) CHILDHOODS

Both the DSM-IV-TR and ICD-10 include categories for disorders that usually have their onset during childhood or adolescence. Since several of these disorders continue to manifest themselves in some form over the course of the lifespan, the wise assessor will be particularly careful to obtain a full history based on as complete a set of records as can be assembled.

MENTAL RETARDATION

This is a condition in which the mind has failed to develop completely, with the result that normally acquired skills that contribute to 'intelligence' are not attained. These include the cognitive, motor, language, and social skills. In addition to deficiencies of intelligence, mentally retarded individuals are more than three to four times more likely to suffer from co-morbid mental disorders than the rest of the population (DSM-IV-TR, p. 45).

A formal diagnosis of mental retardation requires that onset occurs before age 18. It is stipulated that there be below-average intellectual functioning and that there be major limitations in adaptive functioning. These deficiencies can show up in several areas like communication, self-care, social and interpersonal skills, academic accomplishments, work, and so on. Functioning is defined by intelligence as measured in standard ways.[2] Obviously, in cases where there are profound communication difficulties, it is difficult to obtain a comprehensive history and there will be greater than usual reliance on information provided by others. Retardation can be associated with biological or psychosocial factors (or both). Determining precise etiology is often difficult. Factors to be considered include heredity, problems *in utero*,[3] trauma to the head in childhood, poisoning, infection, and so on. With levels of severity ranging from mild to profound, mental retardation of some degree of impairment likely affects about 1% of the population.[4]

ATTENTION-DEFICIT/HYPERACTIVITY DISORDER

This condition, called hyperactivity disorder in ICD-10, affects boys more than girls, and is estimated in the DSM-IV-TR to occur in 3 to 7% of school-age children. It is marked by failure to give close attention to details, inability to sustain effort, difficulties organizing tasks, resistance to schoolwork, forgetfulness, fidgeting, excessive talking, restlessness, and impulsivity (see DSM-IV-TR, pp. 92–102 for full listing of diagnostic criteria). These characteristics are normally displayed widely: at home, at school, at work, and in social situations. McMurran (2001) refers to the 'constellation of hyperactivity/inattention/impulsivity behaviours' (p. 483), noting that 'This characteristic may be called different things across the lifespan – difficult temperament in babies, hyperactivity in childhood, sensation-seeking in adolescence, and personality disorder in adults' (p. 483).[5]

CONDUCT DISORDER

In DSM-IV-TR, the age of onset and at least one criterion of conduct disorder must be identifiable before 10 years of age in order for an individual to qualify for the childhood-onset type. If certain criteria are met after age 10, the person will be diagnosed as adolescent-onset type.[6] Those with the childhood-onset type have a poorer prognosis than those in the adolescent-onset category in the sense that they are at enhanced likelihood of evolving into antisocial (Or 'dissocial' in ICD-10) personality disorder as adults. The disorder is described in DSM-IV as 'A repetitive and persistent pattern of behavior in which the basic rights of others as major age-appropriate societal norms or rules are violated' (p. 98). The list of diagnostic criteria includes items like: bullies, threatens, intimidates, fights, uses weapons, is cruel to people or animals, steals, forces sexual activities, sets fires, destroys property, breaks into houses and cars, lies, stays out late, runs away, and is truant. Assessors can specify the severity of this condition as 'mild', 'moderate', or 'severe'.

OPPOSITIONAL DEFIANT DISORDER

This disorder is marked by 'a recurrent pattern of negativistic, defiant, disobedient behavior toward authority figures' (DSM-IV-TR, p. 100). The ICD-10 indicates that this disorder is typically seen in children under 10 years old. Although a certain amount of such rebellious behavior can safely be anticipated from many children as they grow up, children who qualify for the diagnosis show it in an extreme form. This will include loss of temper, argumentativeness, disregard of rules, being annoying to adults, blaming others, being angry and irritable or spiteful and vindictive. There must also be impairment in social, academic, or occupational functioning. Such children, relative to others of their age, persistently test limits and fail to negotiate. Some children with oppositional defiant disorder develop conduct disorder, but many do not.

NOTES

1 Steve is hard to reach at the moment. He seems determined to place himself on an aggression-centered trajectory. The key phrase, three lines from the bottom, is 'most studies'. Although we ourselves find statistical correlations between EARL-20B scores when the children are under 12, and eventual outcome years later (Augimeri, 2005), there are plenty of individual cases where such boys do *not* lead aggressive lives in adulthood.
2 Mild retardation is set at intelligence quotients of 50–55 to about 70; moderate at 35–40 to 50–55; severe at 20–25 to 35–40, and profound at below 20 or 25 (see DSM-IV-TR, 2000, p. 42). The ICD-10 uses rather similar ranges.
3 Examples might be infections, toxic effects of alcohol consumption by mother, etc. Although the DSM-IV-TR does not mention 'fetal alcohol syndrome' as such, it gives weight to 'fetal malnutrition, prematurity, hypoxia, viral and other infections, and trauma' (p. 46).

4 The DSM-IV-TR and ICD-10 list many childhood disorders which may have association with later violence. Examples include learning disorder, reading disorder, mathematics disorder, disorder of written expression, motor skills disorder, developmental coordination disorder, expressive language disorder, phonological disorder and stuttering. It is worth noting, though, that 'Stress or anxiety have been shown to exacerbate stuttering' (p. 67) and that 'Impairment of social functioning may result from associated anxiety, frustration, or low self-esteem. In adults, stuttering may limit occupational choice or advancement' (p. 67). An appalling act of lethal workplace violence in Canada was committed at OC Transpo in Ottawa by Pierre Lebrun, a man seemingly afflicted with stuttering and low self-esteem. At the inquest it was revealed that he was greatly teased about this by his co-workers. In this way it is not only the condition that may play some role in helping induce violence in particular circumstances, but the way circumstances and other people single out their 'victims'. Excessively persecuted in such ways, a few people will occasionally act out their frustrations in the form of more or less indiscriminate killings.

5 McMurran notes that this characteristic 'is a risk factor independently for both substance abuse and crime' (p. 483). She refers us to a study by Klinterberg, Anderson, Magnusson, and Stattin (1993) who followed teacher-rated 13-year-old hyperactive boys for 13 years (i.e., until they were 26). These boys, grown into men, were three times more likely to have alcohol difficulties and eight times more apt to be violent. An alcohol problem in violent offenders potentiated violence risk by a factor of about 10.

6 In practice, this distinction can be hard to make since many children will conceal information and caregivers can underestimate symptoms and think age of onset was later than thought (DSM-IV-TR, 2000, p. 95).

FELIX

He stabbed his own mother
Not knowing what he did
And feels as we do, horror
That this could have happened.
What next? We'll wait and see
He might get better
But even if he does
How can we and he be sure
His brother won't get stuck
Next time around?
No simple answer
Comes to mind.[1]

(B) PSYCHOSES

The weight of evidence to date is that although a statistical relationship does exist between schizophrenia and violence, only a small proportion of societal violence can be attributed to persons with schizophrenia.

(Walsh, Buchanan, & Fahy, 2002, p. 494)

The DSM-IV-TR notes that the term 'psychosis', or 'impaired contact with reality', though useful, resists an exact description and that the meaning changes somewhat from one specific condition to the next. In general, though, it includes delusions, prominent hallucinations, and disorganized speech and behavior.

We now consider some psychiatric disorders especially relevant to the issue of violence risk. These are drawn from the DSM-IV-TR section on schizophrenia and other related disorders.[2] Schizophrenia is characterized by 'delusions,[3,4] hallucinations,[5] disorganized speech,[6] grossly disorganized or catatonic[7] behavior' and 'negative symptoms[8]' (p. 298). There are several subtypes of schizophrenia. The paranoid type has some particular pertinence to the main topic of this book. Persons so afflicted may present reasonably normally in ability to think and may display appropriate emotions. Yet there may be prominent delusions or auditory hallucinations. These may have to do with jealousy, or religiosity. Some delusions may be persecutory or grandiose. According to the DSM-IV-TR 'the combination of persecutory and grandiose delusions with anger may predispose the individual to violence' (p. 314).

Delusional disorder rests on the presence of persistent nonbizarre delusions (e.g., that the person is being followed, infected, deceived, poisoned, etc.). There are several subtypes, two of which have particular relevance to this text. Persons afflicted with the erotomanic subtype are deluded by insistent thoughts that another person is in love with him or her. Sometimes the person makes efforts to contact the other individual by letter, telephone, email, visits, and so on. This can extend to surveillance and stalking (Mullen, Pathé, & Purcell, 2000). Some such men come into contact with the law over their inappropriate efforts to save or protect the person whom they believe to be in love with them.[9] Another condition of importance in the context of possible violence is the persecutory subtype. Persons suffering from this disorder believe that they are being conspired against. They may think that they are being cheated, maligned, or obstructed and they may exaggerate small slights. Often they want to remedy unfairnesses against them by legal means. DSM-IV-TR suggests that: 'Individuals with persecutory delusions are often resentful and angry and may resort to violence against those they believe are hurting them' (p. 325). Psychotic states may be induced by intoxication with or withdrawal from alcohol and certain drugs (substance-induced psychotic disorder).

NOTES

1 Felix had no idea he was killing his mother as he did so. He thought he was saving her from a terrible fate.

2 ICD-10 employs similar, though not identical categories to DSM-IV-TR but, for simplicity, the latter is used in this section. Shared psychotic disorder arises only very rarely for clients within the CJS, the CMHS, and the FMHS. One person with a long-standing delusion comes to influence another person who comes to share that delusion.

3 DSM-IV-TR defines a delusion as 'a false belief based on incorrect inference about external reality that is firmly sustained despite what almost everyone else believes and despite what constitutes incontrovertible and obvious proof or evidence to the contrary' (p. 821).

4 Delusions were examined in the MacArthur Study (Chapter 7D). Although a few aspects associated significantly with violence, the correlations were quite low and in a *negative* direction (e.g., persecutory delusions −0.07, religious −0.08). In other words, against expectation, having such symptoms seemingly protected against violence very slightly.

5 DSM-IV-TR defines an hallucination as: 'A sensory perception that has the compelling sense of reality of a true perception but that occurs without external stimulation of the relevant sensory organ' (p. 823). It differs from an *illusion* in that the latter is based on a real external stimulus but with misperception or misinterpretation.

6 In some cases speech is so badly disorganized that it becomes incomprehensible, resembling 'word salad' (DSM-IV-TR, p. 300).

7 DSM-IV-TR defines a catatonic subtype of schizophrenia. This centers on motor immobility, stupor, purposeless motor activity, mutism, bizarre posturing, and the like.

8 DSM-IV-TR defines positive and negative symptoms as follows: 'The positive symptoms appear to reflect an excess or distortion of normal functions, whereas the negative symptoms appear to reflect a diminution or loss of normal function' (p. 299). It is not uncommon to find seriously mentally ill persons in prisons and penitentiaries. Such persons are apt to receive little care and attention. Negative, withdrawing symptoms are easy to overlook.

9 It is worth noting that DSM-IV-TR makes the interesting comment that: 'Most individuals with the subtype in clinical samples are female; most individuals with this subtype in forensic samples are male' (p. 324). This shows how base-rate levels for different psychiatric conditions can vary according to basic demographic data like gender (see Chapter 8).

ERNIE

Little fellow, wiry and pretty jumpy
Wild jumbled stories of fabulous deals
And politics in the Bahamas
A sometime operator
But they're moving in on him
He's most definitely in debt
Odd thing is that his wife really wants him
Is willing herself to
Try to pay it all off
Not crazy
But not exactly typical either
Just can't live on a small scale, like us.[1]

(C) MOODS

The DSM-IV-TR and ICD-10 list several disorders of mood. Not infrequently, persons in the CJS, FMHS, and CMHS, suffer from a major depressive episode (simply depressive episode in ICD-10 with mild, moderate, and severe subtypes). The key feature for such a diagnosis is a depressed mood or 'loss of interest or pleasure in nearly all activities' (DSM-IV-TR, p. 349). This must be present for at least two weeks. Adults with this condition may feel 'depressed, sad, hopeless, discouraged or 'down in the dumps'' (p. 349). Children or adolescents in a major depressive episode may be irritable or cranky. This condition can be accompanied by suicidal thoughts or attempts. So, within each of the three systems there may be issues of violence towards the self. Not infrequently the major symptoms of a depressive episode are overlooked in detention centers and prisons. In contrast, the DSM-IV-TR lists manic episode during which the individual shows 'an abnormally and persistently elevated, expansive, or irritable mood' (p. 357). To meet criteria, such elevated mood must last for at least one week and be accompanied with some additional symptoms like inflated self-esteem or grandiosity, reduction in sleep, speaking in a pressured way, ideas which fly in different directions, distractibility, or motor agitation. There may also be excessive involvement in pleasure-giving activities, often with disastrous results (e.g., 'unceasing and indiscriminant enthusiasm for interpersonal, sexual, or occupational interactions', p. 357). Importantly, 'child abuse, spouse abuse, or other violent behavior may occur during severe manic episodes' (p. 384).

When two or more major depressive episodes have occurred at least two months apart, along with some other criteria, it may be appropriate for qualified clinicians to diagnose a major depressive disorder. According to DSM-IV-TR (2000), persons with this disorder are perhaps 1.5 to 3 times more likely than the general population to have first-degree relatives who also suffer from it. Dysthymic disorder, another classification in this grouping, rests on there being 'a chronically depressed mood that occurs for most of the day, more days than not, for at least two years' (p. 376). One of the criteria is that 'The symptoms cause clinically significant distress or impairment in social, occupational, or other important areas of functioning' (p. 381). Such symptoms can, of course, seriously impede attempts to help the individual integrate into society. Bipolar disorder, formerly called manic depressive disorder, is characterized by the successive and alternating occurrences of manic and depressive episodes.

When mood is affected directly by street drugs, medications, exposure to toxins and the like, it would be appropriate to diagnose substance-induced mood disorder. Mood in some women can also be affected by giving birth. DSM-IV-TR thus includes a postpartum onset specifier. Among the listed symptoms are fluctuation in mood and preoccupation with the infant's well being. Occasionally thoughts may become delusional and, if so, can elevate risk of harm to the child (p. 422).

The DSM-IV-TR (2000) and ICD-10 both include sections on anxiety disorders. Many people in the CMHS, FMHS, and CJS suffer from these kinds of disorders. These include panic attacks, agoraphobia (i.e., anxiety about being in crowded places from which it might be hard to escape), panic disorders, social phobia (social anxiety disorder), obsessive compulsive disorder, acute stress disorder, generalized anxiety disorder, and substance-induced anxiety disorder. There is also post-traumatic stress disorder, which may merit application in instances where persons have experienced or witnessed 'actual or threatened death or serious injury, or a threat to the physical integrity of self and others' and where the individual has responded with 'fear, helplessness, or horror' (p. 467). Symptoms that can be associated with this disorder include irritability or outbursts of anger (p. 468). A few people in the three main systems of interest in this text will be possible candidates for such a diagnosis, which, as has been noted, could carry some elevation of violence risk under particular circumstances.

NOTES

1   Ernie is in a highly energized state. It is hard for the assessors to sort out what is actually occurring in his life and what is not. His wife is suffering greatly as a result of his manic actions.

CHRIS

He's a street kid, scarcely seventeen
No point in being in the office today
He's hyped-up on something, can't stand still
So we sit outside on a wall
He's in a lot of trouble
With dealers
Amazing he comes here
All he wants from me
Is money, or at least a meal
Hardly amenable to 'psychotherapy'
Which is for more settled clientele[1]

(D) SUBSTANCES

DSM-IV-TR (2000) devotes slightly over 100 pages to 'substance-related disorders'. In fact, this set of disorders receives more space than any other.[2] Substances refer to a drug of abuse, or medication, or a toxin. Alcohol, sedatives, hypnotics, and anti-anxiety drugs tend to fall together as do amphetamines, cocaine, and some other sympathomimetics. Polysubstance dependence merits a separate category.[3] Readers will know that some prescribed and over-the-counter medications like antihistamines and muscle relaxants can induce substance-related disorders. When gasoline and such products are used for the purpose of becoming intoxicated they are called 'inhalants'. The DSM-IV-TR (2000) makes a distinction between substance-use disorders and substance-induced disorders. The former refers to substance dependence and substance abuse; the latter to substance intoxication, substance withdrawal, and a wide range of substance-induced disorders (including delirium, dementia, psychotic disorder, mood disorder and sleep disorder).

Persons with substance dependence consume repeatedly and this can result in tolerance and withdrawal. It can also lead to a compulsion to use the substance or substances. Dependence applies to almost all substances.[4] It normally means 'craving'. Tolerance is a phenomenon whereby an individual requires more of the substance to achieve the same effects (or fails to gain the same effect with repeated doses of the same size). The many varied substances now fairly readily available produce markedly different rates of tolerance. According to the DSM-IV-TR, for example, persons who take opioids and stimulants can develop as much as a 10-fold increase. Such a final dose would be fatal to a person intolerant to the drug. Such mishaps sometimes occur in formerly drug-dependent individuals after a period of abstinence. Of course, it is hard to determine levels of tolerance in those who use street drugs simply because the substances tend to be mixed and impure. It is also difficult to get accurate reports of actual levels of consumption.[5]

Withdrawal is 'a maladaptive behavioral change, with physiological and cognitive concomitants, that occurs when blood or tissue concentrations of a substance decline in an individual who had maintained prolonged heavy use of the substance' (DSM-IV-TR, p. 194). To relieve those highly unpleasant effects the person is inclined to take more of the substance. Not uncommonly, heavily addicted persons devote all of their waking energies to avoiding the effects of withdrawal.

Since substance abuse is so pervasive a phenomenon and since its effects vary so much according to the individual's physical constitution (e.g., gender, race) and history (e.g., levels of tolerance to particular drugs), mental health professionals are challenged first to obtain reliable information and second to integrate it into an overall picture (i.e., including, importantly, the presence of other possible mental disorders). They are also often hard pressed to come up with interventions and treatments which will interrupt a firmly entrenched pattern of substance abuse (see Chapter 15).[6]

NOTES

1 The counselor has to accept that today, at least, Chris is beyond reach.
2 ICD-10 runs to 13 pages, still a substantial proportion, The DSM-IV-TR manual has some 700 pages devoted to the various disorders. Disorders usually first diagnosed in infancy, childhood, or adolescence has slightly under 100 pages.
3 It is a fact that, over time, most individuals who abuse substances have come to consume a wide range of them. In the mid-1970s, the government of the Canadian province of British Columbia eventually learned that the passing of an Act to force treatment for abuse of a single drug, under the Heroin Treatment Act, was in vain. It turned out that 'pure' heroin addicts were rare and that most were polysubstance abusers (Webster, 1986). There is also the fact that over time substances initially considered benign, like nicotine, have gradually been noted to possess the potential for highly adverse effects not only on physical health but on potential for physical aggressiveness (e.g. in the DSM-IV-TR the heading Nicotine Withdrawal lists 'irritability, frustration, or anger' and 'restlessness' as two of eight criteria, p. 266).
4 The exception is caffeine.
5 This is why some boards and tribunals, with authority to do so, sometimes impose random urine and blood checks as a condition of provisional release. The legality of this can sometimes be challenged.
6 It ought to be clear that physicians whose practice centers on people with polysubstance abuse problems and mental disorders need a near encyclopedic knowledge of how prescribed medications will likely interact with the illicit use of street drugs (see Law & Nutt, 2000).

RED

He was completely wasted so now he tells me
When years ago   he took a shovel to someone
Who happened   to be in the way when he
Was doing a   routine break and enter
But lifers do get out   some anyway
In his case he went on to get parole and a job
Yet there's a tradition to drink when work is done
I fear one day he'll   get plastered and it'll happen again
And Julia whom he   met on the inside is a treat
Their first kid died   though and I doubted he'd cope
But somehow he's   managed to hang on
And so has she   though it can't be easy[1]

(E) IMPULSES

The DSM-IV-TR contains a section on 'Impulse control disorders not elsewhere classified' and ICD-10 has a similar category of habit and impulse disorders. Impulse control[2] is a key feature of many disorders already described (e.g., schizophrenia, substance-related disorders, and mood disorders) and others to be considered below (e.g. antisocial personality disorder and paraphilias). It is an item in its own right in the Hare Psychopathy Checklist–Revised (PCL-R, 1991) described in Chapters 6 and 7C. Wishnie (1977) and Wishnie and Nevis-Olesen (1977) provide clear descriptive pictures of impulsive personalities, people with destructive character disorders. There is also a useful recent text on the topic (Hollander & Stein, 2006).

Four specific, named, impulse control disorders are of particular relevance to the present text: intermittent explosive disorder, kleptomania, pyromania, and pathological gambling. Intermittent explosive disorder rests on a 'failure to resist aggressive impulses that result in serious assaultive acts or destruction of property' (DSM-IV-TR, p. 663). In common parlance it is sometimes called 'road rage'. Based on a nationally representative sample of over 9 000 persons aged 18 or over, it has recently been concluded that intermittent explosive disorder was estimated to be a fairly common disorder, with a lifetime prevalence of 5.4 % and 12-month prevalence of 2.7 to 3.9 % (Kesler et al., 2006). Few correlates were found between the disorder and various sociodemographic variables, meaning that the condition is widespread. It was also evident that the condition tends to begin in childhood. Kleptomania is the 'recurrent failure to resist impulses to steal items even though the items are not needed for personal use or for their monetary value' (p. 667). Pyromania is the 'presence of multiple episodes of deliberate and purposeful fire setting' (p. 669).

Individuals suffering from this latter condition experience tension or arousal before they set a fire and they tend to have interest in all things having to do with fire. Frequently, they return as bystanders to fires they have themselves have set. Pathological gambling is 'persistent and recurrent maladaptive gambling behavior' (p. 671), which affects family and work life negatively. One of 10 criteria listed is 'restless or irritable when attempting to cut down or stop gambling' (p. 674). Another is 'has committed illegal acts such as forgery, fraud, theft, or embezzlement to finance gambling' (p. 674). These clearly have pertinence to some persons who come within the ambit of the FMHS and the CJS. Other criteria link to CMHS issues (e.g. preoccupation with gambling, lies to family members, therapists, and others).

NOTES

1 Red did not plan to commit this murder. It seems to have occurred on the spur of the moment. His seeming abstinence does not really allay the assessor's worry that further impetuous violence might occur in the future. His wife is viewed as a positive, protective, influence. Yet the climate and culture of his work in the moving industry remains a concern.

2 As an example, a specific piece of legislation in Canada, Part XXV of the *Criminal Code*, referring to dangerous and long-term offenders, rests heavily on the notion of 'impulsivity'. The Part is replete with references to the concept, e.g., 'failure to restrain his or her behaviour', conduct that 'in the future is unlikely to be inhibited by normal standards of behavioural restraint', and 'likelihood of causing injury, pain, or other evil to other persons through failure to control his or her sexual impulses' (s.752).

ERIC

Each week I talk to this man
About the fact that paedophilia is
Not only against the law but damaging
To Boys
Each week he agrees reluctantly to think it over
But nothing really changes here and he wants
Me to take a look at the book he's writing
On Boys
Each week he reminds me that all would be well
If only he'd been born in earlier happier times
In Greece perhaps where all things were possible
With Boys[1]

(F) PERVERSIONS

Both the ICD-10 and the DSM-IV-TR include sections on sexual and gender identity disorders. They do occur with some frequency among forensic and correctional populations and are often central in the assessment of risk for future violent or sexual reoffending. Those with the most forensic or correctional importance will be included among the paraphilias, a subsection of this broader grouping.

DSM-IV-TR defines the paraphilias as characterized by 'recurrent, intense sexual urges, fantasies, or behaviors that involve unusual objects, activities or situations and cause clinically significant distress or impairment in social, occupational, or other important areas of functioning' (p. 535). This requirement has been controversial as many would contend that individuals who, for example, fantasize having sex with dead bodies, even if it causes no distress or impairment in their functioning, are nonetheless abnormal enough to be considered sexually deviant.

The main paraphilias of interest in this text are exhibitionism, fetishism, transvestitic fetishism, frotteurism, pedophilia, sexual masochism, sexual sadism (ICD-10 combines these two as 'sado-masochism'), and voyeurism. Here we venture a few remarks on each. Those interested in more detailed information should consult the DSM-IV-TR (pp. 566–576). Both ICD-10 and DSM-IV-TR include categories that cover disorders not otherwise given specific names in their classification schemes. Thus, necrophilia, the sexual arousal to corpses, is subserved under this category.

Exhibitionism centers on the exposing of genitals to strangers. This may be accompanied by masturbation. The onset of the disorder usually occurs before age 18. *Fetishism* is a form of sexual activity that involves the use of non-living objects (e.g. in the case of males, female underclothes, shoes, etc.). Fetishistic transvestitism refers to the wearing of the clothes of the opposite sex and is accompanied by sexual arousal. DSM-IV-TR requires that the fantasies or actual behavior cause 'significant distress or impairment in social, occupational, or other important areas of functioning' (p. 570). *Voyeurism* (or peeping) is diagnosed when the fantasies or behaviors involve 'the act of observing an unsuspecting person who is naked, in the process of disrobing, or engaging in sexual activity' (p. 575). As with the other paraphilias, this must cause the individual, who must have acted on the urges, 'marked distress'. *Frotteurism* involves touching a non-consenting person or rubbing up against him or her. It commonly occurs in trains, buses, crowded streets, and the like, so that arrest can easily be evaded. *Pedophilia* involves sexual activity with children, usually age 13 or younger. For the diagnosis to be applied as required by DSM-IV-TR, the person must be 16 or older and at least five years older than the victim. Some pedophiles prefer males, some females, and some are drawn to both. Pedophilia with male victims appears to be more common than with female ones. Pedophilic acts can cover a wide range from the relatively innocuous (e.g. looking, undressing) to the distinctly forceful (e.g. penetration of vagina, mouth, anus, with objects, fingers or penis). Commonly, those who commit such acts will produce rationalizations and cognitive distortions to justify their behavior to themselves or others. Some pedophiles perform their acts on their own children, stepchildren, or relatives; some abuse children beyond their own families. Some will marry a woman in order to gain access to her child or children. The 'course is usually chronic, especially in those attracted to males' (p. 571). When males are the target, recidivism rates are higher than when it is females.

A diagnosis of *sexual masochism* requires that the individual be beaten, humiliated, bound, or made to suffer in some way. Examples would include being spanked, urinated on, obliged to crawl, and being shocked by electricity. The sexually masochistic individual may or may not include a partner. The DSM-IV-TR draws attention to one especially dangerous form of the condition known as 'hypoxyphilia' (also referred to as 'asphyxiophilia' or sexual asphyxia). This entails gaining sexual arousal apparently by oxygen depletion (i.e., through use of nooses, ligatures, plastic bags over the head). The risk is obviously that of failure of a safety mechanism intended to ensure survival.

Sexual sadism has considerable pertinence to a select few sex offenders most likely to be found in the CJS and FMHS. The diagnosis officially depends upon the fact that the individual gains sexual pleasure from inflicting psychological and physical suffering on a victim. In some cases the person with the paraphilia will have the fantasies during sexual activity yet not act on them. In other cases the partner may be consenting (and might be sexually masochistic). In yet other instances the sexual sadist chooses to act out their sadistic sexual urges on non-consenting victims. The central feature is the inflicted suffering. Unfortunately, the disorder is often chronic. When it takes place on non-consenting persons it is likely to persist until police intervene. The DSM-IV-TR comments that 'When sexual sadism is severe, and especially when it is associated with antisocial personality disorder, individuals with sexual sadism may seriously injure or kill their victims' (p. 574).[2] It should be noted that some researchers have questioned the utility of separating sexual sadism from other extreme forms of sexual aggression (Marshall & Kennedy, 2003).

NOTES

1   Eric's ideas are firmly entrenched and this seems to be frustrating the counselor.
2   To an extent, Part XXV of the *Criminal Code of Canada*, Dangerous and Long-Term Offenders, is designed to deal with extreme cases of pedophilia and sexual sadism.

BEATRICE

Last week she threatened to kill her ma
Who this week has brought her in for care
Now the big issue is her boyfriend's gone off
So she tells me with the proceeds of her paycheck.
It would help a little if just for once
The weekend hadn't left her dead drunk
She threatens suicide but how am I to know
Whether she means it or has ever meant it?[1]

(G) PERSONALITIES

The DSM-IV-TR describes a personality disorder as 'an enduring pattern of inner experience and behavior that deviates markedly from the expectations of the individual's culture, is pervasive and inflexible, has an onset in adolescence or early adulthood, is stable over time, and leads to distress or impairment' (p. 685). Both ICD-10 and DSM-IV-TR include a number of such disorders plus a 'not otherwise specified' condition. In the ICD-10 the categories are paranoid, schizoid, dissocial, emotionally unstable, histrionic, anankastic, anxious (avoidant), dependent, and other specific types (including narcissistic and passive-aggressive). In DSM-IV-TR these are: paranoid, schizoid, schizotypal, antisocial, borderline, histrionic, narcissistic, avoidant, dependent, and obsessive compulsive. These 10 disorders can be grouped according to Cluster A (paranoid, schizoid, and schizotypal – the 'odd or eccentrics'), Cluster B (antisocial, borderline, histrionic, and narcissistic – the 'dramatic, emotional, or erratic') and Cluster C (avoidant, dependent, and obsessive compulsive – 'the anxious or fearful').[2] We now consider the three clusters in turn. In ICD-10 the schizotypal subtype is included instead among the schizophrenic disorders because of its affinity to that group.

CLUSTER A (THE ODD OR ECCENTRICS)

Persons with *paranoid personality disorders* are distinguished by patterns of 'pervasive distrust and suspiciousness' (p. 690). They do not trust others and as a result cannot work with them. It is interesting to note that 'Their combative and suspicious nature may elicit a hostile response in others, which then serves to confirm their original expectations' (p. 691). Such people tend to draw out angry and aggressive responses from others. Individuals with *schizoid personality disorder* are 'detached from social relationships' (p. 694) and display a limited range of emotional expression. Those with *schizotypal personality disorder* are also commonly socially detached but, as well, they tend to be afflicted with cognitive or perceptual distortions and tend to behave in unusual or eccentric ways (p. 700).

CLUSTER B (THE DRAMATIC, EMOTIONAL, OR ERRATIC)

The four personality disorders which make up Cluster B, taken together, have been construed as psychopathy (Wulach, 1988; psychopathy is discussed further in Chapters 6 and 7). Many persons with antisocial personality disorder find themselves in the CJS, the FMHS, and even the CMHS. To meet criteria for antisocial personality disorder a person, since age 15, must have demonstrated 'a pervasive pattern of disregard for and violation of the rights of others' (p. 706). To qualify, the person must be at least 18 years old and there must have been evidence of conduct disorder beginning before age 15 (subsection A). The person must show three or more of the following seven behaviors: (i) failure to conform to the law and committing acts for which arrest could be possible; (ii) deceitfulness, conning; (iii) impulsivity and failure to plan; (iv) irritability and aggressiveness; (v) recklessness in matters of safety; (vi) irresponsibility; and (vii) lack of remorse.[3] It is important to realize that persons with florid mental disorders are not immune to having a coexisting antisocial personality disorder. Oftentimes, though, this can be masked on initial assessment by the extreme nature of the psychosis, mood disorder, substance use, or other mental disorder. The *borderline personality disorder* diagnosis is reserved for persons with marked emotional instability usually due to response to stress. In treatment they often surprise their therapists by behavior which works against themselves. Such patients show marked impulsivity and often make suicidal gestures. They feel empty and tend to be easily bored. Often their anger is intense and inappropriate. One key feature of *histrionic personality disorder* is the need to be the center of attention. Initially, persons with this condition may charm others with dashing and dramatic actions but their audiences tend to wear down quite quickly. Their friends are inclined to vanish because of demands imposed on them. Emotions are often shallow and superficial. Persons diagnosed with *narcissistic personality disorder* have a 'pervasive pattern of grandiosity (in fantasy or behavior), need for admiration, and lack of empathy' (p. 717). They are often exploitive and arrogant, believing themselves to be 'entitled' and superior to others.

CLUSTER C (THE ANXIOUS OR FEARFUL)

Cluster C personality disorders are marked by anxiety and fearfulness. The *avoidant personality disorder* diagnosis is applied to persons who are pervasively socially inhibited, feel inadequate, and react to criticism with oversensitivity. Such individuals tend to avoid social situations like work and school settings. They require much support if they are to join in social activities.[4] As the name implies, *dependent personality disorder* may be a suitable diagnosis for persons who have 'a pervasive and excessive need to be taken care of' (p. 721) and who may also show 'submissive and clinging behavior and fears of separation' (p. 721). The final category listed in Cluster C is *obsessive-compulsive personality disorder*. This is characterized by a 'preoccupation with orderliness, perfectionism, and mental and interpersonal control, at the expense of flexibility, openness, and efficiency' (p. 725). A great difficulty for persons with the condition is that, because they insist on achieving perfection at every stage, tasks and projects tend not to reach completion.

NOTES

1 Beatrice has some of the characteristics of borderline personality disorder. Again, the narrative brings out some of the counselor's frustrations.

2 The manual makes it clear that this grouping, which may have value for research or educational purposes, likely has 'not been consistently validated' (p. 686).

3 Hare (2003a) has argued that antisocial personality disorder (ASPD) is often confused with psychopathy as defined by his PCL-R. He noted that ASPD is 'a disorder that applies to the majority of criminals and that has only tenuous implications for treatability and the likely violent reoffending' (p. 6). He remarks that many persons on death row in the United States are treated as if they have 'the personality structure of the psychopath' when, in fact, they might meet ASPD criteria only. The same may sometimes apply in Canada with respect to designations of dangerous offender and long-term offender status by courts.

4 That persons with this disorder require so much support is worth noting when it comes to applying violence risk-assessment schemes like the HCR-20 (see Chapter 11). Item R3 is called 'Support'. The criteria under R3 need to be viewed through a diagnostic lens. For example, persons with avoidant personality disorder would almost certainly require more-than-average help if they are to make an adequate community adjustment (which could be one factor in future violence risk).

IRV

He's from down east
From crushing poverty
Punches to the head
No schooling really
No serious crime record
But put it all together
And its many summers missed
No call for 'psychotherapy'
Hard to fill up an hour
Looks like he can't read
We go to 'manpower' together
A big waste of time
So we try reschooling
We sit there doing the tests
Even with my help
He'll start at the bottom
Which is a bit of a blow
To both our esteems
His and mine
But the teachers try
And he hangs on
Until oddly a job shows up[1]

(H) CONCUSSIONS

A cluster of symptoms that may follow a head injury is called, in ICD-10, post-concussional syndrome though the accompanying text recognizes that its nosological status is controversial. The DSM-IV-TR (2000) lists it as 'post-concussional disorder' among a number of 'proposed categories' which, though not officially recognized, appear as aids to further study. The central feature of the proposed post-concussional disorder is 'an acquired impairment in cognitive functioning, accompanied by specific neurobehavioral symptoms, that occurs as a consequence of closed head injury of sufficient severity to produce a significant cerebral concussion' (p. 760). This may include loss of consciousness, amnesia after the trauma, and, occasionally, onset of seizures. Included in the tentative criteria are deficits in cognition, attention, and memory. Also for consideration are items like 'irritability or aggression on little or no provocation', 'affective lability', and 'social or sexual inappropriateness' (p. 760). It is important to note that 'substance-related disorders are frequently associated with closed head injury', and that 'closed head injury occurs more often in young males and has been associated with risk-taking behaviors' (DSM-IV-TR , 2000, p. 761).

Although it is the case that several group-based statistical studies have shown a link between neurological impairment and violence (e.g., Ferguson & Smith, 1996),[2] it needs to be remembered that such persons may be particularly likely to be identified by police or staff members at psychiatric facilities (see Blumenthal & Lavender, 2000, pp. 68–69).

NOTES

1   The assessor wonders about the effect of 'punches to the head'. In an earlier DSM psychiatric classification, use was made of the term 'minimal brain dysfunction'. It was applied to children when the assessor, often in the absence of hard evidence, nonetheless thought that brain damage might be a factor of note.
2   The MacArthur Study (see Section 7D) showed a significant correlation between any head injury and subsequent violence ($r =$. 10, see Table B.1, p. 165).

6

PSYCHOPATHS

BARNEY

He did twenty five long years
Some of them even on death row
For winning a shoot-out with a cop stateside
And a few   other things which we needn't go into
But he bade   his time and built his case
Which was   that at sixty he's burnt out
And deserves   another shot at the street
A sloppy file review helps
Reduce his perceived risk
And a couple of shrinks agree his force is spent
So out he   goes into, well, just about nothing
Except of   course B & E's and gun possession
So to our   amazement and the shoppers in the mall
He's again   involved in a shoot out
With a cop who happened by
Who said Barney was too old?[1]

In Chapter 5 it was made clear that mental health professionals rely heavily on either the ICD-10 or the DSM-IV-TR for making diagnostic decisions. It is the language through which clinicians communicate. Attention to symptomatologies of the many kinds can greatly sharpen treatment formulations and, in the context of the present book, help in assessing future risk for violence. It may therefore come as a surprise that perhaps the risk-assessment concept in most current common use within forensic and correctional practice is not part of the present behaviorally oriented DSM or ICD scheme.

Psychopathy was included as a major heading as sociopathic personality disturbance in the first edition of the *Diagnostic and Statistical Manual* of the

American Psychiatric Association (1952).[2,3] It stated that 'Individuals to be placed in this category are ill primarily in terms of society and of conformity with the prevailing cultural milieu, and not only in terms of personal discomfort and relations with other individuals' (p. 38). Yet the manual urged that psychiatrists realize that 'sociopathic reactions are very often symptomatic of severe underlying personality disorder, neurosis, or psychosis, or occur as a result of organic brain injury or disease' (p. 38). Only some components of the construct are captured under the antisocial personality disorder classification (see Note 3, Sub-section 5G).

More often than not, individuals qualify for not just one diagnosis but two or more categories concurrently. Having one disorder does not preclude having another. Often the clinician, acting as diagnostician, has to build a picture by 'ruling in' some disorders and 'ruling out' others, always being cognizant of the fact that diagnoses may change over time and according to altered circumstances. In the same way, it is possible, when the need arises, for the skilled clinician to 'build' the construct of 'psychopathy' from four listed DSM-IV-TR personality disorders – antisocial, borderline, histrionic, and narcissistic (Wulach, 1988, see Cluster B under Subsection 5G).

An easier and more direct approach to assessing psychopathy is to employ Hare's measure of psychopathy, the Psychopathy Checklist – Revised (PCL-R, 1991, 2003b). Hare's scheme was originally based on a text published by psychiatrist Hervey Cleckley in 1941 called *The Mask of Sanity*. Cleckley's very large contribution to present-day understanding of the term psychopathy derives in part from his ability to describe cases. He gives 13 of these in the fourth edition (1964) of his book. One of these is Max. Max is a small man. He is constantly in trouble with the law and with his wives (some of whom were acquired bigamously). Physically fit and agile he has ability as a boxer. His second wife, who keeps a first rate and highly reputable brothel, is his consistent support (though even she cools off for a period when he breaks her jaw). Mainly, he exists by fraudulence. He is constantly on the move. When he gets into a particularly tight corner he gains admission to the psychiatric hospital. Therein he is agreeable most of the time. When he gets bored he threatens to leave (until the doctors point out that if he does go anywhere it will be to prison). Although he is constantly in fights he does not get hurt much and, broken jaw to the wife aside, does not greatly injure others. He is often grandiose and his alleged history of having been at university in Heidelberg is open to challenge. From the file it looks as if he has a knowledge of the classics and Shakespeare but, according to Cleckley, this illustrates only the ignorance of the professionals who have been taken in by Max's pseudo-knowledge. Cleckley remarks about Max that he is lacking 'in the ability to see that others are moved. It is as though he were colorblind, despite his sharp intelligence, to this aspect of human existence. It cannot be explained to him because there is nothing in his orbit of awareness that can bridge the gap with comparison. He can repeat the words and say glibly that he understands, and there is no way for him to realize that he does not understand' (p. 58).[4]

Some several years later it fell to Robert Hare to carry on where Cleckley left off (see Hare, 1998a, for a description of how this came about). Hare set out to produce a measurement scheme based on Cleckley's compelling clinical observations along with his own. At one point his scheme contained 22 items (Hare, 1985). When finally formally published in 1991 this had been reduced to 20 on the basis of extensive statistical analysis. These 20 items remain unchanged in the latest 2003 version. The Hare PCL-R uses a scoring scheme of 0 (not present), 1 (possibly present), or 2 (definitely present). The items in the scheme are as follows: (1) glibness/superficial charm; (2) grandiose sense of self-worth; (3) need for stimulation/proneness to boredom; (4) pathological lying; (5) cunning/manipulative; (6) lack of remorse or guilt; (7) shallow affect; (8) callous/lack of empathy; (9) parasitic lifestyle; (10) poor behavioral controls; (11) promiscuous sexual behavior; (12) early behavior problems; (13) lack of realistic, long-term goals; (14) impulsivity; (15) irresponsibility; (16) failure to accept responsibility for actions; (17) many short-term marital relationships; (18) juvenile delinquency; (19) revocation of conditional release; and (20) criminal versatility. Readers will recognize that an assessment for psychopathy requires much more than use of a list of the kind given here.[5] With 20 items each possibly scored 2, the scale has an upper limit of 40. According to the manual, a score of 30 is required before the term psychopathy is applied.

The Hare PCL-R has been tested extensively on correctional, forensic, and general psychiatric populations. Although originally not intended as a risk-assessment device, its scores have shown remarkable correspondence with subsequent aggressiveness and violence (see Dolan & Doyle, 2000). A 12-item screening version (PCL:SV, Hart, Cox, & Hare, 1995) was developed in association with the MacArthur Study (discussed in Subsection 7D).[6] This is intended primarily for use with psychiatric populations. It has shown promise as part of violence-assessment schemes (e.g., Skeem & Mulvey, 2001).

Statistical and conceptual analyses have shown that the 20 items of the Hare PCL-R can be subsumed under two main dimensions: (1) affective/interpersonal and (2) antisocial/criminal dimension. Another analysis, based on the MacArthur data, has yielded three such dimensions: (1) arrogant and deceitful interpersonal style; (2) deficient affective experience; and (3) impulsive and irresponsible behavioral style (Cooke, 1999).[7] As well, one influential commentator, Sheilagh Hodgins (2003, personal communication), has argued that the 20 factors fall into five fairly distinct groups. These are: (1) history of criminality; (2) history of antisocial behavior; (3) impulsivity/sensation-seeking; (4) arrogant and deceitful interpersonal conduct; and (5) defective emotional experience. Clearly, more work remains to be done on isolating the key constructs within the psychopathy umbrella.[8]

NOTES

1   Barney had the motivation and skill to 'build his case' for parole. The 'sloppy file review' actually refers to some 'untidiness' in the administration of the G-SIR and its reporting. There is no reason to presume that all psychopaths 'burn out' as they age. Some may, but not all do.

2   DSM-I was 144 5.5 × 8.5 inches pages long. The definition section consisted of 32 pages. The balance was taken up mainly with how to record and report conditions. The DSM-IV-TR is 943 7 × 10 inch pages long. Some 700 of those pages are devoted to descriptions of disorders. DSM-I listed about 200 conditions; DSM-IV-TR offers about double that number.

3   The DSM-I category of 'antisocial reaction' referred to 'chronically antisocial individuals who are always in trouble, profiting neither from experience nor punishment, and maintaining no real loyalties to any person, group or code. They are frequently callous and hedonistic, showing marked emotional immaturity, with lack of sense of responsibility, lack of judgment, and an ability to rationalize their behavior so that it appears warranted, reasonable and justified' (p. 38). This description has considerable correspondence to the modern-day Hare Psychopathy Checklist – Revised (1991, 2003b).

4   Cleckley's inclusion of 'specific loss of insight' is of some interest. He says 'In a special sense the psychopath lacks insight to a degree seldom, if ever, found in any but the most seriously disturbed psychiatric patients ... He has absolutely no capacity to see himself as others see him. It is perhaps more accurate to say that he has no ability to know how others feel when they see him or to experience subjectively anything comparable about the situation' (1964, p. 383).

5   That is, assessors must follow carefully the item definitions provided in the manual. Most would-be evaluators these days accept specific instruction in the form of a two-day workshop on psychopathy led by the authors of the scheme or other clinicians well versed in it.

6   The 12 items in the screening version are as follows: (1) superficial; (2) grandiose; (3) deceitful; (4) lacks remorse; (5) lacks empathy; (6) doesn't accept responsibility; (7) impulsive; (8) poor behavioral controls; (9) lacks goals; (10) irresponsible; (11) adolescent antisocial behavior; and (12) adult antisocial behavior.

7   Cooke's model deletes items to do with offending (e.g., early behavioral problems, juvenile delinquency, criminal versatility). In this view, such a move 'has the advantage of removing items which could add circularity to the argument that psychopathy influences violence' (1999, p. 303).

8   Babiak and Hare (2006) remark that 'just having a psychopathic personality disorder does not make one a criminal. Some psychopaths live in society and do not technically break the law – although they may come close, with behavior that usually is unpleasant for those around them' (p. 19).

7

STUDIES

The important early work of Steadman and Cocozza (1974) which followed upon the release of Johnny Baxstrom was mentioned in Chapter 4. These authors showed that through actual follow-up in the community of persons earlier presumed 'dangerous' it is possible to detect 'false positive error'. In fact, of course, civil patients, those contained within the forensic mental health system, and prison inmates are not followed routinely after having been assessed for violence potential and data tend not to be amassed statistically. It is usually only when specific research or administrative studies are launched, often at great expense, that information is gained about rates of various kinds of recidivism. Such base-rate data, when they do become available, can be extremely helpful in guiding the conduct of risk assessments (Chapter 8 following). The point that needs to be stressed is that, whereas previous to the 1980s it was often presumed that base rates for many types of violence were too low for it to be possible to achieve much predictive accuracy, most modern studies based on all three settings of interest including those described in this chapter, show that base rates for violence are much higher than earlier thought.

In this restricted review, we concern ourselves with brief mention of four studies: two from the forensic field (Menzies & Webster, 1995; Quinsey, Harris, Rice, & Cormier, 1998, 2006); one drawn from the correctional literature (Hare, Clark, Grann, & Thornton, 2000); and one involving released civil psychiatric patients (Monahan et al., 2001). An international study is now beginning to contribute to the understanding of violence risk assessment and management (Hodgins et al., in press).

EDDIE

He thinks the shrink's a soft touch
And maybe he's right in a sort of way
Since he's obviously not really crazy
Just another 'personality problem'
Which is to say
Drinks too much
Has no job
Or any friends in particular
Not a great matrimonial bet
At fifty he's in bad shape
Sort of foggy in his thinking
Has no teeth
But here he is and it's cold outside
'Where next?' he asks and so do we.
There really isn't a great deal for him
Here or anyplace much else.[1]

(A) METROPOLITAN TORONTO FORENSIC SERVICE

The Metropolitan Toronto Forensic Service (METFORS) began providing assessment services to Toronto and area courts in 1977. Located in separate quarters within a large civil psychiatric hospital, it offered a multidisciplinary Brief Assessment Unit (BAU) and a 23-bed inpatient unit. The BAU at METFORS made it possible for the courts to remand from detention centers individuals whose fitness to stand trial[2] was in question. With some 600 persons sent for such one-day remands each year, METFORS was an ideal research site. This was especially so because some individuals could be studied in depth during the course of subsequent 30- or even 60-day inpatient assessments.

Although perhaps not vital to its main responsibility, 'dangerousness' emerged as a topic of keen interest at METFORS. It was possible to have members of the interdisciplinary team offer global judgments about possible future violence risk and to check those opinions against actual follow-up obtained two or more years later. Such studies revealed that, generally, prediction data averaged across clinicians could, if nothing else, exceed chance in their forecasts of subsequent violence (e.g. Sepejak, Menzies, Webster, & Jensen, 1983). Yet the correlations between predicted and actual outcome tended to be low, around 0.30 at best. Moreover, it became evident that some clinicians were more accurate predictors of subsequent violence than others (see especially Menzies & Webster, 1995). Much of this work was summarized in a book devoted to the topic (Webster, Menzies, & Jackson, 1982).

In an attempt to get beyond global predictions, interdisciplinary assessment schemes were devised at METFORS to ensure some consistency in ratings and to try to find out if particular factors might be shown to have power in this forensic remand population. The two schemes, which will not be described in much detail here, were the Dangerousness Behaviour Rating Scheme (DBRS) and the Interview Assessment Scheme (IAS). The former contained 23 items (many of which were originally proposed by Megargee, 1976). All of the DBRS and IAS items were defined in manuals. The DBRS items included 'passive aggressive', 'hostility', 'anger', 'rage', 'emotionality', 'guilt', 'capacity for empathy', 'capacity for change', 'control over actions', 'tolerance', 'environmental support', 'environmental stress', 'dangerousness increased with alcohol', and 'manipulativeness'. The 13 IAS items included 'greeting behavior', 'grooming appearance', 'eye contact', 'posturing', 'agreeability', 'verbal responses', 'patient control over interview', 'level of tension', and 'level of rapport'. Items from both devices were rated on some 160 remanded persons both by clinicians within the interdisciplinary team and by trained, uninvolved coders.[3] A seven-point scale was used for both schemes. After an interval of first two years (Menzies, Webster, & Sepejak, 1985a) and later after six years (Menzies, Webster, McMain, Staley, & Scaglione, 1994), the remandees were traced according to criminal justice, mental health, coroners' and other records.

These studies demonstrated that, in the main, items can be sufficiently well defined so that participating clinicians can use them reliably.[4] As was found in the other three studies covered in this chapter, violence levels were high. Of the nearly 160 subjects in the six-year follow-up, 140 engaged in at least one incident in the community, a prison, or a hospital (87 %). Thirty-nine were involved in 20 to 49 incidents and nine between 50 and 99.[5] Base rate figures for violent offenses were, of course, somewhat lower. Even so, nearly two-thirds (62 %) had at least one such violent incident. One person had 50. From the data it was also possible to find out *where* these violent incidents had occurred. These showed that per patient per year 3.4 occurred in hospital, 0.5 in prison, and 0.3 in the community. Of course, these levels will reflect not only actual occurrences but will also depend on the level of surveillance and scrutiny that was likely applied in the three different kinds of contexts.[6]

Generally speaking, the trained coders showed greater predictive accuracy than the interdisciplinary clinicians (with averaged prediction outcome correlations across the six years as follows: 0.16, 0.24, 0.18, 0.18, 0.16, and 0.15).[7] The best global prediction–outcome correlation achieved was +0.33. This was attained by pooling the scores of the three coders using data at year three of the six-year follow-up, a level almost exactly the same as that achieved after a two-year follow-up (Menzies et al., 1985a).

Although Menzies et al. (1994) and Menzies and Webster (1995) were aware of various limitations in their studies, the fact that they could not achieve a correspondence between prediction and outcome beyond 0.34 or so seemed a cause of some disappointment (Menzies et al., 1985b).[8] Yet the project did show that 'multiple-item prediction instruments (DBRS and IAS), though generally limited in predictive power and exceedingly low in clinical utility, did nevertheless in almost all instances, inspire more accurate forecasts than those offered by single-item clinical judgments alone' (Menzies et al., 1994, pp. 18–19). That is, the results seem to promise that if only the 'right' predictor items could be pinned down they would likely foster greater clinical predictive accuracy than simple low, medium, or high types of global clinical judgments.

Another finding of importance concerned the IAS scale. As will have been evident from the item titles noted above, these were posited as somewhat oblique possible predictors of violence. Yet, in fact, the scheme fared as well as did the DBRS. Menzies et al. (1994) say of this that: 'Certainly the IAS instrument, for all its 'indirectness', was no weaker than the to-the-point DBRS' (p. 18).[9] It needs to be recognized that the IAS items have a fugitive resemblance to the affective/ interpersonal (factor 1) items of the Hare PCL-R. Of course, the Hare PCL-R was not in formal existence in the late 1970s when the METFORS studies were laid down.

In stating it to be 'perhaps the most noteworthy findings of the entire study' (p. 19) Menzies and Webster drew attention to the context specificity of the obtained correlations. Considering only DBRS and IAS data from the clinically uninvolved coders, it was found that, over the six years of follow-up, there was not a single statistically significant effect[10] with respect to violent transactions occurring in the community. Respecting follow-up in prisons, there was only *one* significant effect. This was in a negative direction. Yet the two scales achieved far better results with respect to the prediction of *in-hospital* incidents. Over the six-year period the IAS showed positive correlations around 0.50 for general hospital incidents and 0.40 for violent transactions. The DBRS was not far behind with comparable correlations of 0.40 and 0.35. These levels peaked at the end of the second year. For the IAS these were 0.53 for general incidents and 0.39 for violent ones; for the DBRS they were 0.24 and 0.35. Results about context specificity from the METFORS studies allow us to reinforce a point about prediction specificity (see Chapter 3). The investigators had presumed that one set of variables would likely suffice for all three contexts. As already noted, the ideal prediction statement clarifies the nature of the context (i.e., specifies under what conditions violence should be anticipated). The DBRS and IAS variables, on re-examination, seem well suited to hospital-type settings. There is the additional point that, for these variables in a hospital-type context, the six-year time frame may have been altogether too long.[11] To an extent, then, the promise of the DBRS and IAS might have been more fully realized had all effort been applied to the hospital setting. Yet, coupled with findings from the study described immediately following, the METFORS studies had a large bearing on the development of structured assessment guides (Chapter 11).[12]

NOTES

1   Eddie is fairly typical of persons remanded by the courts for brief psychiatric assessments. The charge, unspecified here, was likely not particularly serious. He is probably at high risk for continued low-level violent conduct and, regrettably, he will continue to drift between the civil, forensic, and criminal justice systems.

2   In actual fact, METFORS also gave opinion about criminal responsibility status, 'dangerousness' (in Dangerous Offender hearings), sentence suitability, etc.

3   The clinicians did not rate the IAS, only the DBRS. The three coders rated persons according to both schemes.

4   By 'reliability' it is meant that Clinician A will score an item in the same way, or close to the same way, as Clinician B. It is *always* important to be able to show reliability when constructing and actually using rating schemes. Yet it can be a mistake to jettison a promising clinical construct, one with possible links to future violence, too prematurely. The obtainment of low inter-clinician agreement on an item might, in some circumstances, more properly signal the need for more concentrated efforts at description and measurement. Hare (2003a) would argue that this has been a failing in the DSM-IV-TR description of antisocial personality disorder, that the clinical indicators in psychopathy were jettisoned because they were more difficult to measure than were the behavioral aspects.

5   As well as this, there were 74 *threats* of violence while in the community. Most necessitated hospital contact (Menzies et al., 1994, p. 15).

6   In actual fact, the great preponderance of general incidents and violent transactions occurred in the community. Adjustments must though be made to take into account the opportunities available to commit violent acts. When these are made, the hospital came out as the most 'dangerous place'.

7   'Correlation' is a term in common use in the medical, health, and social sciences. It is an index of how closely two sets of scores relate to one another. Height, for example, correlates with weight and ingestion of sugar correlates with resting levels of blood glucose. A perfect positive correlation is defined as +1.0. That value cannot be exceeded. If there is absolutely *no* correlation between prediction and outcome (i.e., there is only a random relation between the two sets of scores), the correlation is zero. It is also possible to find *inverse* relations between prediction scores and outcome scores. These, at the extreme, reach −1.0 (for a perfect negative correlation). Some individual clinicians are capable of achieving such negative correlations between risk prediction and actual outcome.

8   Though in fact one influential commentator, Lee Robins (1991), noted that, all things considered, and given the complexity and difficulty of the prediction task, such correlations should be seen as encouraging starts for inspiring new research and clinical projects.

9   The quotation continues, though, as 'Whether it would be effective used singly, rather than in combination with the DBRS is unknown' (p. 18).

10 'Statistical significance' is a term used by researchers to indicate the level of probability that a result they have found would likely recur were the study to be repeated. When it is said, for example, that the level of significance is 0.05 it means that the chances are that the obtained result would occur 95 times out of 100. A higher standard would be 0.01, meaning that the obtained result would likely occur 99 times out of 100 repeated tests.

11 This is to say nothing of the possible unfairness to clinicians when researchers extend, as was done in the METFORS study, the duration of follow-up periods (i.e., clinicians should surely know well in advance what intervals they are predicting over, as well as the circumstances under which assessees will be living).

12 Referring to a related study based on a different group of remanded persons and published shortly after this one, Menzies and Webster (1995) offered the following comment: 'The comparative impotence of clinical assessments and actuarial instruments and the relatively superior predictive power exhibited by a handful of sociodemographic variables arguably represent the most compelling findings of this study' (p. 776).

BOB

His record is appalling
Takes your breath away
Stabbing and strangling
Sixteen year old boys
Is his greatest joy
Lots of other stuff too
Even escapes from prison
Not actually mentally ill
'Sadistic personality disorder'
Is what they've settled on
'Humane containment'
Will have to do
For now[1]

(B) OAK RIDGE, PENETANGUISHENE MENTAL HEALTH CENTRE

In 1993 Harris, Rice, and Quinsey published a paper which demonstrated clearly the potential predictive power of a dozen variables most of which are easy to obtain from the clinical record. They examined the fate of some 600 men, all of whom had been assessed for serious violent offenses within the Oak Ridge (high security) Division of the Penetanguishene Mental Health Centre in Ontario. About half of the men in this forensic sample were evaluated only. Once evaluated, they were returned to court and were dealt with by the CJS. The other half were retained in Oak Ridge and treated for at least two years. The investigators were at pains to collect outcome data from mental health, criminal justice, and other sources first at seven years post release and later at 10 years. The study is reported fully in Quinsey, Harris, Rice and Cormier, 1998 and more recently, (2006).

The predictor variables were compiled in the course of thorough file reviews. Research assistants, separate from those dealing with the outcome data, coded the files to extract information on a wide range of variables. With the two data sets complete it was then possible to correlate them and to perform a variety of other statistical manipulations. Out of this large array of data, the investigators were able to pinpoint 12 variables[2] which, taken together, showed reasonably acceptable correlations with outcome (around 0.45, and up to 0.53 in some subsamples).[3] As has been found in other similar studies, the overall level of violence was high during the follow-up periods (31 %). First to be noted is that the Hare PCL-R score topped the list of individual items with a correlation of 0.34. Next in line was elementary school maladjustment at 0.31 (see Quinsey et al., 2006, Exhibit 8.1, p. 162). Third was meeting criteria for any DSM-III[4] personality disorder at 0.26. Age at index offense was, as would be expected, negatively correlated with index offense (−0.26). A second childhood variable, separation from either parent except by death, showed the fifth highest correlation at 0.25. The sixth highest placed variable was failure on prior conditional release (0.24). Seventh was score on a nonviolent offense history scale (0.20). The other five variables achieved somewhat lower, though still significant, correlations with violent recidivism.[5,6]

The VRAG is generally thought of as being a 'prediction instrument' (see Blumenthal & Lavender, 2000, pp. 108–109). This is because, once the 12 items have been weighted according to results from the Oak Ridge research, it is possible to ascribe an individual to a particular future violence probability level according to his score. Harris et al. (1993) use nine 'bins' ranging from very low to very high VRAG scores. When actual violence during follow-up is plotted against the bins there is a striking effect, meaning that the graphed line shows that the higher the VRAG bin number, the higher the amount of violence detected during follow-up.[7]

Shortly after the Harris et al. (1993) paper was published, the main findings mentioned above were incorporated into a small text (Webster, Harris, Rice, Cormier, & Quinsey, 1994). This book discussed many of the same topics as the present one. But as well as offering what amounted to a 'repackaging' of the basic Harris et al. (1993) paper it laid out a scheme which clinicians might use to modify the VRAG probability level upward or downward but by no more than 10 % (p. 57). The so-called ASSESS-LIST scheme contained 10 items such as self-presentation, expectations and plans, symptoms, supervision, institutional management, and treatment progress. Although the idea of using dynamic, clinical, variables to adjust the VRAG-obtained future violence probability level seemed sensible at the time, it was correctly and emphatically retracted in the eventual book-length treatment of the VRAG research (Quinsey et al., 1998, 2006). There it was argued that the actuarial prediction is what it is and needs no modification (see Quinsey et al., 1998, p. 163; 2006, p. 197). Although the Penetanguishene group has made important contributions to the understanding of dynamic, clinical factors (e.g. Quinsey, Coleman, Jones, & Altrows, 1997; Quinsey et al., 1998, pp. 217–220; 2006, pp. 385–390), its main and uncompromising emphasis has been on the actuarial side.[8,9,10,11]

NOTES

1   The Oak Ridge Division of the Penetanguishene Mental Health Centre is a maximum security facility for men in Ontario. Bob is likely to be sent there by the court. It is a made-up vignette, representing no one in particular. It is included only to portray the kind of case for which there is no immediate solution beyond detention. Although he will be treated, it is unlikely, in view of his violence record, he will achieve some form of conditional release in the near future.

2   This does not mean to say that only 12 of the variables associated statistically with subsequent violence, only that these 12 were the most powerful.

3   Although this figure may seem high to some readers, it needs to be remembered that a correlation of 0.50 accounts for only 25 % of the total variance. It is also worth noting from the description in the previous section of the METFORS research that these investigators were able to demonstrate DBRS and IAS prediction–outcome correlations of this approximate magnitude in the hospital context.

4   Readers will note that the VRAG calls for DSM-III not DSM-IV-TR diagnoses. This is simply because the DSM-III, published in 1980, was the document then in official use.

5   The remaining five items are: never married (or equivalent) at 0.18; meets DSM-III criteria for schizophrenia at −0.17; most serious victim injury at −0.16; alcohol abuse score at 0.13; and finally, female victim in the index offense at −0.11. Full details are given in Quinsey et al., 2006 (see especially Chapter 8, Exhibit 8.1, p. 162). The fact that diagnosis of schizophrenia was negatively correlated with violence at outcome may have been due to the fact that, among other possible explanations, the group contained a large number of psychopathic patients and that, relative to them, those with a history of schizophrenia were less apt to recidivate violently.

6 It could also be that persons suffering from schizophrenia were at reduced risk for violence because of medications and other help they were receiving in the community. It is worth considering that, because by no means all schizophrenic patients were released from Oak Ridge, those retained had paranoid and other highly aggressive thoughts and tendencies (i.e., if released, might have been at elevated chance for violent recidivism). However this may be, we prefer to assume, along with Monahan et al. (2001), that some forms of schizophrenia carry with them at least minimal violence-enhancing potential (see Walsh et al., 2001).

7 While this is true, it needs to be remembered that the bulk of cases tended to have, as would be expected, moderate VRAG scores (i.e., bins 3, 4, 5, and 6). Such scores may not be as much use in prediction exercises as very high ones (e.g., bins 8 or 9) or very low ones (e.g., bins 1 or 2). Yet as would be expected from a normal distribution, the bins at the extremes contained relatively few cases. It is an example of how, sometimes, actuarial information is of little practical help to clinicians.

8 To address criticism that the VRAG's predictive power is limited largely to the long term. Harris, Rice, and Cormier (2002) published the results of a 'prospective' study based on a population entirely different from that reported formerly. Here they attempt to show that the VRAG's usefulness is not necessarily restricted to male accused persons who have committed highly serious offenses. Although some merit attaches to this supplementary venture, it still seems that they are attacking a 'straw clinician'. Nothing is said at all about the possible, admittedly not certain, value of *structured* clinical assessment procedures (see Chapter 11). Moreover, to call this study a prospective one is a stretch insofar as the results were extracted from previously compiled file information.

9 In fact, some of the publications from this group tend to be highly critical of clinical opinion. They argue, for example, that members of the Criminal Code Review Board making release decisions are too much influenced by the views of senior clinicians participating in hearings and too little by VRAG probabilities (Hilton & Simmons, 2001).

10 Another example of an actuarial scheme, one based on probationers, uses just six variables; (1) age in years; (2) gender; (3) number of youth custody sentences; (4) time in years since first conviction; (5) total number of court appearances and (6) type of offence (the Reoffender Group Recidivism Scale, OGRS, Copas & Marshall, 1998). These authors are able to demonstrate clear associations between OGRS scores and subsequent reoffending. Yet they remind would-be users, and us as authors of the present text that an actuarial 'score is not a prediction about an individual, but an estimate of what rate of recidivism might be expected of a group of offenders who match the individual on the set of covariants used by the score' (p. 170). And, helpfully, they add that the OGRS 'is a benchmark against which probation officers can check the subjective estimates that they have made in a particular case'

(p. 170). Finally, they put it well when they say that actuarial information can supply 'objective aid' and that 'The human mind, it seems, tends to give too much weight to anecdotal evidence and the individual instance, rather than a broad range of cases (p. 171).

11   See Hilton, Harris, and Rice (2006).

DAVE

Nice chap but got a fix on his daughter
All well and good and perhaps no harm done
But in fact he's been through all his women
She's just the last in the line or so it seems
Actually she and ma now wish they'd not turned him in
He's needed and loved at home so it would appear
And he sure doesn't see what all the fuss is about
No, definitely not nuts, no doubt about it
But the fact is it's against the law
So the poor sod of a judge can decide[1]

(C) ENGLISH PRISON SERVICE

The Hare et al. (2000) study centered on the predictive validity of the PCL-R but included use of other possible predictive scales and devices (i.e., the Level of Supervision Inventory – Revised, LSI-R, Andrews & Bonta, 1995; the Offender Group Reconviction Scale, OGRS-2, Taylor, 1999). The project, led by prominent internationally known researchers, was based on a population representative of the entire English prison system. In all, 728 adult males from seven different prisons were included. The PCL-R scores were made by prison psychologists trained by Hare and colleagues.

The study was reported in two parts. The first dealt with institutional infractions, the second with reconvictions following release into the community. Data on misconducts and infractions were available for some 650 men. Nearly half of the men, 46 %, had at least one reported misconduct (i.e., the base rate was high). Total PCL-R scores correlated significantly with total number of prison misconduct reports ($r = 0.31$). The correlation dropped progressively for assaults on staff ($r = 0.24$), property damage ($r = 0.18$), and assaults on inmates ($r = 0.15$). Those with institutional misconducts had significantly higher PCL-R scores than those without (mean scores were about 19 versus about 14. Of those with a PCL-R score of 30 or higher

75 % were responsible for at least one misconduct -42 % of these committed one or more assaults. Comparable figures for those with scores less than 30 were 44 % for misconducts and 16 % for assaults.[2]

The second part of the Hare et al. (2000) study was based on 278 offenders, members of the sample examined in the already-described first part, who were released into the community. Fifty-five of those scored 24 or higher and belonged to a high PCL-R group[3] and the remainder (223) were assigned to a low PCL-R group. The follow-up period was at least two years. During that time 48 % were convicted of at least one new offense. With respect to general offenses, the reconviction rate was 85 % for the high PCL-R group, contrasting with 40 % for the low PCL-R group. When it came to violent offenses the respective rates were 38 % versus 3 %.

It is now possible to ask how well the PCL-R fared relative to the LSI-R and the OGRS. Adding the PCL-R scores made a small (but significant) improvement in predictive power. Neither the LSI-R nor the OGRS associated significantly with violence. Yet the PCL-R did so. An important point from this research is that the affective/interpersonal dimension of the Hare PCL-R made as much or more contribution to predictive accuracy as the antisocial/criminal dimension (see Chapter 6).

There remains one more vital point to be made from the Hare et al. (2000) study. Some of these men were treated, others not. Generally speaking, treatment had little effect on either of the two groups. Yet if only factor 1 (interpersonal affective) scores were considered[5] a significant effect did emerge. Assuming, though, that the purpose of treatment is to reduce recidivism, the outcome was disquieting. Those persons who had *not* been treated achieved a reconviction rate of 59 %; those who *had* achieved a rate of 86 %. The result, in other words, though significant, was significant in the 'wrong' direction.[4,5]

NOTES

1 The narrative description draws out the awkwardness sometimes found in aligning values enshrined in the law with those bound in some family cultures.
2 When *all* types of misconduct were considered, however, the best predictor was not the PCL-R. Age and number of previous convictions were superior. Yet the PCL-R was the best predictor for *assault*, the variable of central interest in this text.
3 It is not unusual to use a PCL-R score of 25 as a cut-off for research purposes. In addition, British samples tend to score slightly lower than North American ones (see Hare et al., 2000, p. 634).
4 A similar result has been reported by Rice, Harris, & Cormier (1992).

5   Hare et al. (2002) comment 'It appears that prison treatment or vocational training served to increase the reconviction rates of offenders who were particularly callous, glib, deceptive, grandiose, manipulative, and remorseless as reflected in high Factor 1 scores' (p. 638). It may also be that 'psychopaths learn less about themselves than they do new ways of manipulating and deceiving others, and that they are able to convince therapists and staff that they have made good progress when in fact they have not' (p. 638).

IRMA

We've all told her
To get a grip on herself
These near daily threats
Of mutilation and suicide
Seems she's got everything
She could possibly need
Why then this insistence
On not deserving to live?[1]

(D) MACARTHUR

The project by Monahan et al. (2001) is fully prospective and based on over 1 000 psychiatric patients released from three separate American cities (Pittsburgh, PA; Kansas City, MO; and Worcester, MA).[2] Great attention was paid to the selection of possible predictor variables and the reliability and completeness of data collection. Patients ranged in age between 18 and 40 and had to have at least one diagnosis of the kind largely outlined in Subsections 5B, 5C, and 5D. Research interviewers were responsible for collecting data from patients admitted to hospital. Research clinicians used the DSM-IIIR (1987) to confirm diagnoses. Once released to the community the patients were interviewed by researchers up to five times during the year post discharge (i.e., about every 10 weeks). Most of these interviews were face to face.[3] As well as meeting with patients, the researchers also interviewed 'collaterals' (i.e., persons familiar with the individual such as family members, friends, professionals, and co-workers). Outcome information was obtained from hospital and arrest records. The most common incidents of violence involved patients hitting or beating another person (49 %). Weapon use and threats accounted for 29 %. Recipients of this violence tended to be spouses, other family members and boyfriends or girlfriends (p. 19). A full 75 % of incidents occurred in patients' residences or the homes of other persons (p. 21). Monahan et al. (2001) comment that 'it is striking that about one-fourth of the violent incidents (54 % of the 49 % where the patient reporting having a medication prescribed) involve a situation in which the patient was not taking a prescribed medication' (p. 22).

For the purposes of this summary, attention is restricted to simple correlation coefficients between the various predictive elements and violence outcome. With a sample of nearly 1 000 it is possible to achieve statistical significance with quite low correlations.[4] The highest single correlation listed in this study was 0.26 and was between outcome violence and score on the 12-item Hare PCL:SV. Next in line came various measures of previous violence history (e.g., adult arrest – seriousness at 0.25, adult arrest – frequency at 0.24, recent violent behavior at 0.14; official report of any arrest for a person crime at 0.13; any arrest for another crime at 0.11). A third variable was chart diagnosis of antisocial personality disorder at 0.19. A fourth set of variables related to family, sociocultural factors (e.g., father ever used drugs = 0.16; father ever arrested = 0.15; father ever excess drinking = 0.11). A fifth group related to early childhood experiences (e.g., seriousness of abuse as child at 0.14; frequency of abuse as child at 0.12). A sixth category related to recorded substance abuse[5] at the time of admission (0.14). Any drug at time of admission yielded 0.12 and cocaine specifically correlated at 0.11. A seventh category was any head injury at 0.10.[6]

One of the intriguing findings of the MacArthur study was that delusions while in hospital largely did not correlate with post-release violence. This held for any delusions and various specific ones. Where there were weak associations they were small and in a negative direction. This Monahan et al. (2001) finding flies in the face of 'popular wisdom'. The authors, though, point out that their recent observation 'should not be taken as evidence that delusions never cause violence. It is clear from clinical experience and from many other studies that they can and do' (p. 77).

Some of the MacArthur findings were against expectations. Earlier work by this group has suggested the possible importance of a phenomenon called 'threat-control override', TCO (see Link, Monahan, Stueve, & Cullen, 1999). A TCO delusion is said to be present if persons have ever reported having a belief that other individuals were attempting to harm them or that outside forces were in control of their minds. Yet in the actual MacArthur study this yielded a significant though small negative correlation with subsequent violence (−0.10). Another unanticipated finding was that violence was enhanced by having more, not fewer, mental health professionals in the social network (−0.10). These two last-mentioned findings point up difficulties entailed even in large-scale undertakings. Seemingly sound hypotheses not only fail to be supported but in fact can yield results opposite to those expected.[7]

An extremely important finding from the MacArthur study centered on the relationship between diagnosis of mental disorder and substance abuse taken together and pitted against subsequent violence. There were nearly 400 patients who had a diagnosis of mental disorder (schizophrenia, depression, delusional disorder, etc.) without a diagnosis of substance abuse or dependence. A similar-sized group had both diagnoses. A third group of about 140 had a diagnosis of 'other mental disorder' (e.g., personality or adjustment disorder and 'suicidality') with substance abuse or dependence. The rate of violence over the one year of follow-up was 18 % for the group with major mental disorder but no substance problem. The group with both reached 31%. But the third group showed a rate of 43 %. This observation points to the utter necessity of considering possible predictor variables *in combination*, not singly. While it may well be true that, broadly, violence risk factors are additive in the sense that the more the number identified the higher the risk (Hall, 2001), it remains vital to be able to consider how specific candidate factors not only apply but also interact with one another in the particular case. A simple additive model will likely not suffice. It is this reality that has drawn the MacArthur group to espouse complex approaches to violence decision making (i.e., interactive classification tree, ICT, see Monahan, Steadman, Robbins et al., 2005).

Although future violence can be to some limited extent forecast through reliance on the 'additive principle', it seems more and more likely that some way will have to be found to integrate a large number of potentially highly *fluctuating* variables (see Monahan et al., 2001, p. 142). The MacArthur solution has been to suggest that this task is one ideally suited to computer programming. If the 'right' variables can be selected in the first place, measured accurately and consistently, then it ought to be possible to create and test 'multiple models' that would have not just general scientific interest but would have pertinence to the individual clinical case at hand. Certainly, Monahan et al. (2001) are of the view that, given our emerging understanding about the complexity of the violence prediction and assessment tasks, clinicians in the future 'will need to have computer support available' (p. 143). And they remind us that 'At best, predictions will involve approximations of the degree of risk presented by a person, presented as a range rather than a single number, with the recognition that not every person thus classified, even one accurately determined to be in a high risk group, will commit a violent act' (p. 143). The MacArthur group has now published its own violence risk assessment device (Monahan et al., 2005). This they classify as an 'actuarial' device and call it the Classification of Violence Risk (COVR). Based on their ICT work, they offer a software program to assist in the violence assessments of about-to-be released civil patients in the United States. The authors see this as a work in progress, one that needs additional support from research studies.

NOTES

1   Irma reminds us that, aside from trying to prevent violence against others, clinicians who work with patients, prisoners, and parolees also have to worry about suicide risk.

2 A four-country study by Hodgins involving both civil and forensic patients awaits final publication (see Hodgins et al., in press).

3 It is most interesting to note that it took an average of seven contacts to get the first interview done. This speaks partly to the heroic efforts required in studies of this kind. It is also a commentary on the fluidity of these persons' lives. A total of 951 completed one or more follow-up interviews. Only 564 completed all five. From the starting total of 1 136, 185 were lost to follow-up, yielding a follow-up sample of 951 (see Table A.2, p. 160). This points to the issue of how difficult it is to collect base rate data (Chapter 8).

4 That a correlation is small does not mean that it does not describe an important effect. The correlation between smoking and lung cancer is very small and would not likely be detected statistically without the aid of very large samples. Although the overall effect size is small from a statistical point of view, it is one with potentially crucial implications for individuals trying to decide whether to smoke or not.

5 More specific analyses based on research clinicians' DSM-III diagnoses of alcohol or drug abuse yielded a 0.18 correlation with violence during follow-up.

6 It is of some interest to try to link the MacArthur findings to the HCR-20 scheme discussed more fully in Chapter 11. Some of the HCR-20 items received support, some did not. Some HCR-20 items were not addressed (N/A). Appendix B of the MacArthur report allows rough comparisons (pp. 163–168). In the following we cite what seems to be the highest listed correlation and refer it to the HCR-20 item:

H1, Previous Violence (0.25, $p < 0.001$);
H2, Young Age at First Violent Incident (N/A);
H3, Relational Instability (Ever Married, not significant, NS);
H4, Employment Problems (NS);
H5, Substance Use Problems (0.14, $p < 0.001$);
H6, Major Mental Illness (-0.19, $p < 0.001$);
H7, Hare PCL:SV Psychopathy (0.26);
H8, Early Maladjustment (0.14, $p < 0.001$);
H9, Personality Disorder (0.19, $p < 0.001$);
H10, Prior Supervision Failure (N/A);
C1, Insight (N/A, though it should be noted that the Mini Mental Status, and the Global Assessment of Functioning yielded no significant correlations). The Brief Psychiatric Rating Scale of Overall and Gorham (1988) showed small effects, some in a negative direction;
C2, Attitudes, Non Violent Aggression in the record (0.06);
C3, Symptoms (paranoid delusions, hallucinations, decompensation and bizarre behavior from the record yielded small but significant negative correlations around -0.09);
C4, Impulsivity (Barratt Motor Impulsivity, 0.07, $p < 0.05$).
C5, Treatability (N/A);

R1, Plans (N/A);

R2, Destabilizers (living alone, -0.07, $p < 0.05$);

R3, Support (percentage of mental health professionals in social network, -0.10; number of negative persons in social network, 0.07, both $p < 0.05$);

R4, Noncompliance with Remediation Attempts (medicine noncompliance -0.07, $p < 0.05$ but note that violent incidents were apt to occur when persons were not taking prescribed medication – see p. 22 of the Monahan et al. 2001 text); and

R5, Coping (perceived stress, 0.08, $p < 0.02$).

7   A strong point of the MacArthur write-up is that, throughout, the authors do not overassert their findings and give weight, where due, to clinical experience and opinion. They also offer useful explanations for negative results. For example, with respect to the small negative correlation between number of persons in the social network and subsequent violence, they follow Estroff, Zimmer, Lachicotte, and Benoit (1994) in suggesting that 'delusions are often associated with chronic psychotic conditions, which are frequently attended by social withdrawal and the development of smaller networks' (p. 78).

8

BASERATES

INGE

She's been in and out of hospitals for years
Still young and decidedly good looking
    Four marriages
      Two kids.
      But wants
      A lot
    Out of one relationship
And her men don't seem to match up quite
Which is to say they're like most people
When they don't come through she gets mad
Invents queer schemes which come back on her
That's why she's under lock and key right now
'Prognosis guarded' which means she might make it[1]

> A wide variety of clinical, theoretical (both basic and applied) statistical, and operational skills are required to conceptualize, operationalize, design, conduct and analyze the kind of research that would give new life to the field of actuarial risk assessment.
>
> (Monahan, 1981, p. 12)

From the preceding chapter it is evident that the METFORS study, the Penetanguishene study, the English Corrections study, and the MacArthur study all yielded higher rates of violence for particular subsamples than might have been expected. As already noted, it has been this realization that has made it possible to move toward the creation of practical assessment and prediction devices. These four studies are, of course, merely representative of the vast amount of information that is accumulating on the topic of violent recidivism in civil, forensic, and criminal justice populations.

Trying to establish the 'true baserates' for persons with different mental and personality disorders is a very difficult task.[2] People continually move back and forth between the civil, forensic, and criminal justice systems. Since record-keeping systems are rarely interlinked, it takes mammoth undertakings to 'capture' the right records for the right time periods. As was found in the MacArthur study, the attrition rate over one year of post-discharge follow-up was high. There can then be difficulties due to inaccuracy, vagueness, and incompleteness in diagnosis.[3] We learn, for example, that even highly seasoned clinicians tend to miss substance abuse disorders in the course of diagnosing major mental disorders (Bryant, Rounsaville, Spitzer, & Williams, 1992). Changes in law alter the types of persons inducted into the three main systems considered in this book. It had an effect in Canada when in 1992 the Mental Disorder provisions of the *Criminal Code* were altered. Since far more persons have subsequently become forensic 'accused persons' on the basis of relatively less serious offenses, earlier baserates might or might not have applicability in the present. There is, as well, the problem that diagnostic categories change over time (e.g., as with the progression from DSM-I to DSM-IV-TR). Theoretical influences wax and wane. In a few cases, newly available medications can definitely reduce the prevalence of some disorders.[4] There is, too, the fact that some 'diagnoses' are more or less 'attributions', rather than careful matchings of characteristics against clearly stipulated criteria and the exercise of skilled clinical-scientific judgment. Much crime, including violent crime, is concealed and more or less undetected. As infants evolve into childhood, children move into adolescence, and adolescents enter adulthood, the types of factors that might be important at one stage may have little relevance at another. For these and many other reasons, dependable 'baserates', though much called for as part of the decision-making process, are hard to achieve.[5,6]

NOTES

1   With the increasing publication of large data sets and manualized norms, it becomes easier than formerly to use epidemiological data to assist in the assessment process. Yet Inge's case is unusual. Outside postpartum depression, which does not apply in this case, data on samples of women who kill their young infants are hard to come by. This does not mean that the clinician should not locate what studies or case reports are on hand (e.g. Bourget & Bradford, 1990; Resnick, 1970; Spinelli, 2003).

2   One of the best ways of approaching this matter entails carrying out wide-scale longitudinal follow-up studies of large unrelated populations. Several of these have reached fruition in recent years. Readers interested in this approach should consult Hodgins and Janson's (2000) account of the Stockholm Metropolitan Project. This provides an excellent review of similar studies by a variety of researchers in several different countries (see pp. 10–28 in particular). The

Stockholm Project, possibly because of the way records are maintained in that city, is based on over 15 000 persons followed from fetal existence to age 30.

3 Recently Padgett, Webster, and Robb (2005) pointed out reasons why it can be virtually impossible in some cases to retrieve the kinds of information demanded for inclusion in standard devices for actuarially driven violence assessment schemes (e.g., refugees who have no records, 'bureaucratic glaciality', 'sanitization', 'purging', etc.).

4 An example might be the DSM-IV-TR diagnostic category of sexual dysfunctions. At least some of these conditions have recently come to be markedly alleviated by viagra and other such medications.

5 Consider, for example, persons diagnosed with antisocial personality disorder (APD). The DSM-IV-TR places the prevalence of APD in community samples to be around 3 % in men and 1 % in women. This rate is said to be higher in clinical samples, anywhere from 3 to 30 %. The manual goes on to say that: 'Even higher prevalence rates are associated with substance abuse treatment settings and prison or forensic settings' (p. 704). This helps point up the difficulty of establishing, when considering the individual case, a comparison group that is truly equivalent.

6 It is possible, though, to wonder why clinicians or board decision makers should ever improve their predictive capacities in the absence of statistical information about offenses and incidents post release. Consider, for example, a review board which has to grant absolute discharges to some individuals without basic statistical knowledge of the failure rate of persons so discharged into similar situations in previous years.

9

FACTORS

ZACK

At twenty-six Zack's had 'em all, some time or other
Mental handicap, psychotic, immature, unstable, without conscience
And a whole lot more over his short span of life
Incapable of living out there he even tries to break into jail
Once inside he gets beaten up and then lashes out in anger
But then along comes
Staff guy who takes
A special interest
In his terrible plight
Decides to pitch in
Finds him some place to live, organizes his money
Sees him every day, gives him at least a few quick minutes
Weighs in on his behalf, ensures he gets his meds
Strangely, Zack quits fighting, begins to cope in a limited way
Hey, with a little bit of luck he might stay the course.[1]

> The goal is to assess factors that led the individual to be aggressive in the past, ascertain how many of these factors are amenable to change, and then to intervene to alter the triggering factors so that the risk of violence is reduced.
>
> (Pagani & Pinard, 2001, p. 18)

It would be highly surprising if the studies mentioned in the previous section, and others like them, had yielded a set of factors which were strongly and reliably associated with violence across the CMHS, the FMHS, and the CJS. To think that a single factor,[2] or a few factors,[3] might be able to achieve this would be naive. Yet from research conducted over the past two or three decades it has become increasingly clear that some factors simply cannot be left out of account. Several factors, which likely have a bearing on successful release decision making, were discussed over 20 years ago by Monahan (1981,[4] e.g.; sex, age, previous violence, socioeconomic status, opiate or alcohol abuse, etc.). As well, though, as beginning to mark out a structure for violence risk evaluation, Monahan made the key point that 'more information does not necessarily lead to better predictions ... Focusing on a limited number of *relevant* and *valid* predictor items, therefore, is more important than an exhaustive examination that yields much irrelevant and ultimately confusing information' (pp. 125–126). It is necessary, too, not to be overly influenced by information that possesses high accuracy but little actual pertinence to violence prediction generally or to the case at hand in particular (see Haynes, 1985). A major advance in thinking over recent years is related to the idea that caution is required when considering violence risk factors in isolation. As Monahan et al. (2001) have remarked: 'Advances in understanding or predictive accuracy are more likely to come from efforts to assess the interactions among substantial numbers of variables associated with violence' (p. 142). In the same kind of way, in the context of parole supervision, Zamble and Quinsey (1997) put it well when they state 'The amount of drinking or drug use and the way they fit into the pattern of other behavior are more important than just the failure to maintain abstinence' (p. 148). Nonetheless, there is no harm in recognizing that a few variables have shown some consistent ability to relate to subsequent violence. Consider, for example, psychopathy as measured by the Hare PCL-R (1991, 2003b). Although, as noted in Chapter 6, this is a complex variable relying on two (Hare, 1991, 2003b), or three (Cooke, 2006), or five (Hodgins, 2003, personal communication) elements, it does associate with violence in different contexts.[5] Early childhood factors cannot easily be dismissed. The same can be said for a clear diagnosis of antisocial personality disorder. The evidence that the violence potential of persons with schizophrenia is markedly enhanced with a concurrent diagnosis of substance abuse is now incontrovertible. It remains true that a history of violence associates with present and future violence. Studies that fail to show such an effect are in the distinct minority. Such basic information should obviously not be ignored by practicing clinicians and decision makers. Although it may be alluring to think that these awkward decision-making activities will eventually come to be aided by computers and while important strides are being made in this direction (e.g. Monahan et al., 2005), it will be some time before these now-developing schemes are substantiated. In the meantime, there will likely have to be reliance on structured guides and the like (see Chapter 11).

In one of the METFORS projects noted in Subsection 7A, the authors complained that the participating clinicians did not place reliance on such variables as were found in the study to possess predictive power (i.e., they tended to rest their judgments on factors with little or no predictive strength). One reason for writing books on the present topic is to draw out variables which, at the present time,[6] appear to have explanatory or predictive power. This would seem to be necessary as despite what is reasonably well-confirmed published information about risk factors, clinicians may not use it to best advantage. Elbogen, Mercado, Scalora, and Tomkins (2002) obtained responses from 134 CMHS and FMHS professionals on a form that listed 53 possible risk items. These items were derived from several sources including the VRAG, the HCR-20, and the MacArthur study. They found that 'nearly every clinician perceived dynamic, behavioral variables to be *significantly more relevant* than research-based factors' (p. 43, original emphasis).[7] Another observation was that even though psychopathy has been found to be a significantly strong predictive risk factor in the violence literature it 'was *not* perceived by clinicians to be one of the most relevant of risk factors in clinical practice, regardless of profession, psychiatric facility or treatment context' (p. 44, original emphasis). It is also interesting to note that early maladjustment was the lowest rated of the 15 HCR-20 items included in the survey.[8] This is despite the fact that most contemporary wide-scale studies ascribe it great importance (e.g. Hodgins & Janson, 2002).[9]

NOTES

1   This is based on a previously published account by Ryan (1997). Several risk factors seem to be operating. Zack has learning difficulties. This places him at risk for being victimized. He is devoid of support and has very limited ability to care for himself until the psychologist decides to take him on. A key strength factor is the formation of a 'therapeutic alliance' (see Webster et al., 2004). According to the account, much was accomplished by offering small practical steps on the one hard (learning theory) within the context of a supportive relationship (phenomenological point of view).

2   Rodale (1968) is an example of such thinking. He asserts that much criminal behavior is due to the malignant effects of sugar. His book draws together an impressive array of evidence in support of his case. Unfortunately, this is largely anecdotal. High levels of blood glucose levels will be 'causative' of violence in particular instances. There will be at least a few such cases. But inductions from a few limited cases, no matter how startling, will be highly misleading when applied wholesale to large subpopulations.

3   Hellman and Blackman took a step in this direction when, in 1966, they opined in the *American Journal of Psychiatry* that three variables would fit the bill. These were firesetting, enuresis, and cruelty to animals. The 'triad' was purported to have strong associations with violence in adulthood.

4   Monahan considered major mental disorder to be a 'non-correlate' of violence in his 1981 text. In light of his own subsequent findings from the MacArthur project and other recent studies he has had to revise this view. It is instructive to think that after a span of merely two decades on so it has been important and necessary to make such a central revision in light of accumulated scientific findings and professional opinion.

5   It may be that the 'success' of this variable has to do in part with the fact that its items have each been clearly defined, manualized, researched, and 'metricized'. Perhaps if other clinical constructs were to be accorded the

same attention, they would have similar capabilities (e.g. impulsivity, treatability, compliance, supportiveness, etc.).

6   It is hard to see how there ever could be a 'permanent' scheme. The nature of mental and personality disorder changes over time according to cultural, economic, scientific, and other wide-scale influences. Laws change. Diagnostic schemes alter. Dreadful events can more or less create new categories of disorder overnight. The very words 'violence' and 'terror' acquire new meanings as a result of monstrous happenings.

7   Of course, it may well be that clinicians are not wrong in placing their emphases where they do. Just because certain research-based variables have been demonstrated to show this or that correlation with outcome, does not mean that certain more clinical variables, granted better definition and standardization, might not perform in superior ways both with respect to group-based statistical studies and as applied to individual clients. The Elbogen et al. (2002) paper is helpful in showing that clinicians in different settings accord different weights to key variables.

8   By a substantial margin. It had a mean score of 5.1, the next lowest was employment problems at 6.7. Top of this list was previous violence at 9.6.

9   Although not all violence in adults can be traced to difficulties encountered in childhood or adolescence, a good deal of it can. Hodgins and Janson (2002) distinguish three main groups: stable early-start offenders, adolescent-limited offenders, and adult-start offenders (pp. 11–16). These authors describe early starters as those who show a stable pattern of antisociality which persists throughout the child's life. They note that 'While the antisocial behaviours change with age, the persistence is remarkable' (p. 11). Referring to Hodgins' earlier work they say: 'These individuals are at very high risk of becoming recidivistic adult offenders' (p. 11). Hodgins and Janson make it clear that findings from longitudinal follow-along studies conducted in a wide range of countries converge in showing this persistence of antisociality. Generally, the 'baseline level' for such persistent antisociality is around 5 % in boys and much lower in girls. What is truly surprising in this group is the unchanging course of unacceptable conduct over time and circumstances. This is despite rehabilitative efforts and imposition of sanctions. Referring to their own 30-year follow-up study conducted in Stockholm, they tell us that: 'While only 6.2 % of all males in the cohort, these early-start offenders were responsible for 70% of all crimes and 71 % of all the violent crimes committed by males in the cohort' (p. 12). These boys were neither mentally ill nor mentally retarded. The comparable girls, though constituting only 0.4 % of the total early-starter cohort, carried out one-third of all the eventual crimes committed by females (and 30 % of the violent ones). From a violence risk assessment point of view, Hodgins and Janson (2002) can hardly be wrong when they say: 'In our attempt to understand the criminality of persons with major mental disorders, it may be of importance to verify whether they displayed patterns of antisocial behaviour or aggressive behaviour or both in childhood' (p. 15).

The second typology offered by Hodgins and Jansen, adolescent-limited offenders, refers as their term suggests, to more or less expected transitory antisociality. When such adolescents do commit crimes, such infractions tend to be of a minor nature. Family and peer influences seem to be important and, generally speaking, most of this aberrant conduct dissipates on or before entry into adulthood. Those in the third category, adult-start offenders begin their criminal activities after the age of 18. In the Stockholm study, some 13 % of young men and 3.5 % of young women, those without mental retardation or illness, fit the pattern.

10

DEBATES

The computers run numerical models of
  the atmosphere and then spit forecasts
back out to regional offices, where they
  are amended by local meteorologists.
Humans still 'add value' to a forecast,
  as meteorologists say. There is an
intuitive element to forecasting that even
  the most powerful computers cannot
  duplicate.

Junger, S. (1997) The Perfect
  Storm: a true story of Men Against the Sea,   [1]
  pp. 126–127. (New York: W.W. Norton, by permission).

> The dichotomizing of actuarial and clinical approaches to risk assessment, in which
> the clinical approach has been equated with subjective judgement, has been unhelpful.
> (Blumenthal & Lavender, 2000, p. 79).[2]

In this chapter we give brief attention to two rather different kinds of 'debates'. The first,
known as the 'clinical versus actuarial', pits the relative importance of 'static', more or
less unchanging variables, against the more fluid 'dynamic' ones often encountered in
daily clinical practice. We argue that this debate's main importance lies in its ability to
galvanize certain kinds of research and to exert pressure to achieve the highest
professional and ethical standards.[3] The second type of debate refers to everyday
struggles in courtrooms and review boards where one side or party locks in debate over
the relative merits of the evidence being produced in the case as well as other broad-
scale legal and administrative issues. These dialectics are not likely to disappear any
time soon and, in any event, they do have the merit of frequently inducing clinicians to
give their very best thought to the matters at hand (see Ægisdóttir, Spengler, & White,
2006 and related papers for recent extended commentary). Argument in these formal
arenas allows us to make the point that violence potential and its absence are to an extent

'constructed' by opposing parties and that the processes which underlie these constructions have a large practical bearing on the kinds of decisions that are actually made (see Pfohl, 1978; Menzies, 1989).

The word 'actuarial' has a certain appeal, grounded as it is in the world of economics, finance, and insurance. Actuarial analyses can yield information of enormous importance when it comes to making business decisions. Medical insurance premiums are based on experience with hundreds of thousands of cases. The underwriters have come to know what factors to look for in predicting ill health: gender, age, smoking habits, alcohol use, etc. To be able to be profitable, the companies do not need massive amounts of background information. They tend to require, say, a dozen pieces of information for standard out-of-country medical travel insurance. Because of the large numbers of persons involved in the samples at the insurance companies' disposal, and the powerfulness of the effects of certain key variables taken in isolation or combination, they can ensure a profit while remaining competitive with organizations offering similar products. The insurers expect to be 'wrong' in a certain percentage of cases. Although they work to keep claims to a minimum, they are consoled by the fact that the great bulk of people who buy travel insurance do *not* become ill while away from home. That Mr. Smith or Ms. Brown were ones who became ill whereas Ms. Grey and Mr. Jones did not, is of very little if any interest to the company's high-level executives.

The word actuarial used in the context of violence decision making is given, perhaps, a greater 'certainty' than is intended. While it is true that the whole basis of actuarial science is founded on probability theory; the term can be slightly misleading when applied to the kind of complex clinical, forensic, and correctional issues at the core of this text. In the first place, most of the recently published detailed studies on violence prediction are based not on thousands of cases but on hundreds. In the second place, it is becoming ever clearer that violence risk factors operate in concert, that it is very unrealistic and naive to search for a few variables which alone can predict particular types of violence. As was made clear in the previous chapter, it is important, for example, to consider how various kinds of mental or personality disorder interact with particular patterns of substance abuse. In the third place, a point already made in Chapter 3, *assessment* is the foremost task in day-to-day clinical practice. Prediction tends to be a secondary, though often important consideration, if only because it helps sharpen thinking about what strategies might be necessary to minimize violence risk in the particular case. In the fourth place it is not actually possible always to distinguish between actuarial and clinical variables in this sphere. Beyond a few 'tombstone' data, many of the variables which end up in schemes like the VRAG and the H10 scale of the HCR-20 depend completely on data obtained and interpreted clinically (e.g., diagnosis of mental and personality disorder, measures of psychopathy, seriousness of addiction or dependence).

It should not be mistakenly thought that decision makers are here being advised not to use group-based statistical data as a guide to release decision making. It is important to know about base rate data.[4] In violence risk assessment it can be very helpful to be able to estimate an individual's possible failure or success rates relative to individuals with many of the same basic characteristics. It is simply argued that 'the power of the numeric' not overwhelm consideration of seemingly applicable variables that may have a bearing on the case at hand (see Webster, Hucker, & Bloom, 2002).[5] The setting quote to this section by Sebastian Younger is included to emphasize the idea that both actuarial *and* clinical approaches are necessary, a point made more formally by Monahan and Steadman (1996).

NOTES

1 Junger's description of weather forecasting in his novel fits our outlook well. Both actuarial and dynamic factors have to be taken into account when completing violence risk assessments.

2 In their otherwise excellent text, Blumenthal and Lavender (2000) state, correctly or incorrectly, that 'The HCR-20 is probably the best known risk assessment instrument' (p. 105). They are definitely not right, however, in describing the HCR-20 as an 'actuarial scheme' (p. 105). The HCR-20 does not purport to be such. While it may be that at some future juncture, researchers with actuarial leanings will attempt to amass data to produce such a synthesis, this was not an aim of those who proposed the scheme. An incidental point is that Blumenthal and Lavender refer to the HCR-20 as a 'checklist', which, again, it is not (see Webster, Müller-Isberner, & Fransson, 2002).

3 Litwack (1993) was inspired to ask 'what *ethical* principle is violated if, in making the assessment, a mental health professional makes a conscientious effort to obtain and analyze all relevant data (both clinical and actuarial, when the latter is available), is forthright in describing and explaining the facts and logical inferences upon which her or his assessment is based, and is careful not to knowingly exaggerate (or minimize) the degree of risk the person being assessed appears to pose?' (p. 481, original emphasis).

4 As noted in Chapter 8, dependable base rate data are often hard to obtain. These and other matters are helpfully discussed by Hamilton (2001).

5 The point is well made by Dickey (2000) who, after noting the importance of information gained from actuarial devices in formulating opinion about parole-release decision, goes on to say: 'Yet case-specific factors can by no means be ignored. At least occasionally, they give true pause for a quite different level of concern. At other times, they add to effective risk management strategies, one which would not be evident from the statistical scores alone' (p. 170).

GUIDES

PROFESSOR

Staggers into our weekly class
Plunks an armload of books on the table
Each with pieces of paper sprouting out
To mark the important passages
He has a mind to elucidate
[This before the age of yellow stickies]

But the books remain unopened
Instead he talks about what's on his mind today
And invariably succeeds in drawing us in
Using our naïve comments and off-point questions
To open doors yielding unanticipated vistas
[Surely he invented 'lateral thinking']

SERGEANT

Our sergeant who has seen actual enemies
Judging by the proclaiming ribbons
Goes about his much-practiced spiel
Aided by his well-honed 'lesson-plan'
Ideal method for recruits like us
There's only one way of getting a machine gun to bits
Or of extracting a jammed bullet
It's utterly step by essential step
He drills mnemonic devices into us
To aid in this difficult dangerous task[11.]

The guidelines attempt to define the risk being considered, discuss necessary qualifications for conducting an assessment, recommend what information should be considered as part of the evaluation and how it should be gathered, and identify a set of core risk factors that, according to the scientific and professional literature, should be considered as part of any reasonably comprehensive assessment.

(Kropp, Hart, & Lyon, 2002, p. 606)

In 1996 Randy Borum published a highly influential paper on the topic of improving the clinical practice of violence risk assessment in the journal, *American Psychologist*. This paper reviewed the DBRS, the VRAG, the HCR-20, and some other schemes. While not overstating the case, he made it clear that, even at that time, there was evidence that structured approaches to violence risk assessment were beginning to pay off and that, likely, their full potential remained to be exploited. His eventual conclusion, which bears restating here, was: 'Given the ethical and legal obligations to appropriately assess and manage persons at risk for violence, more attention in each of the mental health disciplines needs to be given to improving technology and instrumentation[2] to aid in these assessments, defining clinical practice guidelines, and training professionals[3] in these critical tasks' (p. 954). Recently the American Psychological Association itself has commented at length on evidence-based practice (2006). Its views accord well with those expressed in most structured professional judgment (SPJ) guides that deal with violence risk and management.

The influence of Hare's PCL-R (1991; 2005) on research and practice within the civil, forensic, and criminal justice systems has been remarkable over the past decade or longer. But aside from its originally unforeseen tendency to associate with outcome violence, it has also affected the way violence assessment schemes have developed in recent years. What has been important is that a *manageable* number of *definable* items have been manualized to the point where they can be researched and, with the aid of training sessions, be put at the disposal of clinicians (cf., Kazdin, 1997). Psychopathy, a clinical construct, has been pinned down in a scheme that is actually useable. Without denying that it takes considerable time, effort, and clinical skill to complete a defensible Hare PCL-R evaluation, the fact is that clinical and research experience over recent years has demonstrated that the psychopathy construct 'works'. Part of this likely has to do with 'instrumentation'. Twenty items scored 0, 1, or 2, represent the kind of realistic task which can be completed in routine practice. Just as Hare borrowed from Cleckley, so too did the authors of the original HCR-20 (Webster, Eaves, Douglas, & Wintrup, 1995) borrow from Hare in following his 20-item, 0, 1, 2, layout. The idea of the HCR-20 was straightforward: to include and balance past, historical (H), more or less 'static' factors with current clinical (C) opinion and speculation about future risk (R). The overall violence assessment synthesis was to be left in the hands of the responsible clinician.

The 10 historical items are: H1, Previous Violence; H2, Young Age at First Violent Incident; H3, Relationship Instability; H4, Employment Problems; H5, Substance Use Problems; H6, Major Mental Illness; H7, Psychopathy (according to Hare PCL-R); H8, Early Childhood Maladjustment; H9, Personality Disorder; and H10, Prior Supervision Failure. Readers will note that these items bear some resemblance to the VRAG. As well, they were influenced by research at METFORS (Section 7A). Although these are rooted cast in the past, it should be clear that scores may change as people commit new offences, find stable romantic bliss, give up drinking, and so on.

The five clinical items are: C1, Lack of Insight; C2, Negative Attitudes; C3, Active Symptoms of Mental Illness; C4, Impulsivity; and C5, Unresponsiveness to Treatment. These apply to the present. Scores are expected to change over time. The five risk variables are also dynamic in nature and are future oriented. Here the clinician or researcher is expected to forecast looking a few months ahead. These items are: R1, Plans Lack Feasibility; R2, Exposure to Destabilizers (situational factors); R3, Lack of Personal Support; R4, Noncompliance with Remediation Attempts; and R5, Stress (coping). It is important to note that assessors are expected to offer their ratings on the 0, 1, or 2 scale according to whether the person will be detained within an institution or be allowed to live in the community.

Somewhat to the authors' surprise, the HCR-20 began to attract attention almost immediately following its 1995 publication.[4] One colleague, Henrik Belfrage, though anxious to translate it into Swedish, was interested also in helping to correct some of the scheme's more evident basic flaws before undertaking his task. The result was a 1997 revision of the HCR-20 (Webster, Douglas, Eaves, & Hart). Most of the items were retained, a few were renamed, and the text and the coding scheme were tightened up.

The HCR-20 lists items that are generally within the experience of clinical and correctional personnel. When at the very outset of a workshop or seminar on risk assessment, colleagues in the various disciplines are asked to list possible risk factors for violence on a blank sheet, it is easily possible to 'reconstruct' the HCR-20 from their responses. Even critics who dismiss the scheme on one page often offer a near-identical scheme of their own making on a following page (e.g. Mullen, 2000, see Table 1, p. 2075). What sets it apart is that it is more than a simple checklist (cf. Hare, 1998a, who argues forcefully that checklists are not enough; they need support from item definition). The HCR-20 items are defined[5] and the manual contains detailed scoring instructions. Although it is hard to know where the HCR-20 will eventually 'end up', its seeming usefulness will likely continue for some time provided it is revised periodically and provided that scientific support for it continues to accrue (see Lewis & Webster, 2004; Douglas, Cox, & Webster, 1999). [6,7] Bearing in mind its relative youth, the scheme has attracted considerable research interest. It has been explored in the contexts of the civil, forensic, and criminal justice systems (see Douglas, Webster, Hart, Eaves, & Ogloff, 2001, pp. 41–48). Beech (2001) provides a good explication of how the HCR-20 is intended to be used in practice.

Although, as we have repeatedly stressed, the HCR-20 is a clinical practice violence assessment guide, it nonetheless yields scores that associate with subsequent violence. The size of such effects tends to be in the same general range as those achieved with related schemes (see, for example, Douglas & Belfrage, 2001). The HCR-20 is projected as a framework for the conduct of violence risk assessments in the certain knowledge that, as with the DSM scheme, it will require periodic revision. For the moment it has a role in guiding research and helping in the conduct of individual assessments.[8] Version 3 is now being developed and tested. This is also true of a seven-item scheme based partly on the HCR-20, but limited to inpatient aggression (*Dynamic Appraisal of Situational Aggression*, Inpatient Version, DASA, Ogloff & Dafern, 2005).

The HCR-20 is, as already noted, based on the assumption that all historical, actuarial, static factors[9] and current and future clinical 'dynamic' factors merit careful consideration in risk assessment. It also presumes that the relative salience of one class over the other will vary from individual to individual and according to situational considerations. The scheme leads the assessor through consideration of the 20 factors but, that done, expects her or him to offer a 'theory' of how prior violence might have come about and how projected violence might be averted or managed in the future. The evaluation is expected to indicate an overall projection of violence risk (i.e., low, moderate, or high). Such categorization has been challenged by some (e.g. Quinsey et al., 2006, p. 1999) but seen as helpful and necessary by others (e.g. Monahan & Steadman, 1994, pp. 935–936). Yet the real aim is risk communication should be more specific. A model for 'facet analysis' was described in some detail in Chapter 3. The Risk for Sexual Violence Protocol (RSVP; Hart et al., 2003) uses this approach to good advantage.

One argument for using a scheme like the HCR-20 is that the C and R variables can be reassessed at convenient intervals in order to evaluate response to interventions or treatments (see Webster, Douglas, Belfrage, & Link, 2000). That is, having assessed individuals against the listed definitions, they can be used further to assess change in the individual over time. It can also be employed to 'check' that clients are being detained at the most appropriate level of security (Tengström et al., 2006).

A major development within the HCR-20 project has been the publication of a 'Companion Guide' (HCR-20CG, Douglas et al., 2001). The idea behind the Guide has been to prompt professionals in the various disciplines to think of maneuvers, which conceivably might be introduced to aid in treatment. Item C1,

Insight, for example, asks what procedures or strategies might be used to enhance an individual's self-understanding (assuming a score on this factor of 2, or possibly 1). Item C2, Attitudes, for example, invites assessors to think about how best to approach an individual deemed to hold antisocial attitudes (again, assuming this has been found to be an issue during basic HCR-20 assessment). Similarly, Item C3 sets out some steps which can be taken to reduce the apparent effects of unwanted symptoms of mental or personality disorder. The general idea, then, of the HCR-20CG is to help clinicians identify which issues need to be tackled, to develop concrete strategies concerning procedures that might work, and to offer a scheme for evaluating the effects of the interventions. It is, in other words, a framework for trying to decide 'what might work' in the individual cases.

The *Spousal Assault Risk Assessment* (SARA) guide was developed concurrently with the HCR-20 and was founded on exactly the same principles. It is now in its third revision (Kropp, Hart, Webster, & Eaves, 1999). One departure from the HCR-20 is the use of a 'critical' category which can be applied to each of its 20 items.[10] Another idea was to introduce a write-in category of 'Other Considerations'.[11] Like other members of its family, the SARA has been disseminated extensively by its authors. The SARA is treated in greater detail in Chapter 14 (and the individual items are given in Note 4 to that section).

The *Sexual Violence Risk-20* (SVR-20; Boer, Hart, Kropp, & Webster, 1998) was constructed along lines similar to the HCR-20 and the SARA. Many of the SVR-20 ideas and assessment principles have now been elaborated into a comprehensive and detailed SPJ guide for use with sex offenders. This is called the Risk for Sexual Violence Protocol (RSVP). Next to evolve was the *Early Assessment Risk List for Boys* (EARL-20B; Augimeri, Webster, Koegl, & Levene, 1998). Like the other guides, this one was influenced by clinical experience and clinical necessity. Leena Augimeri and Kathy Levene of the then Earlscourt Child and Family Centre in Toronto, Ontario, had a 56-item Yes/No risk assessment checklist in routine use for children under 12. With effort, this was reduced to 20 items and given a 0, 1, 2 scoring scheme. Several years later after the boys had entered into late adolescence or early adulthood, it was then tested against CJS outcome data using 430 files scored retrospectively. In due course it evolved into Version 2 (Augimeri, Koegl, Webster, & Levene, 2001). Later still, a 21-item scheme was created for under-12 girls (Levene, Augimeri, Pepler, Walsh, Koegl, & Webster, 2001). To fill the age gap between the two EARLS and the HCR-20, Borum, Bartel, and Forth created a *Manual for the Structured Assessment of Violence Risk in Youth*, SAVRY (2002). This contains 10 historical factors, six social/contextual risk factors, and eight individual/clinical risk factors. All of these are scored low, moderate, or high. In a departure, these authors list six protective factors scored on a present/absent basis (i.e., prosocial involvement, strong social support, strong attachments and bonds, positive attitude towards intervention and authority, strong commitment to school, and resilient personality traits). They also allow for inclusion of 'other' risk and protective factors. Like the related schemes, the SAVRY is presented by its authors with suitable caution and once again, as something of a 'work in progress'.

A new area into which the HCR-20 has been extended involves violence in the workplace. This too has brought about some variation from the basic HCR-20 plan. It was here decided to evaluate culture of workplaces themselves in one guide, the systematically oriented *Workplace Risk Assessment-20* (WRA-20; Bloom, Eisen, Pollock, & Webster, 2000), and employees separately in another individual-oriented *Employee Risk Assessment-20* (ERA-20; Bloom, Webster, & Eisen, 2002). This yields 40 items overall. Combined, this scheme looks quite similar to one published independently by Hall (2001) called the *Workplace Violence Risk Assessment Checklist* (WVRAC). Gadon, Johnstone, and Cooke (in press) have now pointed to the importance of situational variables in institutional violence. The topic of antisociality in the workplace has recently been addressed by Babiak and Hare (2006).

The HCR-20 rests on the expectation that assessors will be sensitive to cultural, gender, socioeconomic, and related broad-scale issues as they apply in particular cases. In Chapter 1 it was argued that assessors ignore legal and policy considerations to their peril. In an attempt to deal with these kinds of matters, Boer, Couture, Geddes and Ritchie (2003) have recently published a scheme specifically for use with Canadian Aboriginal offenders. This is called Yōkw'tōl, Risk Management Guide for Aboriginal Offenders (RMGAO, Research Version). It contains 20 items. Some of these are similar to the HCR-20 items but some are different (e.g. Relationship of Offender to Heritage, Support for the Victim). The items are scored Not, Maybe, Yes, rather than 0, 1, 2. The scheme is in a developmental phase and, at the moment, is released as a research document. Two of the four authors are elders, one is a psychologist, and one is a probation officer and therapist.

The HCR-20, as already noted, is designed for use across civil, forensic, and criminal justice systems. Recently Nicholls, Roesch, Olley, Ogloff, and Hemphill (2005) have published a scheme specifically designed to screen for mental illness as people enter jails. This is called the *Jail Screening Assessment Tool (JSAT): Guidelines for Mental Health Screening in Jails*. The manual reviews literature on prevalence rates for mental and personality disorders in prisons and makes clear why it is so important to identify mental illness within corrections. Aside from providing an easy-to-use screening interview, the manual gives helpful advice around safety considerations (pp. 30–33). This SPJ manual, unlike the others mentioned so far, offers the assessors a series of questions that will be helpful during interview. The mental health status items rely to some extent on the Brief Psychiatric Rating Scale (BPRS; Overall & Gorham, 1962). The format, developed from years of experience gained by the authors from undertaking mental health assessment in jails, includes an emphasis on suicide and self-harm issues.

The idea of using an SPJ approach to the assessment of suicide risk in general psychiatry has recently been published by Bouch and Marshall (2005, see also Bouch & Marshall, 2003, for their *Suicide-Risk Assessment and Management Manual*, S-RAMM). These authors take the view that purely clinical approaches to this difficult assessment task 'cannot continue to be supported and that they are unsustainable in risk assessment' (p. 85). Of a purely actuarial approach they say 'the risk statement about patient A may be mathematically 'correct', but it is of limited usefulness, especially in the short term' (p. 85). They see the advantage of an SPJ approach as follows: 'Structured professional judgment asserts but does not replace psychiatric opinion. Clinicians make a structured assessment, which is usually in the formulation of a risk management plan. This by necessity brings risk assessment and management into the domain of multidisciplinary teams' (p. 85).

A similar SPJ venture, but one actually constructed around the multidisciplinary team from inception has recently been published by Webster, Martin, Brink, Nicholls, and Middleton (2004). Although in the past mental health nursing professionals have drawn upon SPJ-type thinking (e.g., Woods, 2001), the Short Term Assessment of Risk and Treatability (START) project was grown directly in nursing soil. Similar in some respects to the HCR-20 it differs in important ways:

1 the time frame is short (days, a few weeks, a month or two at maximum);
2 all of the 20 items are measured not only for risks but also, separately, for strengths (each on a 0, 1, or 2 scale);
3 the focus is not only on risk of violence to others but on multiple risks (self-harm, suicide, risk of being victimized, substance abuse, unauthorized leave, self-neglect, and other case-specific ones);
4 emphasis is placed on 'signature risk signs' (by which is meant that some clients tend to have idiosyncratic ways of signaling that a particular kind of risk is elevated and that a planned intervention may be needed); and
5 some variables treated as historical in the HCR-20 are brought forward for reconsideration in the present and immediate future (e.g., occupational, substance use, rule adherence).

Although conceived as a forum for use in interdisciplinary team meetings, START can be completed by an individual mental health or correctional professional who has access to colleagues in other disciplines. Indeed, it may be possible and helpful in some cases to include patients themselves in the process (Lam & Lancel, 2006). The START is in a 'consultation stage' at present, though one paper reports limited reliability and validity data on a preliminary version (Nicholls, Brink, Desmarais, Webster, & Martin, 2006). The evaluation of the scheme and its characteristics have recently been summarized by Webster, Nicholls, Martin, Desmarais, and Brink (2006). An innovation from the START project has been the development of an *Instructor's Manual and Workbook* (Desmarais, Webster, Martin, Dassinger, Brink, & Nicholls, 2006). The idea here is to offer codable cases and to give would-be teachers of the scheme some additional information about scoring criteria, outcome measurement, and implementation issues.

The authors of START, at the time they were writing, did not know of the existence of *Clinical Practice Guidelines for Violence: The Short-term Management of Disturbed/Violent Behaviour in Psychiatric In-patient Settings and Emergency Departments* (2005). This was commissioned by the National Institute for Clinical Excellence. (See also *Quick Reference Guide*, Clinical Guideline 25, developed by the National Collaborating Centre for Nursing and Supportive Care. The NICE guideline is available at www.nice.org.uk/CG025NICEguideline.) There is considerable similarity of thought between these two documents.

The above discussion of the HCR-20 and the SARA and their progeny might give the impression that all development in the area is of fairly recent origin. This is not so. Perhaps the best example of a device which predated all of the guides mentioned above is the Level of Service Inventory – Revised (Andrews & Bonta, 1995).[12] The main reason that it is not accorded pride of place in this review is that it deals with general recidivism (which, of course, includes violence importantly) rather than specific aggression and violence. A second reason is that it is, unfortunately perhaps, little known in the civil mental health systems.

The general spirit of the LSI-R is similar to that of the HCR-20. In their preface to the *Manual*, the authors remind their readers that 'This instrument is not a comprehensive survey of mitigating and aggravating factors relevant to criminal sanctioning and was never designed to assist in establishing the just penalty' (p. viii). They aim to include factors that are 'supported by research, professional opinion, and a broad social learning on criminal conduct' (p. viii). To the authors there is an 'obvious' value in 'a systematic survey of the domains of criminal history, criminal attitudes, criminal associates, and criminal personality' (p. viii). They are also anxious to point out that 'other dynamic factors such as finances, accommodations, and mental disorder may be highly relevant to level of supervision and level of service decisions that may reduce further victimization' (p. viii). It is intended to assist in getting the right kinds of information assembled and on file, to help allocate supervision and treatment resources, to supplement the monitoring progress while under parole or probation, to facilitate in making release decisions (e.g., to halfway houses), and to estimate the chances of recidivism (p. 3). As with the HCR-20 series, the LSI-R is not 'a substitute for sound judgment that utilizes various sources of information' (p. 3).[13,14,15]

CHALLENGES IN IMPLEMENTING EVIDENCE-BASED CLINICAL PRACTICE

It should be clear by this stage that the HCR-20 and allied devices fit within the tradition of evidence-based clinical practice, that its aim is to achieve the best possible collaboration between clinicians, researchers, and administrators. Although it remains important to be able to demonstrate that these various decision-enhancing guides possess reliability among items, predictive validity, and so on, there is *as well*, good reason to ensure that new knowledge is incorporated into practice and that practice itself using these and other devices is under constant research scrutiny. Increasingly, the challenge is not so much to create new schemes but to verify and refine the ones now on hand. Much needed are studies to find out how best they can be introduced to settings in such a way that they will be understood, accepted, and developed by clinicians.

Organizations like the American Psychological Association have recently expressed strong support for evidence-based practice (2006). This it defines as 'the integration of the best available research with clinical expertise in the context of patient characteristics, culture, and preferences' (p. 273). The report calls for 'a scientific attitude towards clinical work' (p. 277) and expects a 'mutually respectful collaboration between researchers and expert practitioners' (p. 278).

These and related objectives, however laudable, are not easy to achieve. Changing and integrating research and clinical cultures is difficult (Macfarlane & Butterill, 1999). Certainly, this is extremely hard to accomplish if there is little will to seek change in practice on the part of senior clinical and administrative staff. This is particularly so if additional resources are not provided to buttress the implementation exercise. Unless there is a knowledgeable local champion with the necessary expertise, energy, and time to devote to the project, failure is virtually assured. One-shot workshops delivered by 'outsiders,' no matter how well organized and taught, will have little enduring effect. The SPJ device, even if well supported scientifically in research conducted in other settings, cannot be expected to flourish until it has been contextualized. In every case much attention has to be given to practical issues such as *who* in the organization will take responsibility for the accurate completion of the assessment, *how frequently* and under what conditions the scheme will be carried out, *what measures* of outcome will be employed, and so on.

Gauthie, Ellis, Bol and Stolee (2005) say 'Changing practice involves a social learning process; clinicians must synthesize new knowledge with existing knowledge, beliefs, and attitudes, and learn how to function as a community with new practices' (p. 33). These same authors point out that there has to be an initial 'appraisal' phase during which colleagues together examine the evidence for different evaluation approaches and decide what device, if any, to adopt. They point out that even if there is an eventual decision not to change practice, the appraisal process will likely have served a useful purpose. There is too the fact that, in cases where a decision is reached to introduce an already available clinical and research approach, some adjustments will always be required to make it fit the particular local circumstances. It might not be going too far to state that new research on implementation processes are now as much in need as are more studies of basic validity issues. Even when success has been achieved in the implementation phase, much effort is required to ensure continued fidelity to the protocol. 'Drift' away from the published guide will occur without constant vigilance.

NOTES

1   The point of these two excerpts is to suggest that most violence assessments demand a 'down the middle' approach. The Professor is a gifted teacher. But he might not be an ideal expert witness. Courts and review boards do not have unlimited time. As well, members want to 'see' the logic, the connections in an argument. The Sergeant too is a gifted instructor. His rule-following, rote-like method suits his down-to-earth subject. But members of courts and review boards will insist on obtaining some kind of knowledge that goes beyond the 'mere mechanical'. They want a *theory* about a complex problem but one that makes practical sense. The SPJ approach is somewhere between the Professor and the Sergeant. There must be rule adherence but also allowance for the expression of well-informed clinical sense.

2   The word 'instrumentation' is of some note. Clinicians' and researchers' opinions are influenced by the way they organize their data. The mere selection of one kind of 'instrument' over another can probably affect substantially how clients are viewed. This can be so if all scores load in one, usually negative, direction, with no allowance for the expression of the possibly ameliorating effects of protective considerations. Monahan refers to these as 'format effect' (2003, p. 537).

3   Borum reminds his readers of Monahan's (1993) suggestion that large facilities should probably designate a member of staff to be the 'risk educator.' Such a person would keep on top of the literature and conduct periodic training sessions (see p. 954).

4   Considering the large number of requests for the DBRS manual following publication of the first main study (Menzies, Webster, & Sepejak, 1985a), this should perhaps not in fact have been a surprise. These requests came despite the authors' insistence that the DBRS had little predictive validity. What it showed was that there was a heightening demand for some kind of clinically usable scheme.

5   According to the manual 'violence is actual, attempted, or threatened harm to a person or persons. Threats of harm must be clear and unambiguous (e.g., "I am going to kill you!"), rather than vague statements of hostility' (p. 24). The manual devotes a page and a half to this topic (pp. 24–26).

6 A case in point is the use of threat/control override (TCO). Some play is given to this under Item C3, Symptoms. Inclusion of TCO was influenced by early findings from the MacArthur project (Monahan & Steadman, 1994). Since these seem not to have been substantiated in the final published study (Monahan et al., 2001), inclusion of this part of the text will have to be reexamined (also in light of other studies which have addressed the topic and accumulating clinical and research experience with the construct).

7 Kevin Douglas, one of the HCR-20 authors and lead author of the HCR-20CG, keeps track of all information published on the HCR-20. Readers are directed to http://kdouglas.wordpress.com/hcr-20/.

8 The authors advise use of the 0, 1, or 2 scoring scheme not so much because it will necessarily yield 'perfect accuracy' (no matter how well the current scoring scheme is followed) but because it concentrates attention on the issues at hand.

9 The SPJ approach to guide construction has also been criticized on the grounds that it was promulgated before it was scientifically verified (Quinsey et al., 2006, p. 196). In fact, beyond the Hare PCL-R and the PCL:SV which were not originally intended as 'standalone' violence risk assessment devices, the HCR-20 and related schemes have accumulated as much or more evidence in their support than any other such schemes (see Risk Management Authority, 2005). A more important point might be that continued insistence on the 'superiority' of an actuarial approach, one confined to sheer prediction according to normative standards, disquiets clinicians, administrators, and policy makers. As argued in Chapter 15, risk management issues should also enter the frame alongside prediction ones. Of course, it could be that professionals working practically in violence assessment are simply offended by spoken and written assertions such as 'Actuarial methods are too good and clinical judgment is too poor to risk contaminating the former with the latter' (Quinsey et al., 2006, p. 197).

10 It turns out that the number of items marked 'critical' in the SARA may have as much predictive power as summed numerical ratings or global judgments.

11 These are not rated 0, 1, or 2, but can be included as 'critical items.'

12 The LSI-R was originally called the *Level of Supervision Inventory* (LSI). Andrews first published on this in 1982 and, with other colleagues, has been attending to its development and refinement ever since.

13 Two LSI-R items seemingly left out of account in the HCR-20 are Numbers 30 and 31. These are not dealt with directly in the HCR-20, but likely could be subsumed under Item R5, Stress. These two items are fully covered in the START manual. The LSI-R does not, like the VRAG and the HCR-20, place reliance on a formally scored Hare PCL-R. But under Item 50, it is possible to indicate that psychological assessment is required. Among the problems which might signal the requirement of such assessment is 'disregard for feelings of others; possibility of reduced ability or inability to feel guilt; shame; may be superficially 'charming' but seems to repeatedly disregard rules and feelings of others' and 'criminal acts that don't make sense or appear irrational' (p. 11).

14   The LSI-R consists of 54 items scored on a four-point scale (i.e. 0, on one end, represents 'a very unsatisfactory situation with a very clear and strong need for improvement'; 3, on the other end, means 'a satisfactory situation with no need for improvement', p. 5). The 10 items under Criminal History are near ideal for gathering information about HCR-20 Items H1, Previous Violence, and H2, Young age at first violent incident (i.e., 1, Any prior convictions?; 10, Official record of assault/violence?; 5, Arrested under age 16?). Similarly, H10, Prior Supervision Failure relates to the LSI-R (7, Escape history from a correctional facility). The 20 LSI-R items grouped under Education/Employment provide excellent questions (and definitions) all relating to Item H4, Employment Problems, and Item H8, Early Maladjustment. Financial issues are regarded as possible stressors under LSI-R Items 21 and 22. Information under these headings relate to HCR-20 Item R5, Stress. The LSI-R Family/Marital items (23–26) provide more extensive coverage of intimate and family relationships than does H3, Relationship Instability. Accommodation in the LSI-R receives three items (e.g., satisfaction with accommodation; three or more address changes; high crime neighborhood). These would be dealt with under the HCR-20's R2, Destabilizers, as would five items under the LSI-R's 'Companions'. The LSI-R includes nine items under Alcohol/Drug Problems. In the HCR-20 these past such difficulties are addressed under Item H5, Substance Use Problems, and current ones under R2, Exposure to Destabilizers. The LSI-R allows five items for 'Emotional/Personal'. Here the authors place focus on psychological and psychiatric difficulties and allow consideration of how well the individual is adjusting to his or her circumstances. These would correspond to HCR-20 Items C3, Symptoms, C4, Impulsivity, and C5, Unresponsive to Treatment. Three of the four LSI-R items under Attitudes/Orientation link to the HCR-20 item C2 Negative Attitudes. The one remaining LSI-R item, Number 54, Poor attitude toward supervision, is taken up in HCR-20 item R4, Noncompliance with Remediation Attempts.[9,10] Should the fact that there appears to be some considerable correspondence between the LSI-R and the HCR-20 mean that the one should be abandoned in favor of the other? The answer is obviously 'no'. Although similar, they serve different purposes and have different objectives (i.e., to assess for general criminal recidivism, to assess for future violent acts). Would the availability of an already-completed, up-to-date LSI-R be of assistance to an assessor about to undertake an HCR-20 assessment? The answer is obviously 'yes'. Should an expert in violence risk assessment be fully familiar with the LSI-R? The answer, again, is obviously 'yes'.

15   Forth (2003) has provided a review of all of the guides mentioned in this section and many others besides. An even more helpful consolidation has recently been published by Scotland's Risk Management Authority (RMA, 2006). The RMA established a process for rating the various instruments now available (against criteria like validation history, empirical grounding, and interrater reliability).

STARR STORY

Chaotic home
Everyone's violent
Round and round
It goes
Starts drinking
At eight
Smokes and steals
Beaten by father
At sixteen
Runs away
Gets married
Has son
Car smash
While on drugs
Beats wife
Becomes paranoid
Fights at work
Gets divorced
At twenty-eight
Murders mother
While very ill
First to prison
Then to hospital
At thirty-three
Returned again
To the outside world
This time
Marries right woman
Wins a job
Gets on with life[1]

A RETROSPECTIVE HCR-20 ANALYSIS OF ONE MAN'S ACCOUNT OF SELF-ADMITTED EXTREME DYSFUNCTION AND VIOLENCE

Patricia Stefanowska, Christopher D. Webster, and Randy Starr

Practical experience is better than bad theory (there is plenty of that out there), but good theory shaped from evidence is better then practical experience alone.

(Rhodes, 1999, p. 313)

A few words are necessary at outset to explain how the present section came about. Both the second (C.W.) and the third (R.S.) authors were keynote speakers at a 2003 meeting in Cleveland, Ohio. The former talked about risk assessment from a scientific-clinical point of view; the latter as someone who, several years previously, had had the terrible experience of murdering his mother while very ill. After the presentations were over, we had opportunity for discussion. It was agreed that Starr would send Webster a copy of his book, *Not guilty by reason of insanity: One man's recovery* (2000) which by then was out of print. After reading it, Webster passed it and a subsequent article (Starr, 2002) to the first author, then a psychology undergraduate student at McMaster University. She undertook, as an exercise, an HCR-20 (Webster et al., 1997) coding of Starr's book together with his 2002 paper. This included a retrospective analysis of psychopathy via Hare's Psychopathy Checklist-Revised (PCL-R, 1991, 2003b). The second author independently checked the coding. After providing a provisional text to Randy Starr and receiving his comments, it was agreed that he ought to accept a role as a co-author.

This section is intended to make three points:

1 Some persons who have committed very serious offences and who have very high scores on historical, 'static' factors do eventually recover and become able to live as responsible citizens.
2 Structured professional judgment (SPJ) schemes can be used to advantage in the course of retrospective analyses.
3 In some instances, it is helpful to be able to include the patient, or former patient, as a key participant in the assessment process. Expressions of this idea, though hardly original, are actually quite rare in the published literature. Menzies, Webster, and Sepejak (1985a) noted, for example, that it is helpful to establish assessees' perceptions of their own violence potential. Even more to the point, is the value of 'narrative analyses' (see Petrunic & Weisman, 2005).

According to his own reports, Randy Starr's past life was horrific (Starr, 2000, 2002; Athens & Starr, 2003). His childhood was dominated by verbal, substance, and physical abuse. This extraordinary upbringing set the stage for a highly dysfunctional adulthood that made him so aggressive, unstable, impulsive, and generally antisocial that at age 29 he murdered his mother. At that time he was abusing alcohol and drugs heavily. These addictive habits worsened his fixed delusional idea that his family wanted to harm him. In this state he was capable of extreme violence. Given all this, his frank and detailed account notwithstanding, it might never be possible to discount entirely the idea that even today he could again place others at risk. Yet the evaluating clinician's task is 'to assess factors that led the individual to be aggressive in the past, ascertain how many of these factors are amenable to change, and then to intervene to alter the triggering factors so that the risk of violence is reduced' (Pagani & Pinard, 2001, p. 18). In this section we have striven to find out how many negative factors in Randy's past life have truly altered. His account *Not guilty by reason of insanity: One man's recovery* is written with evident sincerity. He recognizes his past 'mental illness, behavioral maladjustments,' the use of 'mind-altering substances' (Starr, 2000, p. vii) and the terrible crime that he committed. His irresponsibility at the time is now a matter of public record and his text details many facts which appear incontrovertible. The book also provides a fair amount of information about his present state of mind, or at least his condition at the time the story achieved formal publication. His writings also point to his ambitions for the future. This emphasis on past, present, and future, align with the HCR-20 (Webster et al., 1997). The purpose of the present section is to use the HCR-20 as a framework for analyzing Starr's risk to others in the past and matters as they now stand.

HCR-20-CODING

Historical Items

As is made clear from the previous section, the 10 historical items in the HCR-20, each scored 0 (not present), 1 (possibly present), or 2 (definitely present), invite the assessor to review the individual's record of violence, employment, mental illness, compliance, and so on. It is, of course, important that the items be coded as faithfully as possible according to the descriptions given in Webster et al. (1997). Scores allotted by the first two authors are given in Table 11.1.

H1   Previous Violence

This item focuses on the number of past violent acts, as well as the seriousness of these acts. By the time Randy reached 16 he had been in as many as 25 fights that he could recall (Starr, 2000, p. xix). This pattern progressed and he became a violent husband at 18 years of age, and a violent co-worker (Starr, 2000, p. 13). The night before his 29th birthday, he decided to visit his mother whom he had not seen for five years. Before this visit he entered a paranoid state while talking with his female friend. He had not slept for a few nights, and had consumed much alcohol and drugs (Starr, 2000, p. 17). His mother was home alone and trustingly let Randy inside. To Randy, she seemed evil and very dangerous. The paranoia seemed to overwhelm him mentally and physically. He felt certain that she was evil and that everyone knew it. He stabbed his mother several times thinking that he was protecting himself (Starr, 2000, p. 17).

H2   Young Age at First Violent Incident

Randy became aggressive at a young age himself. In his early teens he threatened his brother with a sharp butcher knife (Starr, 2000, p. 6).When he was 14 years old

Table 11.1: HCR-20 scoring

Participant		
Name: Randy Starr	Date_____	ID_____

Historical Items	Code (0, 1, 2)
H1 *Previous Violence*	2
H2 *Young Age at First Violent Incident*	2
H3 *Relationship Instability*	2
H4 *Employment Problems*	1
H5 *Substance Use Problems*	2
H6 *Major Mental Illness*	2
H7 *Psychopathy*	1
H8 *Early Maladjustment*	2
H9 *Personality Disorder*	2
H10 *Prior Supervision Failure*	1
Historical Item Total:	17/20

Clinical Items	Code (0, 1, 2)
C1 *Lack of Insight*	0
C2 *Negative Attitudes*	0
C3 *Active Symptoms of Major Mental Illness*	1
C4 *Impulsivity*	0
C5 *Unresponsive to Treatment*	0
Clinical Item Total:	1/10

Risk Management Items In Out	Code (0, 1, 2)
R1 *Plans Lack Feasibility*	0
R2 *Exposure to Destabilizers*	0
R3 *Lack of Personal Support*	0
R4 *Noncompliance with Remediation Attempts*	0
R5 *Stress*	0
Risk Management Item Total:	0/10

HCR-20 Total			18/40
Final Risk Judgment:	Low	Moderate	High

Assessor		
Name P. Stefanowska/C. Webster	Signature_____	Date: 02/01/07

he had his first major fight with his father (Starr, 2000, p. 7). On occasions, his father came home drunk and hostile. Randy was ready to fight and 'pounded the hell out of his [father's] head' (Starr, 2000, p. 8). The two fought hard. Randy lost complete control, until his mother and friends helped to bring him back to reality (Starr, 2000, p. 9).

H3 Relationship Instability

When Randy was 16 years old he ran away from home with his girlfriend to Texas to get married (Starr, 2000, p. 11). They had a son the following year. By the time he was 18, he was already an emotionally and physically abusive husband. This abusive pattern continued, became worse as years passed, and did not end until they separated.

H4 Employment Problems

Past employment problems are coded in the HCR-20 because previous research has shown in a sample of mentally disordered offenders that employment at time of arrest is associated with later violence, at least to some extent (Menzies & Webster, 1995). Randy worked as a construction employee. Though he kept his job, he felt a great deal of uncertainty toward the work setting and his boss (Starr, 2000, p. 28). He admits to work maladjustments; one day while on the job he fought a co-worker sending him to hospital severely hurt (Starr, 2000, p. 13).

H5 Substance Use Problems

Substance abuse affected Randy in many areas of his life. It mainly impaired his physical health, interpersonal relationships, and recreational pursuits. He tasted alcohol at a young age; by the time he reached 15 he would drink himself to oblivion (Starr, 2000, p. 45). At 17, a car accident while on drugs made him decide to take a break from the drinking and drugs. After a few years of being sober, he did, though, go back to his old habits of drinking heavily and doing drugs (Starr, 2000, p. 46). After a day of hard work at the construction site, he would go home and drink (Starr, 2000, p. 46). At one point he had lost all his friends except his 'drugging buddies' (Starr, 2000, p. 47). For many months he took tranquilizers, marijuana, codeine, speed, and cocaine. He could no longer think properly. This did not bother him (Starr, 2000, p. 47). He did not care because 'the booze and the pills [became his] major relationship' (Starr, 2000, p. 47). His maladaptive pattern of substance abuse led him to give up important family and social activities without his realizing or caring that this was happening.

H6   Major Mental Illness

Having a mental disorder can be a risk factor for violence in some instances (Webster et al., 1997). Randy was diagnosed as having schizophrenia. He himself notes that his mental illness began in 1974 at age 24 (Starr, 2000, p. 27). He had symptoms of anxiety, depression, work-related problems, and, most disturbing, definite homicidal thoughts. As years went by, the symptoms of paranoia increased. At a point, he neglected his personal hygiene and had obsessive homicidal thoughts that often led him to call and threaten his family members (Starr, 2000, p. 15). He often worried that he had cancer. He was also bothered by recurrent nightmares and nervous twitches. He became more and more panicky and eventually wanted his parents dead.

Mr. Starr's homicidal thoughts worsened as they became more vivid (Starr, 2000, p. 30). On one occasion he decided to visit a hospital for his stomach problems. He was instead transferred to the psychiatric unit, where he was diagnosed with acute and undifferentiated schizophrenia (Starr, 2000, p. 33). This was nearly five years before his Not Guilty by Reason of Insanity index crime (Starr, 2002). While there, he was put on 'heavy dosages of various psychiatric medications' (Starr, 2000, p. 32). Upon release from the hospital he stopped all medications abruptly. He continued to abuse alcohol, prescription medications, and street drugs (Starr, 2002). Suicidal thoughts continued and worsened. His behavior became more erratic and he perceived his family members increasingly as threats; or as the 'evil ones' (Starr, 2000, p. 16). According to his account, his mental illness was most intense about the time of his matricide. At trial, all parties agreed on Mr. Starr's insanity at the time of the offense (Starr, 2002). He was initially sent to a maximum security psychiatric facility, and later to a less-secure facility. Eventually, he started to respond to treatment consisting of psychiatric medications, counseling, and group therapy (Starr, 2002).

H7   Psychopathy

In Table 11.2 we show the Hare PCL-R (1991, 2003) items along with scores allotted retrospectively to Randy Starr by the first-listed two authors. Although never originally intended to be a device for the prediction of violence risk, there is much evidence to suggest that this SPJ scheme has such capacity (Webster & Hucker, 2003).

Randy's total score of 20 fails to meet the 30 cut-off point for a definition of psychopathy (see Hare 2003, p. 30). A score of 20 does, though, qualify an individual as 'moderate' risk (see Hare, 2003, Table 2.1, p. 31). Generally speaking, very limited retrospective coding, as used in this study will yield lower scores than are obtained when interviews are possible and when information can be obtained from 'collaterals' (Hare, 2003, p. 19).

Table 11.2: Hare PCL-R scores – applied retrospectively to R.S. on the basis of his own published reports

1)	Glibness/superficial charm	0
2)	Grandiose sense of self-worth	0
3)	Need for stimulation/proneness to boredom	0
4)	Pathological lying	0
5)	Cunning/manipulative	0
6)	Lack of remorse or guilt	1
7)	Shallow affect	1
8)	Callous/lack of empathy	2
9)	Parasitic lifestyle	0
10)	Poor behavioral controls	2
11)	Promiscuous sexual behavior	0
12)	Early behavior problems	2
13)	Lack of realistic, long-term goals	2
14)	Impulsivity	2
15)	Irresponsibility	2
16)	Failure to accept responsibility for actions	2
17)	Many short-term marital relationships	0
18)	Juvenile delinquency	2
19)	Revocation of conditional release	1
20)	Criminal versatility	1
Total		20

H8   Early Maladjustment

As a child, Randy would witness his parents' frequent and extreme violent acts of aggression towards other family members and strangers (Starr, 2000, p. 3, p. 5). His father was often verbally, emotionally, and physically violent towards Randy and his brother (Starr, 2000, p. 62). When Randy was 4 years old his father gave him the 'most severe beating of [his] life' (Starr, 2000, p. 7), as already mentioned briefly in H2 above. Violence was the norm, and Randy was involved with as many as 25 fistfights with his peers at a young age (Starr, 2000, p. 9). He had little interest in academic work, was abusing alcohol, and was quick to pick the fights (Starr, 2000, p. xix). He ran away from home at 16 years of age to marry his girlfriend, whom he physically and emotionally bullied (Starr, 2000, p. 9, p. 12).

H9   Personality Disorder

Although it would appear that Randy did not meet criterion for psychopathy, according to the Hare PCL-R (1991, 2003), it would seem highly likely, given his relatively high 'Factor 2' score, that he would at some point have qualified for a diagnosis of antisocial personality disorder. Certainly, traits of this kind are indisputably evident in Starr's own account.

H10   Prior Supervision Failure

The first time Randy was under care of a psychiatric hospital for his mental disorder (prior to the homicide) he left the premises for an hour (Starr, 2000, p. 36). This incident was not serious, since he was willing to be returned to the hospital by his then wife who found him walking on the street (Starr, 2000, p. 36). There is no mention in *One Man's Recovery* of any withdrawal of privileges over this incident or, if indeed, his absence was even noticed at the hospital. It would be scored as 0 since there was no disciplinary action (Webster et al., 1997, p. 46). Yet a score of 1 is warranted because, by his own admission (1997, p. 16) he became noncompliant with prescribed drugs before the index offense and, against agreement, was abusing alcohol and unprescribed medications.

Clinical Items

These are items determined by *present* behavior, thoughts, and attitudes. The present 'clinical rating' is made here as if R.S. had just published his book. The reader must realize that the HCR-20 clinical items are being applied at the end of a period of some years of seemingly successful treatment. Scores would likely have been much higher had they been made shortly after his NGRI finding. It can be presumed these scores would have dropped gradually as time passed and as his treatment progressed.

C1   Lack of Insight

Through the course of the treatment, R.S. began to understand the predicament he was in. Apparently he did not minimize his responsibility for his past acts, whether due to mental disorder or not (Starr, 2000, p. xiii). He acknowledges that during his NGRI time, when diagnosed with schizophrenia, he also was inclined towards mania, paranoia, poor impulse control, inability to cope with stress, and to perceive the world from an antisocial point of view (Starr, 2002). The realization that he had opportunities for recovery from his mental disorder apparently came gradually as he discovered the realities of the illness and came to terms with the murder he had committed (Starr, 2000, p. 56). With work he gained insight into his mental illness and his alcohol and drug abuse (Starr, 2002). By the time of publication of the book he seemingly understood that recovery from mental illness requires a person to be cooperative and to have interaction with supportive people (Starr, 2000, p. 97). It appeared necessary for him to develop his *own* theory about the origins of his mental illness, (i.e. a sequence from isolation to depression, from depression to paranoia, and eventually from paranoia to the homicide). According to his account, he sees the continuing necessity for taking medication to relieve his depression; for monitoring his thinking, and for trying to have healthy interactions with others (Starr, 2000, p. 101).

C2   Negative Attitudes

Randy has, it would seem, learned to deal with others prosocially. His accounts are devoid of pessimistic and antisocial thinking. In one particular treatment session, he reports breaking down with emotions of anguish, pain, regret, and sorrow for the act that he committed (Starr, 2000, p. 22). He speaks of himself as being tormented over the murder of his mother and that giving back to his 'fellow-man helps [him] justify [his] continued existence' (Starr, 2000, p. 25). While still recovering from the mental illness, Randy had numerous setbacks. At one point he wanted to commit suicide by jumping into a lake (Starr, 2000, p. 65). He kept the thought to himself, but then figured that if he did jump into the lake he would have lost hope and let others down (Starr, 2000, p. 67). He did not give up and eventually took charge of his disorder. Afterwards, he met his current wife and this too helped change his outlook towards the positive (Starr, 2000, p. 78). He now seems optimistic about the future and says he gives all people the benefit of the doubt (Starr, 2000, p. 100). He has learned to listen better, interact with and trust others. This he attributes in part to the help he received at the treatment center, especially in learning how to develop sound interpersonal relationships (Starr, 2002). He now focuses on being realistic, confident, and grateful for what he has in life (Starr, 2002). In a sense, the sad death of his mother had the unexpected effect of creating a new path in life for him.

C3   Active Symptoms of Major Mental Illness

Although always mindful that a recurrence of serious mental disorder remains a possibility, he realizes that it is wise to seek professional help even with respect to relatively minor issues (Webster, personal communication, 2003). Randy's mental health is not impeded on a day-to-day basis. He is able to acknowledge the fact that events in his earlier life have caused permanent social, psychological and, possibly, neurological damage. Yet he had found ways to accommodate to these limitations. A clear example is his use of carefully developed videotaped segments which he employs while addressing large professional audiences. These help keep him on track and conceal the fact that, otherwise, he might fail to sustain his line of thought.

C4   Impulsivity

Randy described three situations in detail where he acted in an appropriately restrained way to horseplay and insults from others while in the hospital (Starr,

2000, p. 102). During his stay in Chester Mental Health Center he started to realize that he had the ability to control impulses and that his medications helped in that respect (Starr, 2000, p. 20). He learned to listen attentively, to be patient, and to control his emotions (Starr, 2000, p. 60). He recognizes that, with control, positive change is attainable (Starr, 2000, p. 24). He now teaches and educates others about treatment issues and the formulation of aftercare plans. He advises 'the keys to success' lie in trusting and cooperating with others (Starr, 2000, p. 119).

C5   Unresponsive to Treatment

It took over a year for Randy to realize that his offense was morally wrong. For a long time he believed he was defending himself during the act of killing his mother (Starr, 2002). However, over time, with help of staff members within the hospital, he began to realize what actually motivated the incident. He was changing. The extended account in his book makes no reference to any outbursts or rage episodes while in the hospital. The treatment program was apparently beneficial because he needed rules and boundaries. A locked room gave him a sense of security (Starr, 2000, p. 20). He followed the program actively, started to believe in himself, and learned the difference between aggressiveness and assertiveness (Starr, 2000, p. 21). Apparently, he began to trust in his therapists. He did not escape the hospital when he had chances to do so. As already mentioned, he did at one point have a suicidal thought about jumping into a lake. This he suppressed out of a wish to remain loyal to his primary psychiatrist at the time (Starr, 2000, p. 66). Randy did not want him to think that he had run away from his resolve to start afresh. He states that therapists are coaches whose job it is to help patients control their emotions (Starr, 2000, p. 128) and he points out that the effort put in by members of staff deserves appreciation (Starr, 2000, p. 128). He wanted to change and he did engage in therapeutic alliances.

Risk Management Items

These R items in the HCR-20 are included to help the assessor speculate about how the individual will 'adjust to future circumstances' (Webster et al., 1997, p. 61). Since R.S. was released to the community some several years ago, the present R ratings are made on the assumption that he will continue to live in a way similar to that described in his book.

R1   Plans Lack Feasibility

This item hinges on the individual's acceptance or rejection of a particular treatment program or other intervention plan. Randy received an appropriate treatment program as judged by his favorable response to it. It would appear that he was able to participate in developing the protocol. He showed high motivation to succeed, to obey the rules, to get out of the hospital, and to attain personal goals. It is his opinion that what a person puts into a treatment plan is what they will get out of it (Starr, 2000, p. 137). At the time of writing his book, Randy was proud of his accomplishment of earning a Bachelor of Arts degree majoring in human services, being an addictions counselor, and working in a field with an internationally based mental health organization (Starr, 2002). At present, he works as a consumer specialist and leads responsibility groups to teach people how they too can have successful lives even under adverse circumstances.

R2   Exposure to Destabilizers

The factors that were active in Randy's life before and during the time of the index offense have changed. His previous peer group was constituted largely of people who did drugs with him. He was frequently intoxicated and his mental illness was profound. With treatment, he discovered 'that associating with negative people would be worse than just being by [himself] at times' (Starr, 2002). He now has a highly supportive wife and his new friends appear to be chosen from those who work alongside him in the mental health field (Starr, 2000, p. xx). He is a professional worker, is part of committees and groups. Making many formal presentations before audiences keeps him well occupied (Starr, 2000, p. xx). When first discharged, he moved to an entirely different state and changed his name in order to have opportunity for a fresh healthy integration into the community (Starr, 2000, p. 85).

R3   Lack of Personal Support

Randy has now been married to his second wife for more than 15 years. It is, seemingly, a happy union (Starr, 2000, p. 78). He has had much assistance and encouragement from his wife. This has helped him with his recovery (Starr, 2000, p. xx). Randy states that positive acknowledgment from people is powerful, even 'acceptance and affirmation of one another at a psychiatric hospital can be a source of happiness' (Starr, 2000, p. 95).

R4   Noncompliance with Remediation Attempts

This item focuses on complying with medications and therapeutic treatments. Randy has been accepting of treatments from the start, and remains compliant. He is now able to present advice from the vantage point of someone who has 'been there,' to offer helpful suggestions to individuals who may have challenges in gaining their conditional releases. His stated aim is to teach people with mental illnesses how to improve their lives and to pass on his successful experiences gained over the years with forensic patients and staff (Starr, 2002).

R5   Stress

This item gains admission to the HCR-20 on the grounds that evaluators require license to anticipate what kinds of stressors might be likely to arise in the particular client's life and to estimate how he or she might or might not be able to cope with them. It focuses on pressures from family, peers, and employment. According to his accounts, Mr. Starr could not cope with challenging obstacles when his mental illness was untreated. He was paranoid, frightened, and blamed others for his self-destructive ways (Starr, 2000, p. 99). At present, he seems able to balance his professional and personal responsibilities and can meet the demands of work, travel, and public speaking. Although he appears to have his life in order with a caring wife and a fulfilling career, he remains attuned to the idea that he may require further assistance in the future and, that it is incumbent upon him to seek professional help when it is required.

Conclusion

If R.S.'s NGRI release decision had been based solely on his historical (H) factors, he would probably still be detained in hospital or be under close community supervision to this day. These 'static' scores are very high indeed and will not lower much if any with the passage of time. If, though, this total H score had been compiled from official records, rather than from the author-provided narratives, it is not likely that they would have looked much different. The non-availability of official records and reports to confirm or challenge Mr. Starr's account is, of course, the fundamental weakness of this report.[2,3,4] All modern risk assessment authorities call for 'collateral' information, use of multiple data sources and the like (see Monahan et al., 2001). So in this sense, the present account is deficient.

This much said, the approach should not be entirely discounted (see Robertson, Yaren, & Globerman, 2004). We are not the first to do an HCR-20 based case-level follow-up study based in large measure on the opinions and experiences of persons previously considered to be at risk for violence to others (see Haggård, Gumpert, & Grann, 2001; see Chapter 15). As well as confirmation in statistical terms of the power of individual HCR-20 scales and items, SPJ schemes must be tested against the day-to-day realities faced by individual clients and the professionals and family members who work in their practical support.

Our C and R ratings are markedly low. They are based on a particular time point (the publication of R.S.'s two personal accounts) and, as already noted, lack systematic corroboration. Being now so low, these C and R scores could not drop further. But this does not mean that they could not rise given a particular set of circumstances (e.g., a failure in medication effectiveness, a marital disruption, a serious difficulty in the workplace). Like clinicians who care for him in the present, we would argue that these dynamic factors can come into unexpected play in unexpected ways, and at unexpected times. All we can say, and it is not a small thing, is that the 'Starr case' provides a good example of how the HCR-20 can be used retrospectively to reconstruct the positive as well as the negative. The section emphasizes the idea, usually underacknowledged, that clients themselves can often be brought directly into the practical process of appraising the varied risks that they themselves confront (of substance abuse, of being victimized, and so on) and of helping estimate the potential kinds of harm that they might inflict on others (family members, colleagues, and the like) or indeed, on themselves (Webster et al., 2004). It would seem that a good part of the practical therapeutic challenge lies in helping individuals create the kinds of personal theories which help them accept responsibility, account for their past experiences and actions, and clarify their expectations for the future. The 2003 publication by Athens and Starr, the most recent and perhaps 'blunt' of the three by R.S., is instructive in this respect. It actually shows how a particular theoretical idea, one proposed earlier by Athens (1997), can be enormously helpful to the 'right' client if it comes to his or her attention at the propitious moment.

NOTES

1   The narrative description offers a broad outline of Randy Starr's life.
2   Curiously perhaps, one of the authors of this subsection (C.D.W.) is acquainted with two of the mental health professionals mentioned in R.S.'s text. Considering that both live in the United States, this is an unusual coincidence.
3   Yet it is important to note that, in the 'real clinical world', it is often very difficult to obtain suitable records (Padgett et al., 2005).
4   Although obstructed from obtaining access to the full record, some authors have recently shown what can be accomplished by persistence and attention to detail. Petrunic and Weisman (2005) recently reconstructed the history of Josephs Fredericks, a noted Canadian child sex murderer. Fredericks would score very high indeed on a retrospective HCR-20 analysis of the kind undertaken here.

Obtaining SPJ Guides

HCR-20/HCR-20 Companion Guide/SVR-20/RSVP
    email: info@proactive-resolutions.com
    web orders: www.proactive-resolutions.com/shop

Savry
  email: savryinfo@yahoo.com
EARL 20-B/EARL 21-C
  email: ccco@childdevelop.ca
WRA-20/ERA-20
  email: admin@workplace.calm.to
SARA
  email: info@proactive-resolutions.com
  email: customer_service@mhs.com(MHS version)
START
web orders: http:/www.bcmhas.ca/Research/ResearchSTART.htm

12

COMPETITIONS

Team Lineups for an Imaginary International Soccer Match[1]

ACTUARIALS

VRAG

LSI-R   PCL-R   PCL:SV   OGRS

SARA^{MHS} STATIC-99

ODARA   SORAG   RRASOR   STABLE-2000

JSAT   EARL-20B   WRA-20   START

SARA^{V1,V2} SAVRY

RSVP   SVR-20   RMGAO   S-RAMM

HCR-20

CLINICALS (SPJs)

The inability of any prediction instrument to consistently outperform other instruments does not allow for strong conclusions to be drawn about any particular instrument.

(Kroner & Mills, 2001, pp. 483–484)

It becomes clear that over recent times a variety of violence prediction and assessment 'instruments' have evolved (e.g. LSI-R, GSIR-R, VRAG, HCR-20, PCL-R, PCL:SV). Examination of the various items in these devices would suggest that their content overlaps substantially (see Forth, 2003). Indeed the VRAG and the HCR-20 incorporate the Hare PCL-R (which was not originally conceived as a prediction device). It is therefore not surprising that it would have occurred to researchers to test these and other devices against one another and to try to determine which one produces the most convincing results. Of course, even those researchers who have made such attempts would realize from the start that their results could vary markedly according to the context in which the study was conducted (e.g. civil vs. forensic vs. criminal justice; within institutions vs. in the community).

It is probably fair to say that, when such tests have been carried out, it is hard to show that any one device stands out remarkably over the others. An example of such work has been reported by Kroner and Mills (2001) who applied to 87 consecutively released federal Canadian offenders the Hare PCL-R, the LSI-R, the HCR-20, the VRAG, and a 14-item Lifestyle Screening Form (Walters, 1991). The outcome measures were institutional misconducts and violent and nonviolent reconvictions, and parole revocations. One point made by the authors is that *none* of these devices was able to explain much of the total variance. Correlations tended to be very low (e.g., from 0.11 to 0.19 for violent recidivism).[2] But the main conclusion was that no one instrument consistently outperformed the others.[3]

In another study, a small number (68) of federal offenders were followed for two years after release from penitentiaries. All were given the LSI-R, the GSIR, the PCL-R, and the VRAG. As well, they completed a 67-item true/false self-report questionnaire called the Self-Appraisal Questionnaire (SAQ; Loza, Dhaliwal, Kroner, & Loza-Fanous, 2000). As with the study noted above, the associations between scale scores and eventual outcome scores were modest for all five devices (correlations ranged from 0.19 to 0.32 for violent recidivism, from 0.44 to 0.59 for general recidivism, and from 0.45 to 0.59 for any failure during follow-up). The SAQ score was in fact the 'best performer' (but did not differ significantly from its competitors). Although it should certainly not be concluded from this small study alone, or even others like it, that self-report measures should replace the Hare PCL-R, VRAG, LSI-R, and the like, these findings do at the very least suggest the advisability of taking into account the to-be-released person's opinion about his or her violence potential.[4,5]

Another 'competition' study reports on some 190 released inmates from Barlinnie, Scotland's largest prison (Cooke, Michie, & Ryan, 2001). The aim was to determine the extent to which reconviction could have been 'predicted' from PCL-R, VRAG, and HCR-20 scores. Men were followed for three years. Baseline offending as measured by reconviction for a violent crime was 20 % after two years and 30 % after three years.[6] This report contains a wealth of sophisticated statistical analyses but the essential point, as with the studies noted above, was that scores on all three schemes linked strongly to various violent and nonviolent outcomes. Cooke et al. reach an eventual conclusion that 'While the HCR-20 does not perform any better than the VRAG or PCL-R in this study, it remains the instrument of choice because it provides guidance on how to *manage* risk not merely how to predict risk' (p. 3, original emphasis).

Doyle, Dolan, and McGovern (2002) applied the Hare PCL:SV, the VRAG, and the 10 historical factors of the HCR-20 to 87 FMHS patients followed three months after discharge. Not surprisingly, scores from these three scales correlated highly with one another (0.80 or better).[7] In this study the PCL:R achieved the highest correlation with outcome at 0.52 with the 10 historical variables of the HCR-20 (i.e. H-10) at 0.31 and the VRAG at 0.37. Not surprisingly, the H-10 correlated highly with the VRAG ($r = 0.83$ and $r = 0.78$ when the PCL:SV item was removed from both scales). The authors noted that: 'It is likely that the inclusion of the clinical and risk management components of the HCR-20 would have enhanced the predictive validity of this instrument' (p. 152).

Gray et al. (2003) have tested several schemes against 34 forensic patients held in two Welsh minimum-secure units. These researchers used the H and C scales of the HCR-20 (i.e., HC-15), the BPRS, the Hare PCL-R, and the Beck Hopelessness Scale (BHS). Statistically significant effects were found when violence was measured weekly over a three-month period (BPRS, $r = 0.61$; HC-15, $r = 0.53$; PCL-R, $r = 0.35$). No such effect was found for the BHS. Yet when the outcome measure was self-harm the BHS achieved significance (+0.67), whereas the other three measures did not. This, of course, shows that, to an extent at any rate, scales measure what they are supposed to measure.

Grevatt, Thomas-Peter, and Hughes (2004) used the HC-15 and a scale called the Violence Risk Scale (VRS; Wong, Olver, Wilde, Nicholaichuk, & Gordon, 2000) to determine retrospectively the accuracy of these two devices in predicting risk of inpatient violence over the short term (six months). Neither scheme was successful. Yet closer analysis showed that the *clinical* items of the HC-15 did associate with violence, abuse, and harassment. They make the interesting point that high scores on some historical items may be *protective* for violence at least under inpatient conditions over the short term. It may be, as they say, that 'those who have a previous history of serious violent convictions are appropriately identified by staff, who then implement management strategies and thus prevent violence with high risk patients' (p. 287). Other published (e.g. McNeil, Gregory, Lam, Binder, & Sullivan, 2003) and unpublished (e.g., Ross, Hart, & Webster, 1998) studies have contributed to this necessary competitive experience.

In Chapter 3 the point was made that it is important to distinguish between the task of prediction and the task of assessment. It may be that currently available general instruments for use in these tasks are beginning to reach their possible limits with respect to the pure group-based statistical prediction exercise.[7] It might be that the next challenge is to find ways of using some instruments, especially those containing dynamic elements (e.g., LSI-R, HCR-20), better to plan workable interventions for particular patients, prisoners, and parolees.

NOTES

1   It is worth noting that some members of the Actuarials have enlisted as players schemes which were originally cast clinically (e.g., LSI-R, PCL-R) but later came to 'secure their reputations' by publishing normative data. The Multi-Health Systems (MHS) version of SARA (1999) follows the basic scheme yet is also still published without that statistical support (1995). Referring to the HCR-20 and the SVR-20, Rogers and Shuman (2005) say, 'These guides can be used to organize clinical material according to a checklist format. However, the crucial line is crossed when the forensic clinicians either quantify scores or create scales. At that moment, the structured clinical guide becomes a 'test' according to the offered standards that must be psychometrically validated' (p. 364). Although the originators of SPJ assessment schemes have tended to be wary of publishing normative data, there is nothing to prevent individual organizations collecting and using such data in an attempt to produce local norms which could help guide the particular assessment process. The danger arises though when actual decisions get made with too much reliance on a possibly deficient 'actuarial' score and too little on the prevailing contextual factors.

2   All five scales performed substantially better when parole revocation served as the outcome measure (i.e., from 0.27 to 0.45). Again, though, the scores across the five instruments did not differ statistically.

3   As Kroner and Mills (2001) put it: 'Once a number of items are chosen, together they cover a sufficiently broad array of domains relevant to antisocial behavior, assessing all that can be tapped for purely predictive purposes' (p. 485).

4   Menzies, Webster, and Sepejak (1985a) included 'Self perception as dangerous' as an item in the DBRS (see Section 7A). But they were forced to exclude it from statistical analysis because the trained coders had insufficient data on which to make their ratings.

5   A case report draws attention to the fact that it pays to listen to what patients and prisoners have to say (Litman, 2003). The author describes how a man had a length period of incarceration as his own 'personal treatment goal'. The prisoner's real end by committing armed bank robberies was to 'lead a stress free and 'interesting' existence and to enjoy the free services provided by prisons' (p. 710).

6   This correlation was more or less unchanged (at 0.78) when the PCL:SV scores were removed.

7   Seifert, Jahn, Bolten, and Wirtz (2002) speak to this when they say: 'Even a predictive tool including main clinical parameters cannot be used indiscriminately for all patients. The group of placed patients is too heterogeneous in

terms of disorder pattern, offense leading to placement, socialization, etc. Ultimately an individual prognosis is required, in which particular items play a more important role than others. For instance, questions about the patient's addictive potential are only relevant in terms of prediction, if an addiction actually exists and is causally related to the patient's delinquency' (p. 63).

13

ASSESSING SEX OFFENDERS[1]

CAREY

His ten charges came to us as a bit of a surprise
Rapes pushed through with less than usual courtesy
Just a young chap too
Works for his dad
Girlfriend comes
Very nice too
Now what?
Got no insight
And he's not realistic
Though he's hardly mentally ill
Can't have him on the street as yet
So it's pretty much a foregone conclusion
He'll hook a lot of rugs the next several years.[1]

R. Karl Hanson

Sexual offenses are among the crimes that invoke the most public concern – even a single case of sexual recidivism can lead to careful scrutiny about the adequacy of the risk evaluation. Some jurisdictions have responded to this concern by automatically considering all sexual offenders to be high risk. The intent of such a policy is laudable – increased public protection – but it is not clear that the risk is best managed by treating all sexual offenders in the same way. Sexual offenders vary in the risk posed to the community. Some offenders may need intensive treatment and supervision programs to reduce their risk to an acceptable level. In other cases, the risk for recidivism is sufficiently low that interventions cannot be expected to further reduce their risk. With such cases, the provision of inappropriate services may even have the unfortunate consequence of increasing their probability of reoffending.

So who is a sex offender? Most sexual offenders can be identified by a recent conviction for an explicitly sexual offense. It is not uncommon, however, for an offender to have committed a sexual offense, but have been convicted for a non-sexual offense, such as assault or unlawful entry. For example, the label of the offense may be non-sexual due to plea-bargaining, or an attempted rape may become simple assault due to the victim's resistance. Certain offenses with a sexual motivation rarely result in explicitly sexual convictions. Voyeurs typically get arrested for trespassing; underwear fetishists get arrested for theft. A substantial proportion of murders of unknown women would be expected to have a sexual motivation.

Some judgment is required when considering offenses that occurred many years ago. For example, a 40-year-old offender may have committed a single sex offense when he was a teenager, but is currently serving time for a series of armed robberies. The evaluators' task is to determine whether the factors that motivated the historical sexual offense are still current concerns. In general, the more recent the sexual offense, the more likely it is that the problems contributing to the sexual offense are still present. Offenders with only prior sexual offenses (no index sex offense) are less likely to sexually reoffend than offenders with a current sexual offense (Bonta & Hanson, 1995), but research has not established a time interval after which prior sexual offenses can be safely ignored. Offenders who have ever had a sexual offense on their record are higher risk to commit another sexual offense than offenders who have never been convicted of a sexual offense.

RECIDIVISM BASE RATES

The starting point for any risk assessment is the recidivism base rate, the proportion of offenders who will reoffend after a period of time. Our recent review of the recidivism research found that after 5–6 years, 13.7 % of mixed samples of sexual offenders recidivated with a sexual offense, 14.3 % recidivated with a non-sexual violent offense, and 36.2 % recidivated with any new offense (Hanson & Morton-Bourgon, 2005). As can be seen from Table 13.1, the total proportion of offenders who are caught for a new sexual crime increases as the follow-up period increases: 10–15 % after five years, 20 % after 10 years, and about 25 % after 15 years. Readers should also note that the yearly recidivism rates decline the longer offenders have been crime-free in the community. Only 4 % of sample recidivated for the first time between year 10 and year 15, whereas 14 % recidivated in the first five years after release.

The rates for those who have sexually assaulted adult females (rapists) are similar to the rates for the general population of sexual offenders. Relatively low rates of

Table 13.1:   Sexual recidivism rates (%)

	5 years	10 years	15 years
All sex offenders	14	20	24
Victim type			
Adults (rapists)	14	21	24
Related children (incest offenders)	6	9	13
Unrelated girls	9	13	16
Unrelated boys	23	28	35
Criminal history			
No prior sex offences	10	15	19
Any prior sex offences	25	32	37
Age at release			
Over 50 years old	7	11	12
Less than 50 years old	15	21	26

Source: Reproduced from Harris, A.J.R. and Hanson, R.K. (2004). *Sex offender recidivism: a simple question.* Corrections user report 2004–3. Ottawa: Public Safety Canada.

sexual recidivism are observed for those whose only victims were related children (incest offenders); relatively high rates are observed for child molesters who have offended against unrelated boys. The data in Table 13.1 were based on 10 individual samples from Canada, the United States, and the United Kingdom (total sample of 4724; Harris & Hanson, 2004).

The available data suggest that most sexual offenders do not recidivate sexually. It is important to remember, however, that many sexual offenses are never reported to police. The extent to which the undetected offenses should influence the observed recidivism rates is a matter of debate.

FEMALE SEXUAL OFFENDERS

Most sexual offenders are men, and most of what is known about sexual offenders concerns male sexual offenders. Nevertheless, women do commit sexual offenses and risk decisions need to be made for this subpopulation. The available evidence suggests that the sexual recidivism rate of female sexual offenders is low. Out of a combined sample of 306, only three (1 %) were known to have committed another sexual offense after an average five-year follow-up period (Cortoni & Hanson, 2005). The rate of violent recidivism was 6.3 %, and the rate of any recidivism was 20.2 %. The low number of female sexual recidivists in research samples precludes the identification of reliable risk factors. Consequently, assessment and intervention with female sexual offenders should be guided by what is known about general recidivism among the general population of women offenders.

RECIDIVISM RISK FACTORS

In general, the factors that predict general recidivism are the same for sexual offenders and non-sexual offenders (Bonta, Law, & Hanson, 1998; Gendreau, Little, & Goggin, 1996; Hanson & Bussière, 1998). All offenders are at increased risk for general recidivism if they are young, have criminal friends, endorse attitudes tolerant of crime, lead an unstable lifestyle, and have a history of criminal behavior. The risk factors for sexual recidivism, however, are not identical to the risk factors for non-sexual crime. Criminal lifestyle is important for the prediction of sexual recidivism, but the most important predictors are factors related to sexual deviancy. A priest who is sexually preoccupied with children may be at low risk for stealing or fighting, but high risk for further sexual misbehavior. Consequently, a prudent evaluator should consider separately the offender's risk for sexual recidivism and for general criminal recidivism.

The factors related to sexual recidivism are presented in Table 13.2. The variables on this list are based on the consistent results of at least three different studies (see

Table 13.2:   Established risk factors for sexual recidivism

Sexual criminal history

- Prior sexual offences
- Victim characteristics (unrelated, strangers, males)
- Early onset of sexual offending
- Diverse sexual crimes
- Non-contact sexual offences

Sexual deviance

- Any deviant sexual preference
- Sexual preoccupations
- Attitudes tolerant of sexual assault

Lifestyle instability/criminality

- Childhood behavior problems (e.g., running away, grade failure)
- Juvenile delinquency
- Any prior offenses
- Lifestyle instability (reckless behavior, employment instability)
- Personality disorder (antisocial, psychopathy)

Intimacy deficits

- Single (never married)
- Conflicts with intimate partners
- Emotional identification with children

Response to treatment/supervision

- Treatment drop-out
- Non-compliance with supervision
- Violation of conditional release

Age (young)

Table 13.3:   Characteristics with little or no relationship with sexual recidivism

Victim empathy
Denial/minimization of sexual offense
Lack of motivation for treatment
Clinical impressions of "benefit" from treatment
Internalizing psychological problems (anxiety, depression, low self-esteem)
History of being sexually abused as a child
Sexual intrusiveness of sexual crimes (e.g., intercourse)
Low social class

reviews by Hanson & Bussière, 1998; Hanson & Morton-Bourgon, 2004, 2005). The major factors associated with sexual recidivism are: (a) a history of sexual crimes; (b) deviant sexual interests; (c) lifestyle instability with a history of rule violation; and (d) difficulties forming stable intimate relationships with appropriate partners. Sexual offenders are also at increased risk when they failed to complete treatment programs and are uncooperative with the conditions of community supervision.

Table 13.3 presents factors that have little or no relationship with sexual recidivism. Some of these factors may be surprising. Factors such as victim empathy, denial of the sexual offense, and the sexual intrusiveness of prior offenses are commonly cited as justifications for case management decisions; none of these factors has been found to be related to the probability of sexual recidivism. Although being sexually abused as a child is related to increased risk of becoming a sexual offender, there is no difference in the recidivism rates of sexual offenders who have or have not been sexually abused themselves. There is no evidence that evaluators are able to assess genuine victim empathy or motivation to change in a manner that is related to future behavior.

THE EFFECTIVENESS OF TREATMENT

The empirical evidence suggests that those sex offenders who complete treatment are less likely to recidivate than those who do not start treatment. On average, Hanson et al. (2002) found that the sexual recidivism rate of the offenders treated with current methods was 10 % compared to 17 % for the comparison group (32 % and 51 % for general recidivism). The average follow-up period was about five years. Current treatment programs typically are cognitive-behavioral approaches for adult sexual offenders and systemic treatments for adolescent sexual offenders. Cognitive-behavioral treatments consider offending as a learned pattern, which offenders can control by identifying the personal risk factors associated with reoffending, and by changing their life situations in order to avoid encounters with high-risk situations. Systemic treatments work with the social systems (e.g., school, family, peers, courts) surrounding the offender.

Not all treatment programs are effective. The older, largely psychodynamic treatments were not associated with reductions in recidivism. Even the best treatment model is unlikely to have any effect if it is poorly implemented. Consequently, when evaluators consider the contribution of treatment to the overall risk assessment, they need to carefully consider the quality of the treatment provided. High-quality treatment programs are likely to have an explicit, empirically based model of change, have clearly defined procedures, target factors known to be related to sexual recidivism, and have methods for monitoring treatment integrity (Cook & Philip, 2000). Some jurisdictions have implemented accreditation criteria in order to identity effective correctional programs (Lipton, Thornton, McGuire, Porporino, & Hollin, 2000).

Although completing treatment is associated with a reduction in recidivism, it has been difficult to distinguish between offenders who have done well and those who have done poorly in treatment. In some cases, those offenders who appeared to have done well in treatment recidivate at higher rates than the offenders who appeared to make only minimal progress (Seto & Barbaree, 1998). The evaluations of treatment change with the strongest relationship to recidivism are structured evaluations based on established risk factors (e.g., deviant sexual arousal, attitudes tolerant of sexual crime) rather than factors associated with behavior during treatment (e.g., active participation, quality of victim empathy letters).

OVERALL EVALUATIONS OF RISK

None of the individual risk factors demonstrate sufficient relationship to sexual recidivism that they can be used in isolation. Consequently, evaluators need to consider a range of risk factors in their overall evaluation of risk. The best method of combining risk factors into an overall evaluation remains a topic of debate within the professional community. There are two main approaches to conducting risk assessments, which I will label the pure prediction approach and the understanding approach. In the pure prediction approach, risk factors are selected based solely on their empirical relationships with outcome. The ideal prediction scale would include all relevant risk factors, optimize the weighting of these items, and be used on a sample similar to the samples upon which it was developed. The content of the items is irrelevant, provided that they are related to risk. In contrast, the ideal assessment for evaluators who prioritize *understanding* would be based on a valid model of sexual recidivism. This model would be generally true of sexual offenders and specifically true of the offender who is currently being assessed. For the understanding approach, the ideal items would be those that provide the greatest insight into the characteristics and situations associated with risk for the particular offender.

The most common pure prediction tools are the Static-99 (Hanson & Thornton, 2000), the Rapid Risk Assessment for Sexual Offense Recidivism (RRASOR;

Hanson, 1997), the Sex Offender Risk Appraisal Guide (SORAG; Quinsey, Harris, Rice & Cormier, 2006), and the Minnesota Sex Offender Screening Tool – Revised (MnSOST-R; Epperson, Kaul, & Hesselton, 1998). For the prediction of sexual recidivism, all of these are consistently more accurate than unstructured professional opinion, and there is relatively little difference between them (Hanson & Morton-Bourgon, 2004).

The RRASOR contains four items: any male victims; any unrelated victims; age less than 25; and prior sexual offenses. Each item is assigned one point, except prior sexual offense, which could be accorded up to three points based on the number of prior sexual charges and convictions. The Static-99 contains all the RRASOR items, plus items concerning relationship history, violent offenses, and stranger victims. Both RRASOR and Static-99 were designed to be scored from readily available file information. Given its increased predictive accuracy, Static-99 is recommended over RRASOR.

The SORAG was designed to predict violent reoffending among sexual offenders, and is a better predictor of general violence than the other sexual offender risk measures (Hanson & Morton-Bourgon, 2004). It contains 14 items, the most heavily weighted items being the Psychopathy Checklist – Revised (Hare, 1991) and age at index offense. The MnSOST-R was designed to assess the risk of sexual recidivism among incarcerated rapists and child molesters. It contains 16 items, mostly related to criminal history and offense characteristics.

For evaluators who value understanding their cases, pure prediction scales are unsatisfying. A specific score may indicate high risk, but the score does not explain why the risk is high, nor does it provide any direction as to what can be done to reduce that risk. Consequently, evaluators typically want to 'get to know' the offender, for example, through interviews or reviews of case files. Unfortunately, it is not obvious what evaluators should be looking for; the predictive accuracy of unstructured clinical assessments has been disappointing.

Such concerns have motivated the development of structured professional guidelines. These guidelines provide a framework for understanding risk assessments by specifying the factors that should be considered by prudent evaluators. The factors in these guidelines are selected based on theory and empirical evidence. Not all factors, however, are expected to be equally important in every case; consequently, the overall evaluation of risk is left to the evaluator's own professional judgment. Examples of these structured professional guidelines are the Sexual Violence Risk –20 (SVR-20; Boer, Hart, Kropp, & Webster, 1997), and the Risk for Sexual Violence Protocol (RSVP; Hart et al., 2003).

Another form of risk tool for understanding the risk posed by sexual offenders starts with a list of conceptually derived items (similar to the structured professional guidelines), but goes on to specify how the individual factors should be combined into an overall evaluation of risk. Examples of these *conceptual-actuarial* measures are Stable-2000 (Hanson & Harris, 2004), the Violence Prediction Scheme – Sexual Offender version (VRS-SO; Olver, 2003) and the Structured Risk Assessment procedure developed by Thornton (2002). All these measures contain a range of potentially dynamic (changeable) factors, such as sexual preoccupations, intimacy deficits, and problems with self-regulation.[2]

Compared to the research on the pure prediction schemes, there has been relatively little research on the validity of the professional guidelines and conceptual-actuarial measures. The available research suggests that conceptual-actuarial measures have levels of predictive accuracy similar to those found for pure prediction schemes (McGrath, Cumming, & Livingston, 2005; Olver, 2003; Thornton, 2002). The research on the SVR-20 has produced variable results, with strong predictive accuracy shown in some samples (de Vogel, de Ruiter, van Beek, & Mead, 2004) but not others (Sjöstedt & Långström, 2002). The reasons for this variability remain unknown.

SUMMARY AND CONCLUSIONS

Sexual offenders share many characteristics with general criminal offenders. The chances that the typical sexual offender will reoffend with a non-sexual offense (e.g., theft) is greater than the probability that he will reoffend with a sexual offense. There are certain distinctive characteristics, however, associated with risk of sexual recidivism, such as prior sex offenses and male victims.

Evaluators are likely to increase the accuracy of their assessments when they considered factors empirically related to recidivism risk. A number of specialized sex offender risk scales are available, and these scales are more accurate than unguided clinical judgment. The most well-established risk scales focus on static, historical factors. These scales are useful for long-term risk prediction, but they cannot be used to identify treatment targets or evaluate change. Fortunately, there has been considerable progress in recent years in the identification of dynamic (changeable) risk factors. As well, a number of structured approaches have been developed to help evaluators understand (not just predict) the risk posed by sexual offenders. There is still debate, however, as to how best to combine diverse information into an overall evaluation of risk.

NOTES

1   Carey is in the early stages of assessment. His past conduct and other matters will require close examination before it can be properly concluded that 'he's

hardly mentally ill'. The severity of the charges do suggest that, no matter what, he will be likely detained in either the FMHS or the CJS.

2 In order to use these tools appropriately, it is necessary to have an understanding of sex offenders. I recently conducted a large number of reliability codings for Stable-2000. I found that problems with reliability were most likely when the raters did not share a common vision of the case. In reading through the files, I typically came to a point where I felt I understood the offender, and the rest of the file seemed predictable and expected. Once that understanding was achieved (which may take some time), the specific scoring of the 16 Stable-2000 items could be completed in a matter of minutes.

14

SPOUSAL ASSAULTERS[1]

EUGENE

Tall guy, quite powerfully built, illiterate, mean
Not a thinker, not interested in what's talked over
In our Tuesday meetings
For sex-deranged men
Mainly he's mad as hell because his wife packed up
After he beat the living hell out of her
And took the kids, including the offended-against girls
Can't get it straight
They're not his to violate
He's angry I'll not write it's safe for him to visit
They tell me he's roaming the place, looking for me.[2]

P. Randall Kropp

Spousal violence risk assessment can serve as the cornerstone for offender management in a variety of contexts. Pre-release risk assessments can assist courts, tribunals, and boards to set appropriate sentencing, treatment, and supervision conditions. This brief chapter attempts to review existing knowledge about spousal violence to provide a resource for those conducting or interpreting such assessments. This summary comprises five basic principles.[2]

PRINCIPLES OF SPOUSAL ASSAULT RISK ASSESSMENT

Principle 1: Risk Assessments Should Employ Multiple Sources of Information

The best risk assessment requires the evaluator to obtain multiple sources of information with multiple methods. Of course, this is not always possible, as access to reliable informants and accurate historical information is often restricted. However, if a risk assessment cannot be based on a comprehensive consideration of information, limitations to any conclusions should be appropriately specified. Ideally, a spousal violence risk assessment will include an interview with the accused, a review of official police records, victim and witness statements, criminal history, and collateral records, including an interview with the victim (see Principle 3 below). Although psychological testing is often unavailable and impractical, it can provide valuable information regarding the presence of major mental illness, substance abuse, personality characteristics of the offender, or address specific traits such as anger and impulsivity vital to the assessment of risk. Psychological tests may also provide important information about the types of situations or circumstances within which the offender is likely to be violent (e.g., angry/reactive versus instrumental violence).[3] A review of collateral records is important in evaluating the veracity of information given by the offender, and often provides the evaluator with additional information not offered by the offender.

Principle 2: Risk Assessments Should Consider Risk Factors Supported in the Literature

Those conducting or reviewing risk assessments should only consider risk factors that have some support in the empirical or clinical literature. In recent years a number of comprehensive literature reviews have been published on risk factors for domestic violence (Dutton & Kropp, 2000; Hilton & Harris, 2004; Riggs, Caulfield, & Street, 2000; Schumacher, Feldbau-Kohn, Slep, & Heyman, 2001) and intimate partner homicide (Aldridge & Browne, 2003; Campbell, Sharps, & Glass, 2001). These reviews reflect a burgeoning literature in the past 15 years that has seen hundreds of studies touching on risk issues, and there now appears to be considerable consensus regarding the relevant risk factors. Most risk factor lists include the following: (a) history of violent behavior towards family members (including children), acquaintances, and strangers; (b) history of physical, sexual, or emotional abuse towards intimate partners; (c) access to or use of lethal weapons; (d) antisocial attitudes and behaviors, and affiliation with antisocial peers; (e) relationship instability, especially if there has been a recent separation or divorce; (f) presence of other life stressors, including employment/financial problems or recent loss; (g) history of being the witness or victim of family violence in childhood; (h) evidence of mental health problems and/or personality disorder (i.e., antisocial, dependent, borderline traits); (i) resistance to change and motivation for treatment; and (j) attitudes that support violence towards women (Kropp & Hart, 2000; Pence & Lizdas, 1998; Roehl & Guertin, 1998; Sonkin, 1997; Straus, 1991; Sugarman & Hotaling 1991). These risk factors are generally believed to be associated or correlated with violence and are not necessarily causal in nature.

Principle 3: Risk Assessments Should be Victim-Informed

There are many reasons to believe that those accused or convicted of spousal violence will be less than truthful about their assaultive past. When before the courts, offenders would be ill advised to disclose information that could negatively affect their sentencing disposition or release opportunity. Moreover, offenders are often in a state of denial or they greatly minimize their responsibility for violence. Therefore any assessment based on the accused's self-report only should be made with extreme caution, as the result will likely be an underestimate of risk. It is absolutely critical to make some attempt to interview the victim or gather the victim's version of events from other sources. The importance of victim information has been empirically demonstrated. Weisz, Tolman, and Saunders (2000) reported that survivors' predictions of reassault were significantly associated with the reoccurrence of severe violence. Similarly, Gondolf (2001) found that in a 30-month follow-up of court-mandated batterers, the most significant predictors of reoffense were offender drunkenness and women's perceptions of safety. Whittemore and Kropp (2002) reported a study in which Spousal Assault Risk Assessment Guide (SARA) ratings of risk were made using offender and file information only, and then compared to ratings made with additional victim-reported information. The results revealed that risk ratings made with the added victim information were *higher* than those made without. It seems, therefore, that victims are providing some critical information that is related both to perception of risk and recidivism. It is important to remember, however, that victims' perceptions of risk are not always accurate. Victims can also grossly minimize or underestimate the risk posed by their partners. For example, Campbell et al. (2003) reported the results of an investigation of actual and attempted femicides. Proxy informants were used to gather information regarding the actual homicides. Campbell et al. noted that victims underestimated their spouse's risk in 47 % and 53 % of the actual and attempted femicides, respectively.

Interviews with the victim should ideally cover the same domains assessed with the accused. Information obtained by the victim can then be compared with information presented by the accused. Additionally, some of the same tools used for measuring the type, frequency, and severity of abuse can, and should, also be used with the victim. It may also be beneficial to conduct interviews with relatives and children as they may have valuable insights into the offender's pattern of abusive behavior. Of course, any interview with a victim should be prefaced with appropriate cautions regarding the voluntary nature of the interview and the limits (if any) to confidentiality. The victim should always be completely informed regarding the potential use of the provided information. It is possible, for example, that the risk posed to the victim will increase in the short-term following her participation in a court-related assessment of the abuser.

Principle 4: Risk Assessments can be Improved by Using Tools and/or Guidelines

Risk assessment has become common practice for mental health professionals, and an active debate exists regarding the proper method for assessing risk. Much of this debate centers around the classic actuarial versus clinical prediction controversy (Bonta, Law, & Hanson, 1998; Grove & Meehl, 1996; Litwack, 2001; Meehl, 1996; Quinsey, Harris, Rice, & Cormier, 1998), a debate, it seems, that is still unresolved. In general, there appears to be agreement that some degree of structure is required when conducting risk assessments. Some authors have taken a strict actuarial stand (e.g., Quinsey et al., 1998), while others have argued for a more structured clinical approach (e.g., Kropp, Hart, Webster, & Eaves, 1999). Borum (1996) and Melton, Petrila, Poythress, & Slobogin (1997) observed that despite the debate about the ability of mental health professionals to predict violence, the courts have continued to rely on such assessments. In the absence of perfect prediction instruments, the practitioner must ensure that his or her evaluation is based on the 'best practice' available. In this respect, risk assessment tools and guidelines can provide the necessary structure.

There has been a relatively recent proliferation of instruments designed to assess risk of domestic violence (Dutton & Kropp, 2000; Hilton & Harris, 2004; Kropp, 2004; Roehl & Guertin, 1998). Despite the growth in this area, however, the research on many of these instruments is currently sparse or lacking. Indeed, there are few that are empirically validated. What follows is a review of those instruments for which published reliability and validity data currently exist.

Danger Assessment (DA)

The Danger Assessment (DA) was developed by Jacquelyn Campbell (1995) and colleagues in consultation with victims of domestic violence, law enforcement officials, those working in shelters, and other experts. It is designed to assess the likelihood for spousal homicide, and the original items were chosen from retrospective studies on homicide or near-fatal injury cases.

The DA consists of two sections. The first is a calendar that asks potential victims to record the severity and frequency of violence in the past year (1 = slap, pushing, no injuries and/or lasting pain through 5 = use of weapon, wounds from weapon). This part of the measure is intended to raise the awareness of the woman and reduce the minimization of the abuse. In one initial study, 38 % of women who initially reported no increase in severity and frequency changed their response to 'yes' after filling out the calendar (Campbell et al., 2001). The second section consists of a 15-item yes/no list of risk factors associated with intimate partner homicide. The woman can complete the instrument independently or with the assistance of professionals working in the health care, victim advocate, or criminal justice systems. The number of risk factors is then totaled, although the developer does not recommend using cut-off scores for decision making.

Campbell et al. (2001) summarized the results of 10 research studies conducted on the DA. In those studies, inter-rater reliability coefficients were in the moderate to good range ($r = 0.60$ to 0.86). According to Campbell et al., the DA has also been demonstrated to have strong test–retest reliability in two studies ($r = 0.89$ to 0.94). Construct validity has also been reported, with the DA discriminating between battered women in an emergency department and non-abused controls (Campbell, 1995), and with DA correlating strongly with other measures of abusive behavior such as the Index of Spouse Abuse and the Conflict Tactics Scale (Campbell, 1995). The DA is also associated with the severity and frequency of domestic violence (McFarlane et al., 1998).

Campbell and colleagues (2003) recently completed a multi-site case control study to investigate the relative importance of various risk factors for femicide in abusive relationships. The study included many of the items from the original DA. The investigators interviewed 220 proxies of femicide victims along with 343 abused control women. The results indicated that risk factors discriminating between the two groups included: perpetrators' access to a gun and previous threat with a weapon; perpetrators' stepchild in the home; victim estrangement, especially from a controlling partner; victim leaving abuser for another partner; and the perpetrator's use of a gun in the homicide. Stalking, forced sex in the relationship, and abuse during pregnancy also bore some significance. All but one of the original 15 DA items were significantly associated with femicide, and the measure was subsequently revised to include additional risk factors that were not in the original version. Both the original and revised versions of the DA significantly discriminated between the femicide and abused control groups. This was a retrospective study, and Campbell et al. (2001) have recommended that prospective studies are still needed to evaluate the predictive validity of the DA.

Domestic Violence Screening Inventory (DVSI)

The Domestic Violence Screening Inventory (DVSI) was developed by the Colorado Department of Probation Services. The DVSI was designed to be a brief risk assessment instrument that can be completed with a quick criminal history review. It contains 12 social and behavioral factors found to be statistically related to recidivism by domestic violence perpetrators on probation (Williams & Houghton, 2004). The authors also justified including the risk factors based on a thorough review of the literature, and they consulted judges, law enforcement personnel, lawyers, and victim advocates. The social factors include current employment and relationship status. The behavioral items essentially summarize the offender's history of DV and non-DV criminal history. A copy of the DVSI coding sheet is included in an appendix of the Williams and Houghton (2004) validation paper.

The DVSI was validated on a sample of 1 465 male domestic violence offenders on probation, selected consecutively over a nine-month period. Data on reoffending were collected in a six-month follow-up period from a subsample of the victims ($N = 125$) of these perpetrators and from official records for all perpetrators during an 18-month follow-up period. The results suggest that the DVSI was administered reliably, although the authors acknowledged that the design of the study required that they use multivariate analyses to conduct 'quasi-interrater reliability.' The DVSI also appears to have adequate concurrent validity, correlating strongly with ratings of risk to spouses on the Spousal Assault Risk Assessment Guide (SARA). Finally, Williams and Houghton reported statistically significant predictive validity for the DVSI using a prospective (follow-up) design. The authors used a common method for analyzing effect size in risk assessment research labeled receiver operating characteristic (ROC) analysis. The area under the curve (AUC) using this analysis was 0.60 ($r = 0.18$, $p = 0.00$). One way of interpreting the AUC of 0.60 is as follows: If a recidivist and non-recidivist were randomly chosen from their respective groups, the probability would be 0.60 that the recidivist would have a higher DVSI score. There have been no independent validity studies of the DVSI to date.

Ontario Domestic Assault Risk Assessment (ODARA)

The ODARA is a 13-item actuarial instrument recently developed in Ontario, Canada (Hilton, Harris, Rice, Lang, & Cormier, 2004). The items were empirically derived from an initial pool of potential risk factors gleaned from police files on 589 domestic violence perpetrators. The study followed back the cases for an average of five years and coded the risk factors from archival information in several domains, which included offender characteristics, domestic violence history, non-domestic criminal history, relationship characteristics, victim characteristics, and index offence. Using setwise and stepwise logistic regression, the developers were able to reduce the item pool to 13. The resulting instrument, the ODARA, correlated well with the DA and the SARA (see below), thus demonstrating adequate convergent validity. The instrument was also able to discriminate significantly between recidivists and non-recidivists (AUC = 0.77), and the ODARA total score was also associated with the number, severity, and imminence of new assaults. One shortcoming of the study was that there were no homicides in the construction sample, and the authors have cautioned against using the ODARA for predicting femicide. There is also a need for further cross-validation studies to substantiate the precise probability associated with each ODARA score.

Spousal Assault Risk Assessment Guide (SARA)

The Spousal Assault Risk Assessment Guide (Kropp et al., 1995, 1999) is a set of guidelines for the content and process of a thorough risk assessment. It is composed of 20 items identified by a review of the empirical literature on wife assault and the literature written by clinicians that evaluate male wife abusers. The authors point out that the SARA is not a test. Its purpose is not to provide absolute or relative measures of risk using cutoff scores or norms, but rather to structure and enhance professional judgments about risk. Since the SARA is not a formal psychological test, professionals other than psychologists can use it. The authors list several potential applications of the SARA: pre-trial assessment, pre-sentence, correctional intake, correctional discharge, civil justice matters, warning third parties, and as an instrument to review spousal risk assessments given by others.

The item selection for the SARA was carefully based on relevant factors reported in the literature.[4] The SARA assessment procedure includes interviews with the accused and victims, standardized measures of physical and emotional abuse, drug and alcohol abuse, and a review of collateral records, such as police reports, victim statements, criminal records, and other psychological procedures.

The authors have evaluated the reliability and validity of judgments concerning risk for violence made using the SARA (Kropp & Hart, 2000). SARA ratings were analyzed in six samples of adult male offenders (total $N = 2\,681$). The distribution of ratings indicated that offenders were quite heterogeneous with respect to the presence of individual risk factors and to overall perceived risk. Structural analyses of the risk factors indicated moderate levels of internal consistency and item homogeneity. Interrater reliability was high for judgments concerning the presence of individual risk factors and for overall perceived risk. SARA ratings significantly discriminated between offenders with and without a history of spousal violence in one sample ($t = 27.04$, $p < 0.0001$), and between recidivistic and non-recidivistic spousal assaulters in another ($r = 0.36$, $p. < 0.0001$; or AUC $= 0.70$). Finally, SARA ratings showed good convergent and discriminant validity with respect to other measures related to risk for general and violent criminality (Kropp & Hart, 2000).

Two recently published studies have supported the validity of the SARA. Williams and Houghton (2004), in their evaluation of the DVSI, included the SARA in some of the analyses. Thus, the results also supported the concurrent validity of the SARA, and the AUC for the SARA in the 18-month follow-up exceeded that of the DVSI (0.65 versus 0.60, although the difference was not statistically significant). Similarly, Hilton et al. (2004) reported an AUC for the SARA of 0.64 in a five-year follow-back study. However, the accuracy of the result was limited by the fact the authors could not guarantee the 'integrity' (p. 271) of the SARA scores because they were coded from archival data only.

Finally, due to calls from the field, particularly from law enforcement agencies, to have briefer risk assessment tools to conduct time-limited assessments, the authors of the SARA have developed the Brief Spousal Assault Form for the Evaluation of Risk, or B-SAFER (Kropp, Hart, & Belfrage, 2005). It consists of 10 risk factors, which were derived from the 20 SARA risk items using factor analysis. The B-SAFER has been piloted in Canada and Sweden, but no data have yet been published (Kropp, 2004).

Principle 5: Risk Assessments Should Lead to Risk Management

Effective management of offender risk and victim safety must not end with a risk assessment. Indeed, it is insufficient to report the level of risk posed by the accused without a discussion of how to manage that individual's risk. It is the risk assessment, however, that will guide this process. Risk factors are either static (not changeable through intervention) or dynamic (changeable through intervention or other influences) and it is those dynamic risk factors on which the risk management strategies are targeted. For example, substance abuse is a dynamic risk factor, and may lead to the recommendation of substance abuse treatment as a strategy for managing risk. It is likely that useful risk management will involve a combination of treatment, supervision, and victim safety planning. However, management and safety plans must be tailored to an individual's personal constellation of risk factors. Finally, because risk is dynamic, the evaluator must recognize that part of risk management requires follow-up, recurrent risk assessments. Risk can increase or decrease depending on levels of intervention, passage of time, and circumstances. As discussed by Heilbrun (1997), for a management model to be effective, there must be continuous decision making and the ability to modify previous decisions based on new information.

NOTES

1   This chapter is in part a revision of a paper authored by Whittemore and Kropp (2002) appearing in the *Journal of Forensic Psychology Practice, 2,* 53–64.
2   It is clear that the counsellor is frustrated in trying to get across to Eugene the idea that he is doing harm to his children. Eugene brings to light something not touched on previously in the text: the assessor, perceiving himself to be at risk, wonders what will occur when next he meets Eugene. Provided by C.D.W.
3   'Angry/reactive' violence refers to largely unplanned, unfocussed aggression; 'instrumental' means goal-directed to achieve a particular end.
4   The SARA items are as follows: (1) Past Assault of Family Members (Criminal History); (2) Past Assault of Strangers or Acquaintances (Criminal History); (3) Past Violation of Conditional Release or Community Supervision (Criminal History); (4) Recent Relationship Problems (Psychosocial Adjustment);

(5) Recent Employment Problems (Psychosocial Adjustment); (6) Victim of and/or Witness to Family Violence as a Child or Adolescent (Psychosocial Adjustment); (7) Recent Substance Abuse/Dependence (Psychosocial Adjustment); (8) Recent Suicidal or Homicidal Ideation/Intent (Psychosocial Adjustment); (9) Recent Psychotic and/or Manic Symptoms (Psychosocial Adjustment); (10) Personality Disorder with Anger, Impulsivity, or Behavioral Instability (Psychosocial Adjustment); (11) Past Physical Assaults (Spousal Assault History); (12) Past Sexual Assault/Sexual Jealousy (Spousal Assault History); (13) Past use of Weapons and/or Credible Threats of Death (Spousal Assault History); (14) Recent Escalation in Frequency or Severity of Assault (Spousal Assault History); (15) Past Violation of 'No Contact' Orders (Spousal Assault History); (16) Extreme Minimization or Denial of Spousal Assault History (Spousal Assault History); (17) Attitudes that Support or Condone Spousal Assault (Spousal Assault History); (18) Severe and/or Sexual Assault (Alleged/Most Recent/Index Offence); (19) Use of Weapons and/or Credible Threats of Death (Alleged/Most Recent/Index Offence); and (20) Violation of 'No Contact' Order (Alleged/Most Recent/Index Offence).

15

INTERVENTIONS

Integrated Interventions

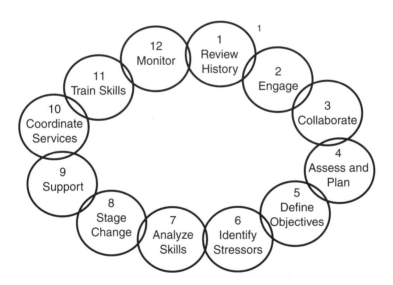

the way out of criminal behavior is probably just as complex as the way in, that desistance from crime is dependent on human agency as well as social structure, and that, these two aspects interact.

(Haggård, Gumpert, & Grann, 2001, p. 1050)

A finding of considerable importance was raised in Section 7C. There it was noted that, in a study by Hare et al., those prisoners with high factor 1 PCL-R scores who had received therapeutic, educational, and vocational programs were *more* likely to recidivate than those who had not. This observation suggests that it is always wise to recognize that the success or failure of a therapeutic or educational program depends critically upon the characteristics of the individual for whom it is being provided. There is very little point in offering expensive and time-consuming programs if there is no effort to determine actual effectiveness and to find out if the intended therapeutic measures are pertinent in the case at hand. This is particularly so because it is becoming clear that some programs can create as many or more problems than they solve. It is also becoming increasingly evident that treatments often need to be combined (e.g. psychopharmacological approaches paired with cognitive behavioral therapy) if treatment stands a chance of being effective (Sammons & Schmidt, 2001).

Readers of this volume will perhaps have noted the point made in Section 7D where recent findings from the MacArthur study were reviewed. One result was that there was a significant negative correlation (− 0.10) between outcome violence and the proportion of social network members who were also mental health professionals (MacArthur et al., 2001, Table B1, p. 165). Although this effect was not a strong one statistically, it does suggest that, in this study at least, it appears that 'more may not necessarily be better'.[2]

The MacArthur study was not intended to assess the effects of treatment interactions. Though in fact providing some illumination on the topic (see pp. 129–143), the authors acknowledge that their project did not include a procedure whereby persons were assigned randomly to treatment conditions. Such a large-scale, multisite, randomized-controlled study has been conducted on over 700 civil patients in the United Kingdom (Walsh et al., 2001). In this project, patients were assigned randomly to one of two conditions: intervention or control. Each group contained about 350 patients. Members of the treatment group received intensive case management for two years (10–15 cases per manager); members of the control group were given standard case management (30–35 cases per manager). Three of the sites were in London, one in Manchester. To be eligible, patients discharged to the community had to be between 18 and 65 and carry a diagnosis of psychosis. Researchers independent of the case managers completed interviews at the point of discharge and at two-year follow-up. Their other task was to elicit information about assaultiveness. Patients in the intensive case management group received more than twice the care given to the controls.

During the two years of the project, about 22 % of the total 700 participants in the Walsh et al. study were physically assaultive to another person.[3] The factors which 'predicted' violence tended to be similar to those noted in Chapter 3. They were: (1) previous violence; (2) young age (19 to 39 years); (3) drug misuse; (4) being victimized in the past year; and (5) learning difficulties. The main finding of interest, though, was that the two groups did *not* differ in terms of assaultiveness over the previous two years (23 % for the intensive case management group and 22 % for the control group).

While doubtless recognizing that violence reduction is only one measure of a case management program's efficacy, the authors of this extensive, difficult-to-conduct study seem puzzled by the lack of treatment effectiveness. They conclude that the 'way of the future' may be to focus 'on the effect of combining community treatment with legally enforceable interventions to reduce violence' (p. 4).[4] To back their point they cite a paper by Swanson et al. (2000).[5]

So far in this highly selective account of the effectiveness of interventions, we have stressed the fact that the 'obvious' cannot always be demonstrated, at least in statistically based studies. It is relatively easy, given the right measures, to show that prior assaultiveness is associated with subsequent violence. Such a finding would be expected and it can indeed be substantiated. But Walsh et al. (2001) were unable to find support for the idea that the more intensive is the supervision and support, the less will be the violence in the community. This does not mean to say, of course, that the results of this one study convincingly demonstrate the absence of the expected association. It could be that the finding is 'there,' but was not discovered in that particular project.[6] There is, in fact, plenty of evidence to suggest that interventions 'work' (e.g., Bellack, Mueser, Gingerich, & Agresta, 1997, 2004; Ashford, Sales, & Reid, 2001; Skeem, Markos, Tiemann, & Manchak, 2006). As well, a good deal of conceptual thought has been given to what must be put in place if treatments and interventions are to be successful (e.g., Farkas, Gagne, Anthony, & Chamberlin, 2005).

A simple, non-statistical, approach to intervention effectiveness might conform better with clinical expectation. Rather than ask patients or former patients to accept this or that treatment, it can sometimes be instructive to ask them, in an organized way, to describe what conditions and circumstances helped them live a violence-free life. This is an approach taken by Haggård et al. (2001). These investigators isolated six individuals who had each scored high on the 10-item historical scale of the HCR-20 but who had not offended formally in the course of a 10-year follow-up involving some 400 violent offenders.[7] Four of the men consented to being interviewed. All lived in or outside small cities. Two were in rural areas. Only one had a full-time job. Two were physically ill.

All four men were 'clean on agency records.' But three of them admitted to some minor offenses during interview. One revealed that he was again criminally involved after a long period of desistance.[8] Some interesting points emerge from this study:

1   'Insight' often takes a long time to come (p. 1055);
2   The experience of being in a forensic hospital is not one some individuals are likely to forget and it can seemingly have a deterring effect on crime;
3   Support from family can be crucial;
4   Medication provided by a trusted physician can be extraordinarily helpful;

5 The pathway toward changing life patterns is a long one and persons may continue in crime for some time after deciding to make the break;

6 Learning the anger management technique of being able to walk away from destabilizing circumstances is essential for some;

7 Reduction in substance abuse is vital but so too is learning how to use alcohol and drugs under conditions where the potential for harm is limited;

8 Some persons tend to be mistrustful of forensic and psychological evaluations;

9 Good relationships established with at least one person while in prison or in hospital can make a big difference in the habilitation process;

10 With institutionalization, persons lose much of their ability to deal with the mundane aspects of life like paying bills;

11 Following release, individuals require a much greater amount of help than is commonly realized; and

12 With a criminal or psychiatric record, or both, stigmatization exerts its effects and it becomes very hard to gain employment, housing, and the like (Sartorius & Schulze, 2005).[9,10,11]

Haggård et al. (2001) put it well when they say: 'It is important to understand individual processes of initiation, maintenance, and desistance from crime to, if possible, develop treatment, risk assessment, and monitoring strategies. Risk assessment has its weakness. For one, it was mainly developed from statistics and used on an individual level in a heterogeneous group. Therefore, it is crucial to gain knowledge concerning subgroups within the offender group and also to combine the actuarial models with a clinical assessment when making judgments about risk' (p. 1061).

NOTES

1 This 'bicycle chain' was created on the basis of the 2001 HCR-20 Companion Guide. It attempts to portray a sequence of events, which often has to occur if transitions are to be successful (i.e., each link intact).

2 Of course, it is possible that the reason that such patients had more mental health professionals in their networks, was that they had relatively fewer other supports and that, under ordinary circumstances, such supports have strong violence-attenuating effects.

3 The authors note that this figure is not much different from that obtained in the MacArthur study during one year community follow-up (27.5 %). Dvoskin and Steadman (1994) outlined the possible value of using intensive case management to reduce community violence by mentally disordered people. They offer compelling arguments for this approach. In their view: 'One important reason for having low caseloads for intensive case managers is that developing a personal relationship with a client takes a great deal of time and individualized attention' (p. 681). They are right to remind us that 'Case management may be

but one piece of a comprehensive mental health care system' but, on the basis of the Walsh et al. study, there as yet seems to be lack of evidence to support Dvoskin and Steadman's expectation that it 'is the key to managing the risk of violence in the community among people with mental illness' (p. 684).

4 It is of course clear that the standard forensic mental health system does in fact combine both approaches. As sitting members on the Ontario Review Board, the authors are constantly reminded that the bulk of accused persons take very seriously the conditions imposed annually by the board. By their formality, these boards seem to be able to exert profound influences in some cases.

5 Parole boards, by way of contrast, make decisions that are very 'big' for inmates. Yet, once made, there tends to be little connection between the boards, the parole officers, the institutions and services involved, and the parolee.

6 Kraemer, Stice, Kazdin, Offord, and Kupfer (2001) also help our understanding of why some programs may be ineffective. They say: 'When there are chains of causal risk factors (all mediators), addressing only one link of that chain may result in treatment effects of minor clinical or policy significance. In the same situation, sequential interventions addressing each link in turn may succeed. Currently, most prevention programs are aimed at multiple risk factors at the same time in blunderbuss fashion. This is not a substitute for understanding how and when individual differences operate' (p. 854). They go on to point out that 'blunderbuss' efforts tend to focus on a wide array of risk factors, both static and dynamic, and that, when this is done, treatment effects may be diluted or diverted. Generally, it seems, as an analogy, that the task is to get the right kinds of oil in exactly the right spots within the machine. More is not necessarily better.

7 It is interesting to note that only six men met all of four criteria: (1) H scale HCR-20 score of 12 or higher; (2) previous violent crimes and at least five convictions for any crime; (3) not been in a forensic unit or prison for the past five of the 10 follow-up years; and (4) not been reconvicted for any crime during the past 10 years.

8 He hoped that participation in the research might help him resist such temptations. Perhaps the influence of research has been underestimated!

9 The point was made by the authors that two of the men 'lived in very isolated rural areas, scared of themselves and how they would react to different situations or how other people would react should they become aware of their pasts' (p. 1059).

10 For a compelling autobiographical account readers are referred to Athens and Starr (2003).

11 For further helpful comments about the study of individual cases using structured professional guides, see Robertson, Yaren, and Globerman (2004) who say on the one hand that 'recently evolved risk evaluation instruments are beginning to provide a solid empirical base, one which was previously completely lacking' but remind colleagues in the next sentence that 'it is a mistake to expect perfection' (p. 13).

16

TRANSITIONS

Mary-Lou Martin

Such incidents are especially apt to occur at transition points, as when, for example, the patient leaves the ward for the first time unaccompanied by staff. It is therefore critical to monitor risk levels systematically and continuously to ensure that patients are neither unduly restricted nor allowed opportunity to aggress against fellow patients and staff members.

(Müller-Isberner, Webster & Gretenkord, submitted, p.18 in draft)

What is transition? Change is an inherent part of life and in practical terms, life is a continuing experience of transition. Transition is a complex and dynamic process that occurs when a person experiences a process or period of change. Transition happens in all aspects of our lives. Transition is not usually a single event, but more often centers on situations that are happening on different levels. Transition is not always under our control and it can be unpredictable. Transition is sometimes tough but not necessarily impossible. Transition can be anticipated but it does not necessarily ensure a positive outcome. Transition can be challenging even when it is something we desire. A person's story of transition is unique to the individual, because people differ in their experiences of transition. The challenge for everyone is to cope, learn, and manage transition successfully.

Transition can be a source of stress and a challenge to many people because of its unpredictability and uncertainty. The perceived loss of control can be frightening and the energy required for coping can be considerable. Transition can be very difficult for clients who suffer from a mental health disorder because they often have fewer resources and supports than others. Transition becomes a problem when it affects the person negatively.[1]

Transitions occur in many different ways. Some examples of transitions include changes in: personal relationships (such as getting married or divorced, having children, alterations in the quality or quantity of social support relation-ships); professional relationships (change in therapist, caregiver or service provider); vocation (change in therapy program, school, volunteer work, or employment); living environment (hospitalization, transfer from one unit to another unit, discharge from hospital, change in housing, change in neighborhood); in mental or physical health (change in capacity for coping); and material resources (change in finances).

How do we prepare the client with a mental health disorder for transition? An important first step to assisting a person to manage transition successfully is assessment. Each person perceives his or her own transition uniquely. It is helpful to anticipate transitions and to recognize them when they are experienced. Assessing the client's experience of transition is not always a simple thing to do. There are many things that clinicians must consider in assessing the client's capacity for transition and for supporting the client during transition. According to Maslow's (1982) theory of hierarchy of human needs, the person will focus on needs that are unmet in any situation. The person will be unable to meet their higher order needs until those lower order needs such as those entailing physiology and safety needs have been satisfactorily met.

Transition can be a source of stress for many clients. Stress can lead to effective or ineffective responses. Signs of stress may include physical symptoms such as fatigue, poor quality sleep, headaches, tension, high blood pressure and changes in appetite. Emotional responses may include feeling vulnerable, powerless, over-whelmed, anxious, unstable mood, withdrawn from other people, and depressed. Cognitive responses may include inability to solve problems, impaired decision making, ineffective coping, poor concentration, confusion, and memory difficulties. Social responses can include impaired social interaction where the quality or quantity of social relationships is negatively affected.

Behavioral responses may include harm to self and others (e.g. aggression, self-harm, suicide, substance use, self-neglect or being victimized).

Clients want to be successful in their transitions. Many clients want to make a transition but are unsure of how to do it. They may want to engage in the transition but sometimes there is also fear of the change. Sometimes transition can be frustrating or painful. Transition may happen too fast as experienced by the client. Other problems inherent in challenging transitions include perceived or real threat, loss of control, surprise or unpredictability, and lack of knowledge or skills. Clients may view transition as empowering because it represents positive change toward gaining something they desire. Others may view transition as overwhelming and negative because it is frightening and chaotic. To assist clients in transition, the clinician's approach must take into account the experience of the transition as seen through their eyes. The clinician needs to understand the client's point of view. The clinician must also be open to hearing about changes in the client's perspective during transition. For transitions to occur successfully, certain conditions must be present and supported.

The clinician must collaborate with the client, explore the client's experience and ask the right questions to facilitate an assessment and to develop a realistic plan. How has the client coped with change in the past? What is the vision of transition? Are there goals to the transition? What strengths are present? What risks are present? How can the client cope with this transition?

When assessing risk to self and others, clinical tools such as the Short Term Assessment of Risk and Treatability (START, Webster et al., 2004) will assist in the assessment process. As already noted (Chapter 11) the START is a clinical guide for assessing strengths and risks for harm to self and others (risk to others, self-harm, suicide, unauthorized leave, substance abuse, self-neglect, being victimized). The START, or some such similar scheme,[2] should be used at regular intervals for case review, for board hearings, or for when the client's experience of transition requires close watching and support because factors contributing to risks to self and others are in flux.

Factors affecting risks of harm to self and others should be considered along with strengths. Clinicians need to be consistently aware of the level of risk the person poses to himself, herself, or others, the types of conditions in play, and the period of time over which it is realistic to make a likely valid forecast (see Chapter 3) and under what period of time. Using the individual's strengths to cope with transition can be helpful and may reduce or assist in the management of the risks. An assessment of the person's strengths as well as risks enables the clinician to view the person holistically in the context of their lived experience.

Long-standing risks for harm to self or others may potentiate in some clients when they are going through a transition. Even clients who have been stable for an extended period may have increased risk when living through a transitional period. For example, psychiatric-mental health clients often find discharge from hospital to the community to be very challenging. When clients are discharged from hospital to the community, their contact with professionals tends to decrease markedly, and their living circumstances will most likely be less structured and less supportive than previously. Many things may change in a transition. The client may be referred to a new case manager, assigned a new psychiatrist, live in a new boarding house and neighborhood, and be without supportive peer relationships.

The Transitional Discharge Model (TDM) evaluated by Forchuk, Martin and others (2005) offers a service that supports the client in their transition from the hospital to the community. The TDM provides the client who is planning for discharge, peer-support volunteers who connect regularly with him or her for a minimum of a year after discharge and a clinician who provides a bridging relationship with the client to the community clinician. The peer-support volunteers are consumers who are living in the community and have been educated to provide such services to another mental health consumer. The bridging relationship by the in-patient clinician continues, until the client and the community clinician establish a therapeutic working relationship. The in-patient clinician then safely terminates the relationship with the community services so that the community clinician provides the assistance.

How do clinicians prepare clients for transition? Planned change can support the clients' transitions. The success of transition normally depends on the clients' and clinicians' ability to predict or anticipate the challenges within the transition and then to create the necessary supports to ensure that the transition is successful. Many clients are dealing with the harsh realities of an uncertain world due to the complexities of their legal, mental health, medical, social, and financial issues etc. They require having informational support about transition (Augimeri, 2001). Being informed about transition can be helpful. It is important for clinicians to assist clients to understand and manage their responses to change and be helped to anticipate the challenges that can be triggered by transition. Transitions have to be tried so that they have the best possible chance of success (Belfrage & Fransson, 2001).

The purpose of planning for transition is to assist and support clients in making positive choices and setting appropriate goals that can be met. Planning for transitions should involve a partnership between the clinician and the client when appropriate. It should also involve the client and other key people in the client's life when possible. The most effective transition plans involve the client, the clinician, and sometimes the family in collaborative activities. If any risks have been identified then a plan must be formulated to address and manage those risks. Planning needs to occur early and continue until the client has emerged from that specific transition. The planning should result in behaviors that will support the client in reaching well-agreed and understood goals. Clinicians can plan appropriate interventions that successfully support difficult transitions. The plan should include strengths and risks, be goal oriented, and should build capacity in the client. Transitions will allow opportunities for the client and clinician to learn new things together and try new ventures under safe conditions.

It is very important to support the client in preparation for the transition and as the transition is occurring. This may involve providing or facilitating many different types of help. The object is to support the client to make decisions, take responsibilities and feel strong and capable, maintain therapeutic relationships, and build social support, peer, spiritual, social service, legal, and health services support. It is important to anticipate that types of risk and degree of risk may fluctuate throughout the transition. Support during transition will most usually help the client be successful in the transition and will help the client maintain optimal health. It goes without saying that clinicians and clients together have to figure out what is to be done in the event that the transition 'fails'. This exercise in itself can have therapeutic benefits.

The success of transition depends on many variables. A vital step is to identify anticipated or current times of transition with the client. Key ingredients to making a successful transition are effective communication, collaborative partnerships, flexibility, and health. A period of adjustment with varied and sometimes unexpected responses to the change can be anticipated. As already noted, there should also be contingency plans in case the original plan does not work. Clinicians can learn from their clients' experience of transition. Clinicians and clients should determine if there are opportunities for further learning or personal development. Successful transition depends on self-awareness, coping, supportive relationships, services, and resources. Knowledge is power for both the client and the clinician.

Stability is something that everyone yearns for, however, transitions in life cannot be eliminated, as they are inherent in our life experience and contribute to our psychological and emotional development as human beings. A transitional process or period of change may be planned or unplanned. Clients respond individually to transition and demonstrate particular responses. It is the role of clinicians to support clients in their transitions by assessing, planning, intervening, and evaluating a plan of care. Risk assessment and management is an important part of developing a plan and supporting clients in hospital or the community. Clinicians can collaborate with, and support clients to make successful transitions (Spaulding et al., 2003).

NOTES

1 Clare Allan's recent novel deals, in a mostly ironic and satirical way, with how people get into the mental health system and how once in, they can find it hard to get out of hospital and into safe circumstances in the community. It also raises, from the client's perspective, how bad bureaucratic systems can be when it comes to allocating material and other resources. Allan takes the view that, too often, senior management attempts to administer by use of slogans, bogus accreditation, and other such crass devices. As depicted in this humorous but bleak book, the 'real' relationships are among the patients. Therapeutic relationships, the theme of this chapter, do not enter the picture.

2 The START manual contains an appendix specifically devoted to a review of similar measures (pp. 145–152).

17

TEAMS

JANE

She is one of our small team
Handles the nursing piece
Of court-diverted 'mental health examinations'
Our chief-of-operations
The one who makes it happen
Always there, always responsible
Offering the sensible and practical opinion

One day she doesn't show up
That's pretty unusual, no call
She's gone for a couple of days
Without reason or explanation
With unease settling around us
Inquiries start to be made
To our great shock we learn
She's excused herself permanently
Had gone to a cottage and overdosed

Now you tell me if you can
Why this attractive young mother did this
To herself, to her family, to us?
And how did we as 'experts'
Fail to notice
What was happening
Before our
Very eyes?[1]

At the beginning of this text we made reference to the idea that clinicians and their administratively inclined colleagues hold theoretical perspectives of different stripes and that these perspectives bear directly on how different kinds of violence risks will be assessed and managed (see Chapter 2). Whether or not clinicians consciously acknowledge the positions they hold, there can be no dispute that these ideas guide the way they approach the task of evaluating and managing risk. It is therefore somewhat surprising that little concerted effort has been directed to the important task of finding out how to optimize disinterested decision making by clinical groups containing members of different disciplines.

This topic has recently been treated in some detail by Burns (2004). What he has to say is directed to community mental health teams but it is likely applicable to teams working in institutions. Burns points out that when multidisciplinary teams first came into being in the UK in the 1960s there tended to be very clear role divisions among the mental health disciplines. Perhaps to some extent influenced by the 'therapeutic community movement' then in vogue at the time (Jones, 1952), it became an expectation that staff members were called upon to bring to their work not just technical competence but also their personal attributes. Although this expectation was perhaps somewhat overemphasized at the time, there remains the point that people entering the mental health field tend to be conscious of their 'ability to understand and enjoy relationships' and that they tend to 'prioritize empathy and curiosity' (p. 23). Burns goes on to remind us that 'Working with individuals struggling with mental illnesses is no job for rigid conformists. A genuine respect for diversity and different world views is needed. Nor is it a rewarding job for the morally conscious – our patients do dreadful things when ill and it is our job to be able to see beyond that to the distressed person' (p. 23).

Teams meet regularly, usually face to face. Different team members, while attending to overall therapeutic objectives, will bring particular kinds of expertise to bear (see Burns, 2004, Figure 2.1, p. 26). Members require support, education, and opportunities for advancement. Unless this is forthcoming, the team will likely not be capable of operating in the interests of patients. Yet conflict is common among team members. Burns traces these to professional allegiances, personality differences, and susceptibility to unhealthy team dynamics like projection and splitting (p. 29). Because of the changeable nature of mental and personality disorders and the blurring of roles among team members, what might be a good division of labor on one day might not be appropriate on another. It takes some effort to keep inherent professional differences balanced.

At its extreme, members of different mental health disciplines can compete against one another to an extent that seems almost farcical and to the detriment of clients (Pfohl 1978; Menzies 1989). Personality differences can be a source of tension if some members characteristically opt for a laissez-faire approach and oppose acting with urgency while other colleagues act quickly and forcefully. Strong personalities can intrude in ways that are adverse to care and treatment. Bad habits unchecked can seriously impede the process (e.g., a member who shows his or her impatience and intolerance or displays of outright rudeness throughout meetings, both verbally and nonverbally). Dominant individuals, persons closed to new opinions and suggestions, are a common problem. It is perhaps not going too far to state that in the extreme such behavior is tantamount to bullying. The psychoanalytic concepts mentioned in Chapter 2, though now no longer exercised very often in the forensic mental health and correctional contexts, apply strongly to team functioning. Unless team members know one another well they can easily be split by clients who learn during their formative years to survive by pitting one family member against another. It is also possible for a team member to lose perspective because a client has projected on to him or her some desirable but unattainable quality.

Leadership in interdisciplinary teams is a key issue. Most would agree that it is an essential component for success. Yet it is hard to define the term. Burns suggests that 'In mental health teams the leader's role is one of harnessing the skills of the team and monitoring (and occasionally correcting) the direction of travel with a gentle touch on the tiller' (p. 33). He also points out that there is a distinction between leadership and management. Sometimes these roles are given to different persons. When this is done, it is essential that there be a close working relationship between them. If not, there will be 'splitting.' This is apt to occur when all the tough decisions are left to the manager (who becomes the 'bad guy'). There are, of course, many other important aspects to consider when teams are being composed (e.g., diversity, ethnic variety, etc.).

Burns (2004, p. 42) draws attention to a development relatively new to the mental health field. This is the notion of 'care pathways,' often called 'integrated care pathways' (ICPs). These are structured interdisciplinary plans of care which spell out essential steps for dealing with the client's particular problems. The ICPs must link to evidence-based guidelines. They are completed at 'major transition points' (i.e., admission, discharge, annual reviews by boards or courts). This ICP approach bears strong resemblance to the use of SPJ violence assessment schemes (Chapter 11). As already noted, these guides hinge not only on scientific considerations (e.g., establishing reliability and validity of items) and to practical day-to-day decision making (e.g., to release or detain), but also to professional guidelines and accreditation requirements (e.g., to ensure that services conform to contemporary ethical and practice standards). It is of some interest that the START scheme, which rests on the idea that it will be applied within teams in most cases, has a distinct correspondence to the ICP approach (see Burns, 2004, p. 45, Table 2.2; p. 47, Figure 2.7).[2]

The main advantages of team-based ICPs or START-type projects are that they: (1) offer a way of infusing research-based evidence into routine clinical care; (2) allow the collection and organization of data that can be checked and consolidated for research and audit purposes; (3) enhance multidisciplinary communication and ensure effective case planning; (4) encourage participation of clients in their own programs; and (5) help staff learn and test new interventions on the job.[3]

NOTES

1   Professionals who work in mental health teams are, of course, not immune to personal difficulties. The narrative description makes the point that, while it may be that Mary's particular stressful circumstances arose outside her job, the work can be very taxing. To an extent anyway, colleagues have to scan one another and be on the lookout for emerging difficulties.

2   Readers will be perhaps impressed to examine the START Summary Sheet (2004, p. 175) and compare it to a form published by Burns (2004, Figure 3.2, pp. 65–66).

3   Of course, there will be detractors. Among other things, such persons will bemoan the time 'wasted' in team discussions, come close to stating that a 'flat organizational structure' obscures the opportunity for them to exercise their brilliant clinical insights, insist that the new scheme creates too much paper-work, and so on.

18

COMMUNICATIONS

BERNIE

This fellow's on an assault charge
Turned in by his wife who got scared finally
His father beat him and defected when he was ten
Went to work at fourteen
What he needs is some fancy psychology
Because he's only uneducated, not unsmart.
Even he can see he's got a 'communication problem'
Tried going to the library for a book on the topic
But they sent him to electrical engineering
Got their wires crossed you might say
Anyway he got a mite discouraged
But he's not beyond hope[1]

> In what way is the result of the risk assessment communicated to external decision-makers such as lawyers, and to others, such as for instance the staff, other professionals, the patient himself/herself, and the patients' relatives? Are the receivers of that information able to interpret and act upon this information as intended?
>
> (Grann & Pallvik, 2002, p. 114)

By this stage it will be clear to readers that it requires a great deal of skill to gain, sift, and interpret information necessary to complete a violence risk assessment. Yet the task does not end with the careful collating and considering of information. That information, if it is to be accurately and fairly conveyed to courts, review boards, and the like, must be presented in a form that can be understood and used by judges, parole officers, mental health workers, and others. The report, whether it is presented orally or in written form, must be laid out scientifically so that the recipients can see how the facts have been marshaled and how the conclusions have been reached. This does not mean that the report should necessarily be unduly long, only that it should be written clearly and impartially.

The report should contain a succinct and accurate[2] *history*. It should make reference to any pertinent[3] results from the kinds of *actuarial* instruments discussed in Chapters 7 and 8. *Dynamic* factors must receive detailed attention whether organized under the C and R headings of the HCR-20 or like scheme.[4] The risk management *plan* has to be conveyed with sufficient detail such that, once put in play, its various components can be implemented and monitored. It also needs to be clear from the plan which persons or agencies will be responsible for particular tasks and how overall coordination will be effected and checked.[5] *Recommendations* must be 'structured to meet legislative and policy requirements' (Taylor, 1998, p. 30).

In at least a few individual cases, it becomes clear to clinicians that such persons display what might be called 'signature sign sets' before they decompensate or act violently. These signs can be highly idiosyncratic and, if apparent and seemingly dependable, require to be conveyed to receiving agencies, family members, and the like (Sutton, 2004).

How violence risk is communicated is becoming a topic in its own right (e.g., Heilbrun, Philipson, Berman, & Warren, 1999; Monahan et al., 2002). It is, for example, now known that it makes a difference in release decision making whether the author of a report says that an individual has a 20 % likelihood of committing a violent offense rather than that 20 out of 100 similar persons will act violently. It is easier to visualize frequencies than probabilities (Slovic, Monahan, & MacGregor, 2000). Consequently, when assessors are able to visualize such information they are apt to make relatively conservative release decisions. The general point is that those who write reports must be concerned not only with the issues of accuracy, completeness, and perspicacity but must, at the same time, have an eye toward how such documents will likely be understood and interpreted.

Heilbrun et al. (2004) have recently made an important distinction between predictive and risk management styles of communication. They argue that clinicians may prefer not to use sheer predictive communication especially in high-risk cases. Such communications, it is argued, may be seen to be prejudicial in the context of legal proceedings (e.g., as with a VRAG bin score – see Heilbrun et al., 2004, p. 195). In contrast, 'practitioners may prefer to convey the nature of the risk factors and the possible risk-reducing interventions in an attempt to avoid premature closure on the deliberation of the decision-maker' (p. 195). They argue that the HCR-20 or similar device, which can provide *both* predictive and risk management aspects, may be favored by clinicians.

NOTES

1 This section of the text deals with how clinicians communicate the results of their release decision-making assessments. Yet, of course, there is the whole issue of how clinicians can best communicate their opinions to patients, prisoners, and parolees. Bernie is 'reachable' but has not yet been 'reached.'

2 It is a fact that errors contained in one report are often unwittingly and unfairly carried forward to the next. Evaluators have a responsibility, above all, to ensure that what they say is accurate (Konečni, Mulcahy, & Ebbessen, 1980).

3 Of course, the author of the report must be able to justify application of published statistically grouped data to the particular patient, inmate, or parolee under consideration.

4 It is important for assessors to think of factors not contained in published schemes like the LSI-R and C and R variables of the HCR-20. It should be noted that some structured guides tend to include an 'other' category (e.g. SARA, SAVRY). Many evaluators now add such a category when completing an HCR-20 violence risk analysis. While this can be a helpful practice, it is important to ensure that such an additional item is actually warranted (i.e., that it cannot be subsumed under an existing defined C or R item).

5 These matters have been laid out very effectively by Belfrage and Fransson (2001, see pp. 119–123). In part, these authors say 'Many of the patients at special forensic psychiatric institutions are so-called multi-problem persons . . . Unfortunately, with poor planning and a lack of sufficient cooperation among professionals, these people have a tendency to glide through various service systems such as hospitals, mental health centers, and correctional institutions. It is therefore essential to establish a form of shared responsibility and a close cooperation between all professionals involved' (p. 122).

19

WITNESS

In court the judge is baffled
Legal adversaries on either side are exhausted
No one disputes the fact that Mr. Lee
Murdered his friend most gruesomely
Yet it is by no means exactly clear
What prompted the sudden violent frenzy
We review the patiently-assembled records
Spend hours talking to him, his family
His boss, his doctor, his nurses here
Give him tests to penetrate his psyche
Apply the latest in 'risk assessment devices'
The analysis is organized, thorough, complete
In the end a more-or-less plausible picture
Emerges the way an artist's hand
Brings alive the landscape through subtle shading
We now see a man 'caught in a web'
Of his own miseries, distortions, delusions
[Though it may be that another 'expert'
Will be called upon to use the same palette
To render an opinion rather differently colored]
The court seems glad for our scientific art
Yet it will reserve the right to ask its own set
Of bluntly-put, squirm-inducing, questions
The anticipation of which
Will keep us pacing the night
Even wondering if scores
From the 'actuarial' side
Were correctly added

In the eventual report
And fretting that our basic opinion
Now framed to fit the legal picture
Is intelligible within the law's ambit
Yet beyond a certain point there's comfort
In the fact that the court alone must decide
What's to be done, where John's to be sent
Who takes over from this point forward
In the end, whether he's to live or die?[1]

At the beginning of the text, in Chapter 1, we pointed to the primacy of the law and suggested that, necessarily, the detail concerning violence risk assessments is dictated by the provisions in place and how they are constantly being reinterpreted (see Faigman & Monahan, 2005, for a compelling discussion of how the 1993 Supreme Court decision in *Daubert v. Merrell Dow Pharmaceuticals, Inc.* raised the general American standard for scientific evidence in court).[2] Although most sitting judges are not comfortable in the role of scientific arbitrator, there can be no doubt that the courts over the years have had a marked influence in raising the quality of violence risk assessment (see Ziskin, 1986).

This poses a singular difficulty for experts. Sales and Shuman (2005) remark that most senior clinicians and researchers who testify in court are overwhelmed by the rate of knowledge development. They say 'As new substantive literatures develop based on methods, techniques, and skills that practitioners never studied in school, it is often impossible for practitioners to understand what this new literature proves and teaches without additional formal training or study' (p. 136). Rogers and Shuman (2005) have also remarked in detail about the complicated and difficult role of the expert witness.[3]

Although drawn from study in a different arena, Tetlock (2006) has recently argued that it is fast becoming very difficult to be a 'real' expert, that many if not most experts offer opinions that are more impressionistic than substantively correct. He distinguishes between two types of decision makers: 'hedgehogs' and 'foxes'. Hedgehogs 'know one big thing' and extend the explanatory reach of this 'one big thing' aggressively into new domains. They display impatience with those who 'do not get it' and they try to mow them down. Such experts express considerable confidence that they are perfectly able forecasters, at least over the long term. Foxes, in distinction, know many small things (cf. Scott, 1977) and tend to be wary of big theoretical schemes. They see explanations and prediction not as deductive exercises but as 'flexible ad hockery.' This requires bringing together information from many diverse sources. They tend to be modest about their ability as forecasters. According to Tetlock, the latter kind of expert is liable to be (slightly) more accurate than the former.

NOTES

1   The narrative description aims to show the complexity of the risk assessment task in important cases. It tries to make the point that law and science have different vocabularies and different agendas.

2   These authors stated that the *Daubert* court put forward four factors to be considered in evaluating whether testimony is expert or not: '(1) testing, (2) rate of error, (3) peer review and publications record, and (4) 'general acceptance' (p. 642).

3   In some jurisdictions mental health workers are called upon to testify as to 'fitness to be put to death'. Yet in all cases, even ones where the precipitating event was of a relatively minor kind, there is the challenge of forecasting the risks that might be present in the varied circumstances to which the person might be sent (e.g., as in the case of some sex and other offenders of being killed by fellow inmates if sent to prison; as in committing suicide if sent home from hospital).

20

CONCLUSIONS

> We believe that a complete science and a complete practice of psychology (and the related mental health and correctional disciplines) should include an understanding of suffering and happiness, as well as their interaction, and validated interventions that both relieve suffering and increase happiness – two separable endeavors.
>
> (Seligman, Steen, Park, & Peterson, 2005, p. 410, phrase in brackets added)

A very great deal has been accomplished since John Monahan wrote his short guide to clinical violence risk assessment a quarter century ago (1981). Major studies have subsequently been undertaken in many parts of the world and, as a result, there is now available a reservoir of information about the frequency with which various kinds of violence occur within civil, forensic, and correctional populations (i.e., 'baseline data', Chapter 8). Although not much dealt with in this text (but see Chapter 4) there has been marked improvement in research and statistical methods (e.g., as with the introduction of receiver operating curves, ROCs, mentioned briefly in Chapter 13). Taken together, the new research has indicated that various kinds of measurable violence occur at higher levels than earlier thought. This fact has helped dispel the notion that the topic of violence prediction was almost impossible to research because of the limiting effects of low baserates (i.e., it is hard to predict the occurrence of events that occur only rarely).

The current evidence is now strong that a higher level of prediction accuracy is possible than earlier thought. Certain variables, often in combination, can now be shown to forecast future violence especially over the course of several years (Chapter 9). That this is so has only been possible because of the painstaking follow-up studies that have been conducted of late. Although some of the clinically grounded variables are complex, as is the case of Hare PCL-R psychopathy (Chapter 6), some are not. It turns out that certain simple factors, ones easily coded from the record (e.g., marital status, history of substance abuse, prior supervision failure) associate statistically with subsequent violence at a higher level than might have been expected 25 years ago. If nothing else, these now oft-found results lend support to the outcome from so-called 'actuarial' studies, which link averaged predictor variables to averaged outcome measures. It follows from this point of view that clinical decisions should be strongly, if not completely, guided by the essential 'empirical facts.' The thought is that decisions made on such a basis will be sounder than those based on unsubstantiated, ungrounded, 'clinical judgment.'

While it is certainly true that every effort should be made during the course of violence risk assessments to obtain and take such information into account, especially when it diverges from findings obtained from an examination of current clinical status, it is hard to imagine how the evaluation can end there. Certainly, a lot depends on what is required from the examining clinician or clinicians according to the law or policy under which the risk assessment is being carried out (Chapter 1). Depending upon the relevant law, the court, review board, or other tribunal, will be interested in the circumstances and characteristics of the individual person under consideration. These bodies will understand that 'experts' in this area have their limits (Chapter 19), that not all experts are equally expert. Yet these organizations have to make decisions not only on the limited issue of prediction of future violence but also, again depending on the defining law, on matters having to do with the provision of appropriate levels of security, likelihood of benefiting from particular treatments, the inevitable expiration of a prison or parole sentence, and so on.

Very gradually over time it has been less and less possible for clinicians to satisfy courts and boards with phrases like 'in my clinical opinion.' These bodies increasingly demand a rationale. They want statements that are explicit and which can be challenged. As well, they often want some discussion of diagnoses in the particular case and have interest in how these might or might not bear on issues of future violence risk (Chapter 5). In line with the setting quote to this section, decision-making bodies want to be assured that the matter has been viewed from a positive aspect as well as a negative one.

In light of the slowly increasing demands of decision-making authorities, many clinicians have sought to improve their standard of practice by exploring a variety of structured professional judgment (SPJ) devices. Such SPJ violence risk assessment schemes, which have been tested in civil, forensic, and correctional settings, have achieved fairly wide use in many parts of the world over the past two decades (Chapter 11). These aim to cover general violence, sex offending (Chapter 13), spousal assault (Chapter 14), and they cover children, adolescents, and other 'special' populations (Chapter 11). All are characterized by item definitions, procedures for use, methods of scoring, and so on. They attempt to integrate what is known from the scientific literature with opinion from experienced practitioners. Generally, they tend to emphasize historical factors but, as well, allow for consideration of dynamic variables (i.e., ones expected to show change over the short run). In some recent studies it has been convincingly demonstrated that clinical constructs employed in the present and limited future outperform historical ones (e.g., McNeil, Gregory, Lam, Binder, & Sullivan, 2003). Of late, there has been a tendency to cover outcomes other than risk to others (e.g., of committing self-harm, of suicide, of substance abuse, of being victimized). In addition, a few of these devices have invited assessors to consider clients' strengths as well as risks. This is intended to aid in hypothesis formulation and in treatment planning.

Some of those who adhere strongly to the 'actuarial approach' tend to be dismissive of SPJ. They argue that clinicians, because they have room to interpret the meaning of items and of overall risk scores, might as well be using unstructured judgment. Their idea is that SPJ is not the 'middle road' that it purports itself to be. The debate is not especially productive. Actuarial data can be helpful if applied sensibly to the individual case and if the sample on which the data was standardized is relevant to that case (though it is worth noting that if the derived actuarial prediction score lies in the middle of the distribution of the standardization sample, as is more likely than not, the information may not be especially helpful). There is the point too that sometimes the normative data, which in some cases are built on a mere few hundred cases, were laid down long before laws changed, diagnostic systems were revised, populations altered as a result of immigration patterns, and so on. As well, prediction of violence is not necessarily the only issue. The SPJ approach has tied its wagon to evidence-based practice and is centered to a large degree on the professional and ethical conduct of practitioners. With the purposes being so different between the two approaches, any discussion of the superiority of the one over the other becomes obscure, to say the least. It is sufficient to say that experienced clinicians, researchers, and policy makers should know the strengths and limitations of *both* approaches. Not so much has been learned in the past 25 years that one position should be jettisoned in favor of the other. Indeed, it is easy to lose the positive galvanizing effect of the debate in a pointless struggle for supremacy in which all victories are pyrrhic.

Very likely the next few years will show that both predictive accuracy *and* evidence-based assessment standards will improve with the development of computer programs that will help clinicians with their point-to-point logic as they assess the individual client. This is not to imply that such programs will 'take over' from clinicians any more than on-board airplane computers have now wrested control from pilots. It is simply that computers turn out to be capable of handling large amounts of rapidly shifting information and can offer solutions that are non-obvious, ones that deserve at least to be entertained. In this violence risk assessment field it will be no bad thing for the individual clinician to have a straightforward way of checking his or her opinion about the risk offered by a particular client (see Monahan et al., 2005, for recent innovation of this kind).

Much development work and research will now be needed in this area. Particular attention must be focused on how best to measure dynamic variables. The difficulty at present is that current recording methods are inadequate in the sense that events once captured tend to lose their dynamic quality (i.e., become static).

It can confidently be expected that the current emphasis on trying to find the one 'right' risk assessment device will pass (Chapter 12). With it will come a realization that devices designed to assess likelihood of violence over a span of years are needed, as are schemes to deal with short terms like a few days or weeks, and others to cover almost moment-to-moment changes in the present and very near future (i.e., minutes or hours). The challenge, presumably, will be to figure how best to connect these devices so that risks during transitions (Chapter 16) are minimized and so that levels and types of risk can be conveyed from one individual clinician or agency to another colleague or organization (Chapter 17).[1] As well, there is the related challenge of figuring out how to research the decision-making activities of multidisciplinary teams (Chapter 18). It seems clear, though it remains to be demonstrated, that there is value in having represented in a team the perspectives and expertise of each individual member.

Some authorities have recently noted the violence risk assessment field has suffered from being rather atheoretical, that what is needed are better contructs for guiding decision making. While this may be so, it is also probably true that insufficient attention has so far been paid to how the different perspectives of individual team members can be brought to bear (Chapter 2). Just as oftentimes the client has more potential than is brought into play, so too it seems do the team members have more to offer than is often used.

It is frequently noted that the time has come to apply to treatment planning the same intensity of effort that is usually given to risk assessment. Too often, the evaluation task ends with a statement about various risks presented by the client with little or no indication as to how those risks could be reduced. 'Critical factors' may be isolated by SPJ and other approaches but there can be a failure to show how measurable risks could be decreased through the implementation of specific treatments. There has been a failure, so far, to demonstrate by means of well-described case histories how particular theoretically driven interventions (Chapter 15), staged across time and according to circumstances, yield positive outcomes (or otherwise). As well, by failing to incorporate multiple measures of outcome, it is very likely often the case that treatments have worked without it becoming evident that this was the case.

One of the most encouraging developments over recent years has been the emergence of multidisciplinary international risk assessment networks which include clinicians, researchers, and administrators. Through these collaborations have come translation of many devices. These various schemes have then been researched in particular countries. Generally, it turns out that findings in one jurisdiction are aligned with those from others. Differences in law and custom, though always important, have not impeded a search for basic knowledge about how risk factors express themselves, combine, interact, and attenuate. None of the various schemes espoused briefly in this text will survive untouched the next 25 years. Considering the importance of assessing violence risks, both to individuals and to society, this is no bad thing. Much remains to be found out and, just as important, great strides are now needed in implementing into routine practice some of the knowledge that is already on hand, for example, Hodgins and Müller-Isberner (2004).

NOTES

1   We are indebted to Kåre Nonstad and Roger Almvik for pointing this out.
2   Elbogen and colleagues say 'Future research is needed to replicate findings using longitudinal data measuring violence from multiple sources. Systematic examination of dynamic, malleable variables such as perceived treatment benefit is wanting in the scientific literature (as well as in clinical practice) because information on these variables can point to potential risk management strategies' (p. 14 in draft).

GEORGE

This narrative description is much longer than the others in the text. Because it contains a wealth of clinical information (especially in the form published by Cresswell & Hollin, 1992), it seemed appropriate to place it at the end. It helps draw together some points made in earlier sections. First, it reinforces the fact that, no matter how well constructed may be the plan for release into the community, chance events crop up. It was a fluke that George was interviewed by the police for a crime he did not commit (and that the exchange prompted him to think about killing people). Second, there is the point that, ideally, his gradually increasing violence potential would have been spotted and acted on much earlier. The signs were there. Third, the connection with acne as a kind of 'signature risk sign' (point 4, under START, Chapter 11) is worth noting, It reinforces the idea that factors do not have to be direct to be useful as risk indicators. Most of all, perhaps, the case points up what can sometimes happen with gradual diminution of self-esteem (associated here with major losses, like his mother's death). Insofar as, according to the account, George's evolving violent fantasies do not get brought to light by the mental health professionals who crossed his path, there is here a sense of missed opportunity to prevent actual violence. Had the violence indeed been forestalled, the victim would not have suffered and George, depicted here as a person with some strengths, might have averted jail.

What a childhood!
Cold, rejecting, unattaching parents
Who laugh at him
Reduced to fantasizing the kind of folks
He ought to have had
In adolescence gets terrible spots
Which nothing cures
And nothing stops the way they all laugh
At him
Small wonder he tries to electrocute himself
Three times
All that keeps him going is the idea of a miracle
For the spots
Gradually dawning is the notion of getting revenge
On all and sundry
By slashing them to bits so they know
What it's like
Such thinking, if you've ever tried it, helps a bit
Makes you feel powerful
In the moment
Yet there's a problem with this dodge
The feeling doesn't last
It ought to be possible to 'reinvent' yourself, you know
Be a happier person
The news is not all bad since George can hold a job
In a department store
He sells the stuff alright but figures it's the salesman acting in him
Not him
Not the real deep down George
You'll not be amazed to learn he's had absolutely no success
With girls
Now at twenty-five, the surgeon declares no hope for
The spots
And just then as luck would have it his mum
Expires
It's no surprise in the face of all this he calls up his old crutch
Fantasy

Thinks now of the blokes he'd like to be with
After death
With mum gone, he has to find a place to live
Alone
Feels even more cut off and angry towards
Other people
Begins to think of the joys of
Massacre
Takes knife to work and tells his doc about all this who suggests
Counseling
But gets more relief from carrying his baseball bat around
Than chat
To the counselor to whom he tells some of this stuff it's information
To sit on
Eventually George tries an overdose which gets him
To hospital
Where after six weeks they say he's just
Absolutely fine
Right after he gets home a guy called Ryan in some other city
Massacres twenty people
This is big stuff which helped sell a colossal pile
Of newspapers
George anyway was inspired to think twenty would be a good number
To top
Starts prowling by night looking for nice candidates
To join him in heaven
And maybe some rich folks he feels to be responsible
For his failure
So he begins to watch them getting to know their details
How they live
Starts with being a nuisance just moving things around
Small stuff
Then, oddly, the police question him about a murder
Which he'd nothing to do with
Yet it gives him an idea:
'If someone else has the guts to do someone in, so could I'
And so he gives it a shot, a bit bumbling but pretty good
For a start
Woman must have been mighty tough to survive the bat he broke
On her
Having actually done something, actually asserted himself
For once
George has a good night's sleep resting on his triumph since he saw
'Fear in her eyes'

A couple of nights later, with a serious slash-up in mind
Attacks and stabs a man
So the man will come to realize what if feels like to be
Him, George
This guy's tough too since he survives okay and, mercifully, George is arrested
At the scene

(after Cresswell & Hollin, 1992)

21

QUESTIONS

The following questions may help some readers recapitulate the major 'facts' presented in the text. We recognize that our 'gold standard', 'correct' answers could be disputed in some cases. Part of the aim of this final chapter is to stimulate thought about steps which might be taken in the future by clinicians, researchers, policy makers, administrators, and those who make concrete decisions about violence risk in individual cases.

1. Cognitive behavioral interventions tend to have marked superiority over pharmacological approaches.

   TRUE/FALSE

2. So few clients characteristically signal that they are about to relapse into violent acts or self-neglect that it is hardly something worth entertaining in the course of conducting risk assessments.

   TRUE/FALSE

3. Monahan was right in 1981 to forward the idea that mental illness is a non-correlate of violence.

   TRUE/FALSE

4. 'Psychopathy' is a diagnostic term used in the current DSM-IV.

   TRUE/FALSE

5. When various contemporary risk assessment guides are pitted against one another in formal studies of predictive accuracy there tends to be no obvious 'standout' scale or device.

   TRUE/FALSE

6. Generally, across the world, there tends to have been an increase over recent years in the size and complexity of forensic mental health systems at the expense of their civil counterparts.

TRUE/FALSE

7. A not unimportant observation made occasionally by commentators is that overemphasis on risk assessments drains resources away from risk management issues.

TRUE/FALSE

8. The HCR-20 is nothing more than a checklist.

TRUE/FALSE

9. Psychopaths invariably 'burn out'.

TRUE/FALSE

10. In structured professional judgment guides it is almost impossible for an individual with low overall total numerical score to be classified as 'high risk'.

TRUE/FALSE

11. So far as violence risks are concerned, civil systems, forensic systems, and criminal justice systems are best viewed as different and separate entities.

TRUE/FALSE

12. The general method of the medical model has no bearing or relevance to our understanding of violence risk assessment.

TRUE/FALSE

13. There is at least some evidence that the functioning of particular multidisciplinary teams can work to the disadvantage of some patients.

TRUE/FALSE

14. Research over the past 20 years or so has surprised in showing the relative power of a few easy-to-measure 'static' variables to predict violence over the long term.

TRUE/FALSE

15. 'Structured professional judgment' lines up fairly closely with 'clinical practice guidelines'.

TRUE/FALSE

16. The sole aim of most risk-structured professional assessment devices is to classify individuals according to levels of risk such as low, moderate, or high.

TRUE/FALSE

17. The HCR-20 is indisputably the best violence risk assessment scheme currently available.

TRUE/FALSE

18. Historical factors are always important in the conduct of violence risk assessments.

TRUE/FALSE

19. Psychopathy, as defined by Hare, is a one-dimensional construct.

TRUE/FALSE

20. The role of 'protective' factors has been somewhat underemphasized in the development of contemporary risk assessment schemes.

TRUE/FALSE

21 Psychologists tend to be better predictors of violence than members of other mental health disciplines.

TRUE/FALSE

22. It is usually instructive to search for statistical baseline comparisons against which to evaluate an individual's potential risk for violence.

TRUE/FALSE

23. Overprediction of violence is the error most likely to be made by clinicians, at least so far as has been discovered in long-term, follow-up, statistical studies.

TRUE/FALSE

24. Clinicians doing violence risk assessments should not concern themselves with broad philosophical issues.

TRUE/FALSE

25. Case studies contribute little or nothing to our understanding of the violence risk assessment process.

TRUE/FALSE

26. A primary focus of the Violence Risk Appraisal Guide (VRAG) is clinical practice guidelines.

TRUE/FALSE

27. Interdisciplinary team functioning can often be optimized when there are good working relationships between clinical leaders and operational managers.

TRUE/FALSE

28. Law, be it civil, forensic, or criminal justice, often contains the broad outlines for practical violence risk assessment.

TRUE/FALSE

29. Actuarial predictions are almost invariably more important in decision making than clinical predictions.

TRUE/FALSE

30. Once in a civil stream, a forensic stream, or a criminal justice stream, it is rare for individuals to 'crossover' and begin a new 'career'.

TRUE/FALSE

31. Psychopathy, as defined by Cleckley and Hare, is arguably the single most powerful known predictor of future violence.

TRUE/FALSE

32. The well-known 'triad' of firesetting, enuresis, and cruelty to animals continues to be a key aspect in violence risk evaluations.

TRUE/FALSE

33. The B-SAFER is an adaptation of the SARA (Spousal Assault Risk Assessment Guide) for frontline police and other such workers.

TRUE/FALSE

34. A great deal of 'expertise' on the part of individual practitioners and researchers in the violence risk assessment and prediction field is assumed rather than demonstrated.

TRUE/FALSE

35. Risk assessments, even complex ones, can be done rapidly if evaluators possess the necessary 'know how'.

TRUE/FALSE

36. A prime emphasis on violence risk to others, while of prime interest to courts and review boards, can blind assessors to risks of other kinds.

TRUE/FALSE

37. It is invariably important in violence risk assessment to find out the client's own plans and intentions.

TRUE/FALSE

38. The same factor may be a risk marker for one client and a protective one for another.

TRUE/FALSE

39. Substance abuse coupled with major mental disorder elevates violence risk, but only slightly.

TRUE/FALSE

40. 'Insight', or its lack, tends to be a major preoccupation of clinicians. Attempts are usually made to help clients improve or gain this faculty. Yet once gained, it can occasionally pose unanticipated new risks for some persons.

TRUE/FALSE

41. Very often, two or more specific violence risk estimates are needed for a single individual, depending upon different kinds of circumstances projected into the future.

TRUE/FALSE

42. A well-structured professional judgment risk assessment covers all listed risk items, possibly adds additional case-specific ones, if there is a compelling case to do so, and offers a theory as to how a limited number of especially critical factors have interacted in the past and how they and other factors can be expected to interact in the future.

TRUE/FALSE

43. Mental health practitioners, generally speaking, should find time and seek opportunity to make members of society more aware of stigma and prejudice operating against their clients.

TRUE/FALSE

44. There is so little that can be measured with respect to most individual clients it is hard to see how such persons can be shown to be in the process of making adequate adjustments to life in institutions or in the community.

TRUE/FALSE

45. Despite all that is written, the evidence is not abundant that 'experts' in a variety of fields are as expert as might be imagined.

TRUE/FALSE

46. Generally speaking, Tetlock has it that decision makers characterized as 'hedgehogs' outperform 'foxes'.

TRUE/FALSE

47. Mental health teams sometimes fail, not because the members lack experience or competence, but because they lack manners, patience, and courtesy.

TRUE/FALSE

48. Although little studied to this point, there is some evidence to suggest that projections of violence by individual clinicians vary markedly in their accuracy.

TRUE/FALSE

49. When organizations opt to introduce some new kind of violence risk-assessment device (possibly in connection with upcoming external audits or accreditation surveys), rarely is consideration given to the actual testing of the scheme *in situ*.

TRUE/FALSE

50. There are some studies of short-term violence risk which demonstrate the superiority of clinical over static predictions.

TRUE/FALSE

51. The newly developed COVR by Monahan and colleagues aids clinicians by offering a 'branching' type of computer software intended to enhance logical consistency in decision making.

TRUE/FALSE

52. Hare maintains that his PCL-R rests on three major dimensions: irritability, supremacy, and glibness.

TRUE/FALSE

53. The START differs from the HCR-20 in that it projects over a very short time frame (i.e., days, weeks, a month or two).

TRUE/FALSE

54. 'Facet analysis' helps researchers and clinicians determine the single most important violence risk variable operating in a particular case.

TRUE/FALSE

55. A 'false negative' error has more or less the same consequences as a 'false positive' error.

TRUE/FALSE

56. The scientific study of how violence risk is communicated among professionals and services is getting to be an important topic in its own right.

TRUE/FALSE

57. A limitation of 'actuarial' data is that scores lying in the middle of the range tend not to offer decision makers the guidance they seek.

TRUE/FALSE

58. There is some evidence that when actuarial data are available they tend to overwhelm the influence of opinion offered by senior clinicians.

TRUE/FALSE

59. In the future it may come about that mental health, forensic, and criminal justice personnel will be required to reach certain agreed standards if they are to venture opinion about violence and other risks.

TRUE/FALSE

60. Violence risk assessment can benefit through examination of common 'dangerous' parallels (e.g. air flight, surgery survival, motorcycling, etc.).

TRUE/FALSE

61. The HCR-20 is mainly an 'actuarial' scheme.

TRUE/FALSE

62. There is no particular need for mental health workers involved in violence risk assessment to attempt to become acquainted with legal statutes and precedents. This is work for lawyers.

TRUE/FALSE

63. Once a person is 'captured' in one system of supervision or care (e.g., civil, forensic, correctional) there tends not to be much 'crossover' from one system to another over the course of time.

TRUE/FALSE

64. The 'big philosophies' of the latter half of the twentieth century continue to have important influences on contemporary theories affecting violence risk assessment.

TRUE/FALSE

65. In a statistical study, a significant correlation of $+0.08$ between a factor (e.g., learning disorder) and actual violence at outcome would be a strong effect.

TRUE/FALSE

66. The HCR-20 is very useful in dealing with emergency, urgent, rapidly evolving violence risk.

TRUE/FALSE

67. Concepts arising from the correctional field have virtually no applicability to general or forensic mental health issues.

TRUE/FALSE

68. Since cultural considerations are not discussed in the 1997 HCR-20, they have to be left out of consideration.

TRUE/FALSE

69. The MacArthur study was based on forensic patients followed for many years.
TRUE/FALSE

70. The Penetanguishene study followed both forensic and correctional clients.
TRUE/FALSE

71. Early maladjustment has some connection to subsequent violence but the effect in several studies has been small and rarely reaches statistical significance.
TRUE/FALSE

72. Many authors write that the difficulties faced by clients as they make 'transitions' (e.g., from hospital to community) tend to be exaggerated.
TRUE/FALSE

73. Processes issues can arise when management decides to adopt some kind of violence assessment scheme. Much time can be wasted exploring these issues with clinical staff. The answer is to sidestep such futile discussions and simply institute what seems to be the best-available approach.
TRUE/FALSE

74. Generally speaking, the American Diagnostic and Statistical Manual (DSM) and the European World Health Organization International Classification of Diseases–Amended (ICD-10) have little in common with respect to diagnostic groupings.
TRUE/FALSE

75. Very generally, persons with a primary diagnosis of an antisocial personality disorder of some kind are at an elevated risk of ending up in the correctional system.
TRUE/FALSE

76. Persons who suffer some form of depression are apt not to be correctly diagnosed and treated when placed in the correctional system.
TRUE/FALSE

77. Children diagnosed with conduct disorder rarely attract a diagnosis of antisocial personality disorder in adulthood.
TRUE/FALSE

78. Girls tend to express aggressivity in much the same way as boys.
TRUE/FALSE

79. In all of the many studies to date, the Sexual Violence Risk – 20 (SVR-20) stands head and shoulders above other assessment instruments for the prediction of sexual violence.
TRUE/FALSE

80. It is unlikely that computer software programs could be developed any time soon to help clinicians avoid making some risk decision errors.
TRUE/FALSE

81. Some authorities argue that actuarial predictions of violence are so impressive and clinical forecasts so dismal that only the former should be relied upon. This view is increasingly accepted by practicing clinicians worldwide.
TRUE/FALSE

82. Three factors well known to have a strong relationship with sexual recidivism are: (1) victim empathy; (2) lack of motivation for treatment; and (3) history of being sexually abused as a child.
TRUE/FALSE

83. It makes sense to view all sex offenders as high risk.
TRUE/FALSE

84. It is usually possible to be able to infer sexual motivation from criminal convictions.
TRUE/FALSE

85. Because sex offending in women occurs rarely and little is known about the factors which are important, it probably is best to rely on factors related to general recidivism.
TRUE/FALSE

86. Sex offenders who complete treatment are less likely to recidivate than those who do not start treatment.
TRUE/FALSE

87. The 16-item Stable-2000 for assessing sex offenders can be completed in a matter of minutes if evaluators come to the point that they think they understand the case.
TRUE/FALSE

88. The RRASOR for assessing sex offenders has five items: (1) any male victim; (2) any unrelated victims; (3) age less than 25; (4) prior sexual offences; and (5) demonstrated deviancy shown by phallometric testing.
TRUE/FALSE

89. Generally, women's perception about their own safety or otherwise have been shown to be predictive of further future assaults against them.
TRUE/FALSE

90. The Ontario Domestic Assault Risk Assessment (ODARA) is a good recent (2004) example of a structured professional judgment guide.

TRUE/FALSE

ANSWER KEY

1. FALSE	31. TRUE	61. TRUE
2. FALSE	32. FALSE	62. FALSE
3. FALSE	33. TRUE	63. FALSE
4. FALSE	34. TRUE	64. TRUE
5. TRUE	35. FALSE	65. FALSE
6. TRUE	36. TRUE	66. FALSE
7. TRUE	37. TRUE	67. FALSE
8. FALSE	38. TRUE	68. FALSE
9. FALSE	39. FALSE	69. FALSE
10. FALSE	40. TRUE	70. TRUE
11. FALSE	41. TRUE	71. FALSE
12. FALSE	42. TRUE	72. FALSE
13. TRUE	43. TRUE	73. FALSE
14. TRUE	44. FALSE	74. FALSE
15. TRUE	45. TRUE	75. TRUE
16. FALSE	46. FALSE	76. TRUE
17. FALSE	47. TRUE	77. FALSE
18. TRUE	48. TRUE	78. FALSE
19. FALSE	49. TRUE	79. FALSE
20. TRUE	50. TRUE	80. FALSE
21. FALSE	51. TRUE	81. FALSE
22. TRUE	52. FALSE	82. FALSE
23. TRUE	53. TRUE	83. FALSE
24. FALSE	54. FALSE	84. FALSE
25. FALSE	55. FALSE	85. TRUE
26. FALSE	56. TRUE	86. TRUE
27. TRUE	57. TRUE	87. TRUE
28. TRUE	58. FALSE	88. FALSE
29. FALSE	59. TRUE	89. TRUE
30. FALSE	60. TRUE	90. FALSE

REFERENCES

Ægisdóttir, S., Spengler, P. M., & White, M. J. (2006). Should I pack my umbrella? Clinical versus statistical prediction of mental health decisions. *The Counseling Psychologist, 34,* 410–419.

Agnew, J., & Bannister, D. (1973). Psychiatric diagnosis as a pseudo-specialist language. *British Journal of Medical Psychology, 46,* 69–73.

Allan, C. (2006). *Poppy Shakespeare.* Toronto: Bond Street Books.

American Psychiatric Association. (1994). *Diagnostic and Statistical Manual of Mental Disorders – DSM-IV.* Washington, DC: American Psychiatric Association.

American Psychiatric Association. (2000). *Diagnostic and statistical manual of mental disorders* (4th ed., Textual revision – DSM-IV-TR). Washington, DC: American Psychiatric Association.

American Psychological Association (APA) Presidential Task Force on Evidence-based Practice (2006). Evidence-based Practice in Psychology. *American Psychologist, 61,* 271–285.

Andrews, D. A. (1982). *The level of supervision inventory (LSI): The first follow-up.* Toronto: Ministry of Correctional Services (Ontario).

Andrews, D. A., & Bonta, J. (1995). *The Level of Service Inventory – Revised: User's manual.* Toronto: Multi-Health Systems.

Ashford, J. B., Sales, B. D., & Reid, W. H. (Eds.). (2001). *Treating adult and juvenile offenders with special needs.* Washington, DC: American Psychological Association.

Athens, L. (1997). *Violent criminal acts and actors revisited.* Urbana: University of Illinois Press.

Athens, L., & Starr, R. (2003). One man's story: How I became a "disorganized" dangerous violent criminal. In L. Athens & J. T. Ulmer (Eds.), *Violent acts and violentization: Assessing, applying, and developing Lonnie Athens' Theories* (pp. 53–76). Amsterdam: Elsevier.

Augimeri, (2001). Support. In K. S. Douglas, C. D. Webster, D. Eaves, S. D. Hart, & J. R. P. Ogloff (Eds.), *HCR-20 Violence Risk Management Companion Guide.* Burnaby, BC: Mental Health Law and Policy Institute, Simon Fraser University.

Augimeri, L., Koegl, C., Webster, C. D., & Levene, K. (2001). *Early Assessment Risk List for Boys (EARL-20B),* Version 2. Toronto: Earlscourt Child and Family Centre.

Augimeri, L., Webster, C. D., Koegl, C., & Levene, K. (1998). *Early Assessment Risk List for Boys: EARL-20B,* Version 1, Consultation Edition. Toronto: Earlscourt Child and Family Centre.

Babiak, P., & Hare, R. D. (2006). *Snakes in suits: When psychopaths go to work.* New York: HarperCollins.

Barbaree, H. E., Seto, M. C., Langton, C. M., & Peacock, E. J. (2001). Evaluating the predictive accuracy of six risk assessment instruments for adult sex offenders. *Criminal Justice and Behavior, 28,* 490–521.

Beech, A. R. (2001). Case material and interview. In C. R. Hollin (Ed.). *Handbook of offender assessment and treatment* (pp. 123–136). Chichester, UK: Wiley.

Behnke, S. H., Perlin, M. L., & Bernstein, M. (2003). *The essentials of New York Mental Health Law: A straightforward guide for clinicians of all disciplines.* New York: Norton.

Belfrage, H., & Fransson, G. (2001). Creating fessible plans. In K. S. Douglas, C. D. Webster, S. D. Hart, D. Eaves, & J. R. P. Ogloff (Eds.), *HCR-20 violence risk management guide.* Burnaby, BC: Mental Health, Law and Policy Institute, Simon Fraser University.

Bellack, A. S., Mueser, K. T., Gingerich, S., & Agresta, J. (1997). *Social skills training for schizophrenia: A step-by-step guide.* New York: Guilford.

Bellack, A. S., Mueser, K. T., Gingerich, S., & Agresta, J. (2004). *Social skills training for schizophrenia: A step-by-step guide.* New York: Guilford.

Blaaw, E., Hoeve, M., van Marle, T., & Sheridan, L. (2002). *Mentally disordered offenders: International perspectives on assessment and treatment.* Amsterdam: Elsevier.

Blanton, H., & Jaccard, J. (2006). Arbitrary metrics in psychology. *American Psychologist, 61,* 27–41.

Bloom, H., Eisen, R. S., Pollock, N., & Webster, C. D. (2000). *WRA-20, Workplace Risk Assessment: A Guide for Evaluating Violence Potential,* Version 1. Toronto: workplace. calm, inc.

Bloom, H., & Webster, C. D. (Eds) (2007). Essential writings in violence risk assessment and management. Toronto: Centre for Addiction and Mental Health.

Bloom, H., Webster, C. D., & Eisen, R. S. (2002). *ERA-20, Employee Risk Assessment: A Guide for Evaluating Potential Workplace Violence Perpetrators.* Toronto: workplace. calm, inc.

Blumenthal, S., & Lavender, T. (2000). *Violence and mental disorder: A critical aid to the assessment and management of risk.* London: Jessica Kingsley.

Boer, D., Couture, J., Geddes, C., & Ritchie, A. (2003). Yokwtol. *Risk Management Guide for Aboriginal Offenders: Structured Guidelines for the Assessment of Risk Manageability for Aboriginal Violent Offenders* (Research Version). Harrison Mills: Aboriginal Initiatives Branch, Pacific Region, Correctional Service of Canada.

Boer, D. P., Hart, S. D., Kropp, P. R., & Webster, C. D. (1998). *Manual for Sexual Violence Risk-20: Professional Guidelines for Assessing Risk of Sexual Violence.* Vancouver: British Columbia Institute Against Family Violence.

Bolen, D. E. (1992). *Stupid crimes: A novel.* Toronto: Vintage.

Bonta, J., & Hanson, R. K. (1995, August). *Violent recidivism of men released from prison.* Paper presented at the 103rd Annual Convention of the American Psychological Association, New York.

Bonta, J., Harman, W. G., Hann, R. G., & Cormier, R. B. (1996). The prediction of recidivism among federally sentenced offenders: A re-validation of the SIR scale. *Canadian Journal of Criminology, 38,* 61–79.

Bonta, J., Law, M., & Hanson, R. K. (1998). The prediction of criminal and violent recidivism among mentally disordered offenders: A meta-analysis. *Psychological Bulletin, 123,* 123–142.

Borum, R. (1996). Improving the clinical practice of violence risk assessment. *American Psychologist, 51,* 945–953.

Borum, R., Bartel, P., & Forth, A. (2002). *Manual for the Structured Assessment of Violence Risk in Youth (SAVRY)*. Tampa: University of South Florida.

Bouch, J., & Marshall, J. J. (2003). *Suicide Risk Assessment and Management Manual (S-RAMM)*. Research Edition. Dinas Powys, UK: Cognitive Centre Foundation.

Bouch, J., & Marshall, J. J. (2005). Suicide risk: Structured professional judgment. *Advances in Psychiatric Treatment, 11,* 84–91.

Bourget, D., & Bradford, J. (1990). Homicidal parents. *Canadian Journal of Psychiatry, 35,* 233–238.

Bryant, K. J., Rounsaville, B., Spitzer, R. L., & Williams, J. B. W. (1992). Reliability of dual diagnosis: Substance dependence and psychiatric disorders. *Journal of Nervous and Mental Disease, 180,* 251–257.

Burns, T. (2004). *Community Mental Health Teams: A Guide to Current Practices*. Oxford: Oxford University Press.

Campbell, J. C., McFarlane, J., Webster, D., Wilt, S., Block, C. R., Sharps, P., Campbell, D., Sachs, C. J., & Koziol-McLain, J. K. (2001, November). *The danger assessment instrument: Modications based on findings from the Intimate Partner Femicide Study*. Paper presented at the 2001 American Society of Criminology Conference, Atlanta, Georgia.

Campbell, J. C., Sharps, P., & Glass, N. (2001). Risk assessment for intimate partner homicide. In G. F. Pinard & L. Pagani (Eds.), *Clinical assessment of dangerousness: Empirical contributions* (pp. 137–157). New York: Cambridge University Press.

Campbell, J. C., Webster, D., Koziol-McLain, J., Block, C., Campbell, D., Curry, M. A., Gary, F., Glass, N., McFarlane, J., Sachs, C., Sharps, P., Ulrich, Y., Wilt, S. A., Manganello, J., Xu, X., Schollenberger, J., Frye, V., & Laughon, K. (2003). Risk factors for femicide in abusive relationships: Results from a multi-site case control study. *American Journal of Public Health, 93,* 1089–1097.

Cleckley, H. (1941). *The mask of sanity* (4th ed. 1964; 5th ed. 1976). St. Louis, MO: Mosby.

Cooke, D. J. (1999). Major mental disorder and violence in correctional settings: Size, specificity, and implications for practice. In S. Hodgins (Ed.), *Violence among the mentally ill: Effective treatments and management strategies* (pp. 291–311). Dordrecht: Kluwer.

Cooke, D. J., Michie, C., & Ryan, J. (2001). *Evaluating risk for violence: A preliminary study of the HCR-20, PCL-R and VRAG in a Scottish prison sample*. Occasional Paper Series 5/2001, Glasgow: Scottish Prison Service.

Cooke, D. J., Michie, C., & Hart, S. D. (2006). Facts of Clinical Psychopathy. Toward Clearer Measurement. In C. J. Patrick (Ed.) *Handbook of Psychopathy* (pp. 91–106). New York: Guilford Press.

Cooke, D. J., & Philip, L. (2000). To treat or not to treat? An empirical perspective. In C. R. Hollin (Ed.), *Handbook of offender assessment and treatment* (pp. 17–34). Chichester, UK: Wiley.

Copas, J. B., & Marshall, P. (1998). The offender group reconviction scale: The statistical reconvictions score for use by probation officers. *Journal of the Royal Statistical Society, 47,* 159–171.

Correctional Service Canada. (1997). *Case Management Manual, Annex J: Revised Statistical Information on Recidivism Scale*. (GSIR-R). Ottawa: Author.

Corrections and Conditional Release Act, 1992, c.20, March 1998.

Cortoni, F., & Hanson, R. K. (2005). *A review of the recidivism rates of adult female sexual offenders*. Report No R-169. Ottawa: Correctional Service of Canada.

Cresswell, D. M., & Hollin, C. R. (1992). Toward a new methodology for making sense of case material: An illustrative case involving attempted multiple murder. *Criminal Behaviour and Mental Health, 2,* 329–341.

Daniel, A. (2004). Commentary: Decision-making by front-line service providers – attitudinal or contextual. *Journal of the American Academy of Psychiatry and the Law, 32,* 386–389.

de Becker, G. (1997). *The gift of fear: Survival signals that protect us from violence.* New York: Dell.

de Vogel, V., de Ruiter, C., van Beek, D., & Mead, G. (2004). Predictive validity of the SVR-20 and Static-99 in a Dutch sample of treated sex offenders. *Law and Human Behavior, 28,* 235–251.

Desmarais, S., Webster, C. D., Martin, M-L., Dassinger, C., Brink, J., & Nicholls, T. L. (2006). *START Instructors' Manual and Workbook.* Port Coquitlam, BC: Forensic Psychiatric Services Commission.

Dickey, R. (2000, December). Assessing inmates for risk of future violence. *Canadian Psychiatric Association Bulletin,* 168–170.

Doctor, R. (Ed.). (2003). *Dangerous patients: A psychodynamic approach to risk assessment and management.* London: Karnac.

Dolan, M., & Doyle, M. (2000). Violence risk prediction: Clinical and actuarial measures and the role of the Psychopathy Checklist. *British Journal of Psychiatry, 177,* 303–311.

Douglas, K. S., & Belfrage, H. (2001). Use of the HCR-20 in violence risk management: Implementation and clinical practice. In K. S. Douglas, C. D. Webster, S. D. Hart, D. Eaves, & J. R. P. Ogloff (Eds.), *HCR-20 Violence Risk Management Guide* (pp. 41–58). Burnaby: Mental Health Law and Policy Institute, Simon Fraser University and Louis de la Parte Florida Mental Health Institute, University of South Florida.

Douglas, K. S., Cox, D. N., & Webster, C. D. (1999). Violence risk assessment: Science and practice. *Legal and Criminological Psychology, 4,* 149–184.

Douglas, K. S., Webster, C. D., Eaves, D., Hart, S. D., & Ogloff, J. R. P. (Eds.). (2001). *HCR-20 Violence Risk Management Companion Guide.* Burnaby: Mental Health Law and Policy Institute, Simon Fraser University and Louis de la Parte Florida Mental Health Institute, University of South Florida.

Doyle, M., Dolan, M., & McGovern, J. (2002). The validity of North American risk assessment tools in predicting inpatient violent behaviour in England. *Legal and Criminological Psychology, 7,* 141–154.

Dutton, D., & Kropp, P. R. (2000). A review of domestic violence risk instruments. *Trauma, Violence, & Abuse, 1,* 171–181.

Dvoskin, J. A., & Steadman, H. J. (1994). Using intensive case management to reduce violence by mentally ill persons in the community. *Hospital and Community Psychiatry, 5,* 679–684.

Eaves, D., Douglas, K. S., Webster, C. D., Ogloff, J. R. P., & Hart, S. D. (2000). *Dangerous and Long-Term Offenders: An Assessment Guide.* Burnaby, BC: Mental Health, Law and Policy Institute, Simon Fraser University.

Eisenman, R. (1987). Sexual acting out: Diagnostic category or moral judgment. *Bulletin of the Psychonomic Society, 25,* 387–388.

Elbogen, E. B., Mercado, C. C., Scalora, M. J., & Tomkins, A. J. (2002). Perceived relevance of factors for violence risk assessment: A survey of clinicians. *International Journal of Forensic Mental Health, 1,* 37–47.

Elbogen, E., Van Dorn, R. V., Swanson, J., Swartz, M., & Monahan, J. (in press). Treatment engagement and violence risk in mental disorders. *British Journal of Psychiatry.*

Ennis, B. J., & Litwack, T. R. (1974). Psychiatry and the presumption of expertise: Flipping coins in the courtroom. *California Law Review, 62,* 693–752.

Epperson, D. L., Kaul, J. D., & Hesselton, D. (1998). *Minnesota Sex Offender Screening Tool – Revised (MnSOST-R): Development, performance, and recommended risk level cut scores.* Iowa State University/Minnesota Department of Corrections. Available at: http://psych-server.iastate.edu/faculty/epperson/mnsost_download.htm.

Esses, V. M., & Webster, C. D. (1988). Physical attractiveness, dangerousness, and the Canadian Criminal Code. *Journal of Applied Social Psychology, 18,* 1017–1031.

Estroff, S. E., Zimmer, C., Lachicotte, W. S., & Benoit, J. (1994). The influence of social networks and social support on violence by persons with serious mental illness. *Hospital and Community Psychiatry, 45,* 21–34.

Eysenck, H. J. (1952). *The scientific study of personality.* London: Routledge & Kegan Paul.

Faigman, D. L., & Monahan, J. (2005). Psychological evidence at the dawn of the law's scientific age. *Annual Review of Psychology, 56,* 631–659.

Farkas, M., Gagne, C., Anthony, W., & Chamberlin, J. (2005). *Community Mental Health Journal, 41,* 141–158.

Ferguson, J. S., & Smith, A. (1996). Aggressive behaviour on an inpatient geriatric unit. *Journal of Psychosocial Nursing, 34,* 27–32.

Forchuk, C., Martin, M-L., Chan, Y. L., & Jensen, E. (2005). Therapeutic relationships: From hospital to community. *Journal of Psychiatric and Mental Health Nursing, 12,* 556–564.

Forth, A. (2003). *Risk assessment tools: A guide* (Draft). A report to Professional Standards and Development, National Parole Board.

Foucault, M. (1978). About the concept of the dangerous individual. In D. N. Weisstub (Ed.), *Law and psychiatry: Proceedings of an international symposium held at the Clarke Institute of Psychiatry, Toronto.* Canada, February, 1977.

Gadon, L., Johnstone, L., & Cooke, D. (in press). Situational variables and institutional violence: A systematic review of the literature. *Clinical Psychology Review.*

Gauthie, N., Ellis, K., Bol, N., & Stolee, P. (2005, Winter). Beyond knowledge transfer: A model of knowledge integration in a clinical setting. *Healthcare Management Forum,* 33–36.

Gendreau, P., Little, T., & Goggin, C. (1996). A meta-analysis of the predictors of adult offender recidivism: What works! *Criminology, 34,* 575–607.

Gondolf, E. W. (2001). *Batterer intervention systems: Issues, outcomes, and recommendations.* Thousand Oaks, CA: Sage.

Grann, M., & Pallvik, A. (2002). An empirical investigation of written risk communication in forensic psychiatric evaluations. *Psychology, Crime and Law, 8,* 113–130.

Gray, N. S., Hill, C., McGleish, A., Timmons, D., MacCulloch, M. J., & Snowden, R. J. (2003). Prediction of violence and self-harm in mentally disordered offenders: A prospective study of the efficacy of HCR-20, PCL-R and psychiatric symptomatology. *Journal of Consulting and Clinical Psychology, 71,* 443–451.

Grevatt, M., Thomas-Peter, B., & Hughes, G. (2004). Violence, mental disorders and risk assessment: Can structured clinical assessments predict the short-term risk of inpatient violence? *Journal of Forensic Psychiatry and Psychology, 15,* 278–292.

Grove, W. M., & Meehl, P. E. (1996). Comparative efficiency of informal (subjective, impressionistic) and formal (mechanical, algorithmic) prediction procedures: The clinical-statistical controversy. *Psychology, Public Policy, and Law, 2,* 293–323.

Haggård, U., Gumpert, C. H., & Grann, M. (2001). Against all odds: A qualitative follow-up study of high-risk violent offenders who were not reconvicted. *Journal of Interpersonal Violence, 16,* 1048–1065.

Hall, H. V. (2001). Violence prediction and risk analysis: Empirical advances and guides. *Journal of Threat Assessment, 1,* 1–39.

Hamilton, J. D. (2001). Do we under utilize actuarial judgement and decision analysis. *Evidence-Based Mental Health, 4,* 102–103.

Hanson, R. K. (1997). *The development of a brief actuarial risk scale for sexual offense recidivism* (User Report 97-04). Ottawa: Department of the Solicitor General of Canada.

Hanson, R. K., & Bussière, M. T. (1998). Predicting relapse: A meta-analysis of sexual offender recidivism studies. *Journal of Consulting and Clinical Psychology, 66,* 348–362.

Hanson, R. K., Gordon, A., Harris, A. J. R., Marques, J. K., Murphy, W., Quinsey, V. L., & Seto, M. C. (2002). First report of the collaborative outcome data project on the effectiveness of psychological treatment for sex offenders. *Sexual Abuse: Journal of Research and Treatment, 14,* 169–194.

Hanson, R. K., & Harris, A. J. R. (2001). A structured approach to evaluating change among sexual offenders. *Sexual Abuse: Journal of Research and Treatment, 13,* 105–122.

Hanson, R. K., & Harris, A. J. R. (2002). *Scoring guide for Stable-2000.* Unpublished manuscript. Ottawa: Department of the Solicitor General of Canada.

Hanson, R. K., & Harris, A. J. R. (2004). *Stable-2000/Acute-2000: Scoring manuals for the Dynamic Supervision Project.* Corrections Research, Public Safety Canada.

Hanson, R. K., & Morton-Bourgon, K. E. (2004). *Predictors of sexual recidivism: An updated meta-analysis.* Corrections User Report No. 2004-02. Public Safety and Emergency Preparedness Canada.

Hanson, R. K., & Morton-Bourgon, K. E. (2005). The characteristics of persistent sexual offenders: A meta-analysis of recidivism studies. *Journal of Consulting and Clinical Psychology, 73,* 1154–1163.

Hanson, R. K., & Thornton, D. (2000). Improving risk assessments for sex offenders: A comparison of three actuarial scales. *Law and Human Behavior, 24,* 119–136.

Hare, R. D. (1985). A checklist for the assessment in criminal populations. In M. H. Ben-Aron, S. J. Hucker, & C. D. Webster (Eds.), *Clinical criminology: The assessment and treatment of criminal behaviour.* Toronto: M and M Graphics.

Hare, R. D. (1991). *Manual for the Hare Psychopathy Checklist – revised.* Toronto, Ontario: Multi-Health Systems.

Hare, R. D. (1998a). *Without conscience: the disturbing world of the psychopaths among us.* New York: Guilford.

Hare, R. (1998b). The role of psychopathy in assessing risk for violence: Conceptual and methodological issues. *Legal and Criminological Psychology, 3,* 121–137.

Hare, R. D. (2003a). Psychopathy and antisocial personality disorder: A case of diagnostic confusion. *Psychiatric Times, 13,* 1–9.

Hare, R. D. (2003b). *The Psychopathy Checklist – revised* (2nd ed.). Toronto, Ontario: Multi-Health Systems.

Hare, R. D., Clark, D., Grann, M., & Thornton, D. (2000). Psychopathy and the predictive validity of the PCL-R: An international perspective. *Behavioral Sciences and the Law, 18,* 623–645.

Harris, A. J. R., & Hanson, R. K. (2004). *Sex offender recidivism: A simple question.* Corrections User Report 2004–03. Ottawa: Public Safety Canada.

Harris, G. T., Rice, M. E., & Cormier, C. A. (2002). Prospective replication of the *Violence Risk Appraisal Guide* in predicting violent recidivism among forensic patients. *Law and Human Behaviour, 26,* 377–394.

Harris, G. T., Rice, M. E., & Quinsey, V. L. (1993). Violent recidivism of mentally disordered offenders: The development of a statistical prediction instrument. *Criminal Justice and Behavior, 20,* 315–335.

Harris, G. T., Rice, M. E., Quinsey, V. L., Lalumiere, M. L., Boer, D., & Lang, C. (2002). *A multi-site comparison of actuarial risk instruments for sex offenders.* Submitted for publication.

Hart, S. D., Cox, D., & Hare, R. D. (1995). *The Hare Psychopathy Checklist: Screening Version* (PCL:SV). Toronto: Multi-Health Systems.

Hart, S. D., Kropp, P. R., Laws, D. R., Klaver, J., Logan, C., & Watt, K. A. (2003). *The Risk for Sexual Violence Protocol (RSVP): Structured Professional Guidelines for Assessing Risk of Sexual Violence.* Burnaby: Mental Health, Law and Policy Institute, Simon Fraser University.

Hart, S. D., Webster, C. D., & Menzies, R. J. (1993). A note on portraying the accuracy of violence predictions. *Law and Human Behavior, 17,* 695–700.

Haward, L. R. C. (1981). *Forensic psychology.* London: Batsford Academic and Educational.

Haynes, R. B. (1985). The reliability of psychiatric diagnosis. In C. D. Webster, M. H. Ben-Aron, & S. J. Hucker (Eds.), *Dangerousness: Probability and prediction, psychiatry and public policy* (pp. 53–64). New York: Cambridge University Press.

Heilbrun, K. (1997). Prediction versus management models relevant to risk assessment: The importance of legal decision-making context. *Law and Human Behavior, 21,* 347–359.

Heilbrun, K., O'Neill, M. L., Stevens, T. N., Strohman, L. K., Bowman, Q., & Lo, Y-W. (2004). Assessing narrative approaches to communicating violence risk: A national survey of psychologists. *Behaviour Sciences and the Law, 22,* 187–196.

Heilbrun, K., Philipson, J., Berman, L., & Warren, J. (1999). Risk communication: Clinicians' reported approaches and perceived values. *Journal of the American Academy of Psychiatry and the Law, 27,* 397–406.

Hellman, D., & Blackman, J. (1966). Enuresis, firesetting, and cruelty to animals: A triad predictive of adult crime. *American Journal of Psychiatry, 122,* 1431–1436.

Hillard, R., & Zitek, B. (2004). *Emergency psychiatry.* New York: McGraw-Hill.

Hilton, N. Z., & Harris, G. T. (2004). Predicting wife assault: A critical review and implications for policy and practice. *Trauma, Violence, & Abuse, 6,* 3–23.

Hilton, N. Z., Harris, G. T., & Rice, M. E. (2006). Sixty-six years of research on clinical versus actuarial prediction of violence. *The Counseling Psychologist, 34,* 400–409.

Hilton, N. Z., Harris, G. T., Rice, M. E., Lang, C., & Cormier, C. A. (2004). A brief actuarial assessment for the prediction of wife assault recidivism: The ODARA. *Psychological Assessment, 16,* 267–275.

Hilton, N. Z., & Simmons, J. L. (2001). The influence of actuarial risk assessment in clinical judgments and tribunal decisions about mentally disordered offenders in maximum security. *Law and Human Behavior, 25,* 393–408.

Hodgins, S. (2003, February). Comments on the conceptual structure of the Hare PCL-R to C. D. Webster.

Hodgins, S., & Côté, G. (1995). Major mental disorder among penitentiary inmates. In L. Stewart, L. Stermac, & C. D. Webster (Eds.), *Clinical criminology: Toward effective correctional treatment.* Ottawa: Ministry of the Solicitor General and Correctional Service of Canada.

Hodgins, S., & Janson, C-G. (2002). *Criminality and violence among the mentally disordered: The Stockholm Metropolitan Project.* Cambridge, UK: Cambridge University Press.

Hodgins, S., & Müller-Isberner, (2004). Preventing crime by people with schizophrenia: the role of psychiatric services. *British Journal of Psychiatry, 185,* 245–250.

Hodgins, S., Tengström, A., Östermann, R., Eaves, D., Harts, S., Koonstrand, R., Levander, S., Müller-Isberner, R., Tiihonen, J., Webster, C. D., Eronen, M., Freese, R., Jöckel, D., Kreuzer, A., Levin, A., Maas, S., Repo, E., Ross, D., Tuninger, E., Kotilainen, I., Väänanen, K., Varianen, H., & Vokkolinen, A. (in press). An international comparison of community treatment programs for mentally ill persons who have committed criminal offences. *Criminal Justice and Behavior.*

Hollander, E., & Stein, D. J. (Eds.). (2006). *Clinical manual of impulse-control disorders.* Arlington, VA: American Psychiatric Publishing.

Hull, C. L. (1951). *Essentials of behavior.* New Haven: Yale University Press.

Husted, J. R. (1999). Insight in severe mental illness: Implications for treatment decisions. *Journal of the American Academy of Psychiatry and the Law, 27,* 33–49.

Hrynkiw–Augimeri, L. K. (2005). Aggressive and antisocial young children: Risk assessment and management utilizing the Early Assessment Risk List for boys (EARL-20B). Unpublished Ph.D. dissertation, Ontario Institute for Studies in Education, University of Toronto Ontario, Canada.

Jackson, J. (1997). A conceptual model for the study of violence. In C. D. Webster & M. A. Jackson (Eds.), *Impulsivity: Theory, assessment and treatment* (pp. 223–247). New York: Guilford.

Jones, M. (1952). *Social Psychiatry: A Study of Therapeutic Communities.* London: Tavistock.

Jones, M. B., & Jones, D. R. (2000). The contagious nature of antisocial behavior. *Criminology, 38,* 25–46.

Junger, S. (1997). *The perfect storm: A true story of men against the sea.* New York: HarperCollins.

Kazdin, A. E. (1997). A model for developing effective treatments: Progression and interplay of theory, research and practice. *Journal of Clinical Child Psychology, 26,* 114–129.

Keehn, J. D., & Webster, C. D. (1969). Behaviour therapy and behaviour modification. *Canadian Psychologist, 10,* 68–73.

Kendell, R., & Jablensky, A. (2003). Distinguishing between the validity and utility of psychiatric diagnoses. *American Journal of Psychiatry, 160,* 4–12.

Kennedy, H. (2001). Risk assessment is inseparable from risk management: Comment on Szmuckler. *Psychiatric Bulletin, 25,* 208–211.

Kessler, R. C., Coccaro, E. F., Fava, M., Jaeger, S., Jin, R., & Watters, E. (2006). The prevalence and correlates of DSM-IV Intermittent Explosive Disorder in the National Comorbidity Survey Replication. *Archives of General Psychiatry, 63,* 669–678.

Klinterberg, B. A., Anderson, T., Magnusson, D., & Stattin, H. (1993). Hyperactive behavior in childhood as related to subsequent alcohol problems and violent offending: A longitudinal study of male subjects. *Personality and Individual Differences, 15,* 381–388.

Konečni, V., Mulcahy, E., & Ebbesen, E. (1980). Prison or mental hospital: Factors affecting the processing of persons suspected of being "mentally disordered sex offenders". In P. Lipsitt & B. Sales (Eds.), *New directions in psychological research* (pp. 87–124). New York: Van Nostrand Rheinhold.

Kraemer, H. C., Stice, E., Kazdin, A., Offord, D., & Kupfer, D. (2001). How do risk factors work together? Mediators, moderators, and independent, overlapping, and proxy risk factors. *American Journal of Psychiatry, 158,* 848–856.

Kroner, D. G., & Mills, J. F. (2001). The accuracy of five risk appraisal instruments in predicting institutional misconduct and new convictions. *Criminal Justice and Behavior, 28,* 471–489.

Kropp, P. R. (2004). Some questions about spousal violence risk assessment. *Violence Against Women, 10,* 676–697.

Kropp, P. R., & Hart, S. D. (2000). The spousal assault risk assessment (SARA) guide: Reliability and validity in adult male offenders. *Law and Human Behavior, 24,* 101–118.

Kropp, P. R., Hart, S. D., & Belfrage, H. (2005). *The Brief Spousal Assault Form for the Evaluation of Risk (B-SAFER).* Vancouver: Proactive-Resolutions, Inc.

Kropp, P. R., Hart, S. D., & Lyon, D. R. (2002). Risk assessment of stalkers: Some problems and possible solutions. *Criminal Justice and Behavior, 29,* 590–616.

Kropp, P. R., Hart, S. D., Webster, C. D., & Eaves, D. (1995). *Manual for the Spousal Assault Risk Assessment Guide* (2nd ed.). Vancouver: British Columbia Institute on Family Violence.

Kropp, P. R., Hart, S. D., Webster, C. D., & Eaves, D. (1999). *Spousal Assault Risk Assessment: User's guide.* Toronto: Multi-Health Systems.

Kuhn, T. (1962). *The structure of scientific revolutions.* Chicago: Chicago University Press.

Laing, R. D. (1969). *The divided self.* New York: Pantheon.

Lam, K., & Lancel, M. (2006, January). Patients viewing themselves through the START. Paper presented at Symposium on START, Assen, The Netherlands.

Lamb, H. R., & Weinberger, L. E. (2001). Adult offenders and community settings: Some case examples. In J. B. Ashford, B. D. Sales, & W. H. Reid (Eds.), *Treating adult and juvenile offenders with special needs* (pp. 465–478). Washington, D.C.: American Psychological Association.

Law, F. D., & Nutt, J. D. (2000). Drugs used in the treatment of the addiction. In M. G. Gelder, J. J. López-Ibor, Jr., & N. C. Andreasen (Eds.), *New Oxford textbook of psychiatry* (Vol. 2, pp. 1337–1342). Oxford, UK: Oxford University Press.

Levene, K. S., Augimeri, L. K., Pepler, D. J., Walsh, M. M., Webster, C. D., & Koegl, C. J. (2001). *Early Assessment Risk List for Girls,* Version 1, Consultation Edition. Toronto: Child Development Institute.

Lewis, A. H. O., & Webster, C. D. (2004). General instruments for risk assessment. *Current Opinion in Psychiatry, 17,* 401–405.

Lewis, G., & Appleby, L. (1988). Personality disorder: The patients psychiatrists dislike. *British Journal of Psychiatry, 153,* 44–49.

Lidz, C. W., Mulvey, E. P., & Gardner, W. (1993). The accuracy of predictions of violence to others. *Journal of the American Medical Association, 269,* 1007–1111.

Linehan, M. (1993). *Cognitive-behavioral treatment of borderline personality disorder.* New York: Guilford.

Link, B., Monahan, J., Stueve, A., & Cullen, F. (1999). Real in their consequences: A sociological approach to understanding the association between psychotic symptoms and violence. *American Sociological Review, 64,* 316–332.

Lipton, D. S., Thornton, D., McGuire, J., Porporino, F. J., & Hollin, C. (2000). Program accreditation and correctional treatment. *Substance Use and Misuse, 35,* 1705–1734.

Litman, L. C. (2003). Letter to the Editor: Lengthy periods of incarceration as personal treatment goal. *Canadian Journal of Psychiatry, 48,* 710–711.

Litwack, T. R. (1993). On the ethics of dangerousness assessments. *Law and Human Behavior, 17,* 479–482.

Litwack, T. R. (2001). Actuarial versus clinical assessments of dangerousness. *Psychology, Public Policy, and Law, 7,* 409–443.

Loza, W., Dhaliwal, G., Kroner, D. G., and Loza-Fanous, A. (2000). Reliability, construct, and concurrent validities of the Self-Appraisal Questionnaire: A tool for assessing violent and nonviolent recidivism. *Criminal Justice and Behavior, 27,* 356–374.

Macfarlane, D., & Butteril, D. (1999, Fall). From principles to practice: The management of post-merger integration. *Hospital Quarterly,* 35–39.

Marks-Tarlow, T. (1993). A new look at impulsivity: Hidden order beneath apparent chaos. In W. G. McCown, J. L. Johnson, & M. B. Shure (Eds.), *The impulsive client: Theory, research and treatment*. Washington, DC: American Psychological Association.

Marshall, W. L., & T. Kennedy (2003). Sexual sadism in sexual offenders: An elusive diagnosis. *Aggression and Violent Behavior, 8,* 1–22.

Maslow, A. H. (1954). *Motivation and Personality*. New York: Harper.

Maslow, A. (1955). Deficiency motivation and growth motivation. In M. R. Jones (Ed.), *Nebraska Symposium on Motivation* (Vol. 3, pp. 42–87). Lincoln, Ne: University of Nebraska Press.

Maslow, A. (1982). *Toward a Theory of Being*. New York: Van Nostrand Reinhold.

May, R. (1969). *Love and will*. New York: Delta.

McAdams, D. P., & Pals, J. L. (2006). A new big five: Fundamental principles for an integrative science of personality. *American Psychologist, 61,* 204–217.

McFarlane, J., Soeken, K., Campbell, J. C., Parker, B., Reel, S., & Silva, C. (1998). Severity of abuse to pregnant women and associated gun access of the perpetrator. *Public Health Nursing, 15,* 201–206.

McGrath, R. J., Cumming, G., & Livingston, J. A. (2005, November). *Predictive validity of the Sex Offender Treatment Needs and Progress Scale (TPS)*. Presentation at the 24th Annual Research and Treatment Conference of the Association for the Treatment of Sexual Abusers, Salt Lake City.

McMain, S. F., & Courbasson, M. A. (2001). Impulse control. In K. S. Douglas, C. D. Webster, D. Eaves, S. D. Hart, & J. R. P. Ogloff (Eds.), *HCR-20 Violence Risk Management Companion Guide* (pp. 101–108). Burnaby: Mental Health Law and Policy Institute, Simon Fraser University.

McMurran, M. (2001). Offenders with personality disorders. In C. R. Hollin (Ed.), *Handbook of offender assessment and treatment* (pp. 467–479). Chichester, UK: Wiley.

McNeil, D. E., Gregory, A. L., Lam, J. N., Binder, R. L., & Sullivan, G. R. (2003). Utility of decision support tools for assessing acute risk of violence. *Journal of Consulting and Clinical Psychology, 71,* 945–953.

Meehl, P. E. (1996). *Clinical versus statistical prediction: A theoretical analysis and a review of the literature*. Northvale, NJ: Jason Aronson. (Original work published in 1954.)

Megargee, E. (1976). The prediction of dangerous behavior. *Criminal Justice and Behavior, 3,* 3–22.

Melton, G. B., Petrila, J., Poythress, N. G., & Slobogin C. (1997). *Psychological evaluations for the courts: A handbook for mental health professionals and lawyers* (2nd ed.). New York: Guilford.

Mental Health Act, Revised Statutes of Ontario, 1990, Chapter M.7 as amended.

Menzies, R. J. (1989). *Survival of the sanest: Order and disorder in a pretrial psychiatric clinic*. Toronto, Ontario: University of Toronto Press.

Menzies, R. J. (2002). Historical profiles of criminal insanity. *International Journal of Law and Psychiatry, 25,* 379–404.

Menzies, R. J., & Webster, C. D. (1995). The construction of validation of risk assessments in a six-year follow-up of forensic patients: A tridimensional analysis. *Journal of Consulting and Clinical Psychology, 63,* 766–778.

Menzies, R. J., Webster, C. D., & Sepejak, D. S. (1985a). The dimensions of dangerousness: Evaluating the accuracy of psychometric predictions of violence among forensic patients. *Law and Human Behavior, 9,* 35–56.

Menzies, R. J., Webster, C. D., & Sepejak, D. S. (1985b). Hitting the forensic sound barrier: Predictions of dangerousness in a pre-trial psychiatric clinic. In C. D. Webster, M. H. Ben-Aron, & S. J. Hucker (Eds.), *Dangerousness: Probability and prediction, psychiatry and public policy* (pp. 115–143). New York: Cambridge University Press.

Menzies, R. J., Webster, C. D., McMain, S., Staley, S., & Scaglione, R. (1994). The dimensions of dangerousness, revisited: Assessing forensic predictions about violence. *Law and Human Behavior, 18,* 1–28.

Molden, D. C., & Dweck, C. S. (2006). Finding "meaning" in psychology: A lay theories approach to self-regulation, social perception, and social development. *American Psychologist, 61,* 192–203.

Monahan, J. (1981). *Predicting violent behavior: An assessment of clinical techniques.* Beverly Hills, CA: Sage.

Monahan, J. (1993). Limiting therapist exposure to *Tarasoff* liability: Guidelines for risk containment. *American Psychologist, 48,* 242–250.

Monahan, J. (2003). Violence risk assessment. In A. Goldman (Ed.), *Handbook of psychology* (Vol. 11, pp. 527–540). New York: Wiley.

Monahan, J., Heilbrun, K., Silver, E., Nabors, E., Bone, J., & Slovic, P. (2002). Communicating violence risk: Frequency formats, vivid outcomes, and forensic settings. *International Journal of Forensic Mental Health, 1,* 121–126.

Monahan, J., & Steadman, H. J. (1994). *Violence and mental disorder: Developments in risk assessments.* Chicago: University of Chicago Press.

Monahan, J., & Steadman, H. J. (1996). Violent storms and violent people: How meteorology can inform risk communication in mental health law. *American Psychologist, 51, 9,* 931–938.

Monahan, J., Steadman, H. J., Robbins, P. C., et al. (2005). An actuarial model of violence risk assessment for persons with mental disorders. *Psychiatric Services, 56,* 810–815.

Monahan, J., Steadman, H. J., Silver, E., Appelbaum, P. S., Robbins, P. C., Mulvey, E. P., Roth, L., Grisso, T., & Banks, S. (2001). *Rethinking risk assessment: The MacArthur study of mental disorder and violence.* Oxford, UK: Oxford University Press.

Mossman, D. (2000). Commentary: Assessing the risk of violence – Are 'accurate' predictions useful? *Journal of the American Academy of Psychiatry and the Law, 28,* 272–281.

Mullen, P. E. (2000). Dangerousness, risk, and the prediction of probability. In M. G. Gelder, J. J. López-Ibor, & N. C. Andreasen (Eds.), *New Oxford textbook of psychiatry* (Vol. 2, pp. 2066–2078). Oxford, UK: Oxford University Press.

Mullen, P. E., Pathé, M., & Purcell, R. (2000). *Stalkers and their victims.* Cambridge, UK: Cambridge University Press.

Muller-Isberner, R., Webster, C. D., & Gretenkord, L. (submitted). Measuring progress in hospital order treatment: Relationships between levels of security and C and R scores of the HCR-20. Submitted for publication.

National Institute for Clinical Excellence (2005). *Clinical Guideline 25. Violence: The short-term management of disturbed/violent behaviour in in-patient psychiatric settings and emergency departments.* London: National Institute for Clinical Excellence (www.nice.org.uk/CG025NICEguideline) (see also *Clinical Guideline 25, Quick Reference Guide*).

Nicholls, T. L., Brink, J., Desmarais, S. L., Webster, C. D., & Martin, M-L. (2006). *The short-term assessment of risk and treatability (START): A prospective validation study in a forensic psychiatric sample. Assessment., 13,* 313–327.

Nicholls, T. L., Roesch, R., Olley, M. C., Ogloff, J. R. P., & Hemphill, J. F. (2005). *Jail Screening Assessment Tool (JSAT): Guidelines for mental health screening in jails.* Burnaby, BC: Mental Health, Law, and Policy Institute, Simon Fraser University.

Nuffield, J. (1982). *Parole decision-making in Canada: Research towards decision guidelines.* Ottawa, Ontario: Ministry of Supply and Services of Canada.

Ogloff, J., & Dafern, M. (2004). *Dynamic Appraisal of Situational Aggression: Inpatient Version (DASA:IV).* Victoria, Australia: Forensicare/Monarch University.

Olver, M. E. (2003). *The development and validation of the Violence Risk Scale: Sexual Offender Version (VRS:SO) and its relationship to psychopathy and treatment attrition.* Unpublished doctoral dissertation. Psychology Department, University of Saskatchewan, Saskatoon, Saskatchewan.

Overall, J. E., & Gorham, D. R. (1962). The Brief Psychiatric Rating Scale. *Psychological Reports, 10,* 799–812.

Padgett, R., Webster, C. D., & Robb, M. K. (2005). Unavailable essential archival data: Major limitations in the conduct of clinical practice and research in violence risk assessment. *Canadian Journal of Psychiatry, 50,* 937–940.

Pagani, L., & Pinard, G-F. (2001). Clinical assessment of dangerousness: An overview of the literature. In L. Pagani & G-F. Pinard (Eds.), *Clinical assessment of dangerousness* (pp. 1–22). Cambridge, UK: Cambridge University Press.

Pence, E., & Lizdas, K. (1998). *The Duluth safety and accountability audit: A guide to assessing institutional responses to domestic violence.* Minneapolis, MN: MPDI.

Penrose, L. S. (1939). Mental disease and crime: Outline of a comparative study of European statistics. *British Journal of Medical Psychology, 18,* 1–15.

Pervin, L. A., & John, O. P. (Eds.). (1999). *Handbook of personality* (2nd ed.). New York: Guilford.

Petrunic, M., & Weisman, R. (2005). Constructing Joseph Fredericks: Competing narratives of a child sex murderer. *International Journal of Law and Psychiatry, 28,* 75–96.

Pfäfflin, F. (1979). The Contempt of psychiatric experts for sexual convicts: Evaluation of 963 files from sexual offence cases in the state of Hamburg, Germany. *International Journal of Law and Psychiatry, 2,* 485–497.

Pfohl, S. J. (1978). *Predicting dangerousness: The social construction of psychiatric reality.* Lexington, MA: Lexington Books.

Quinsey, V. L. (1980). The base rate problem and the prediction of dangerousness: A reappraisal. *Journal of Psychiatry and Law, 8,* 329–340.

Quinsey, V. L., Coleman, G., Jones, B., & Altrows, I. (1997). Proximal antecedents of eloping and reoffending among mentally disordered offenders. *Journal of Interpersonal Violence, 12,* 794–813.

Quinsey, V. L., Harris, G. T., Rice, M. E., & Cormier, C. (1998). *Violent offenders: Appraising and managing risk.* Washington, DC: American Psychological Association.

Quinsey, V. L., Harris, G. T., Rice, M. E., & Cormier, C. (2006). *Violent offenders: Appraising and managing risk* (2nd ed.). Washington, DC: American Psychological Association.

Resnick, P. (1970). Murder of the newborn: A psychiatric review of filicide. *American Journal of Psychiatry, 126,* 58–63.

Rhodes, R. (1999). *Why they kill: The discoveries of a maverick criminologist.* New York: Vintage.

Rice, M. E. (1985). Violence in the maximum security hospital. In M. H. Ben-Aron, S. J. Hucker, & C. D. Webster (Eds.), *Clinical criminology: The assessment and treatment of criminal behaviour* (pp. 57–79). Toronto: M. & M. Graphics.

Rice, M. E., Harris, G. T., & Cormier, C. (1992). Evaluation of a maximum security therapeutic community for psychopaths and other mentally disordered offenders. *Law and Human Behavior, 16,* 399–412.

Rice, M. E., Harris, G. T., & deBecker, G. (1997). *The gift of fear: Survival signals that protect us from violence.* New York: Dell.

Riggs, D. S., Caulfield, M. B., & Street, A. E. (2000). Risk for domestic violence: Factors associated with perpetration and victimization. *Journal of Clinical Psychology, 56,* 1289–1316.

Risk Management Authority. (2005). Risk Assessment Tools Evaluation Directory. Paisley: Scotland [www.rmascotland.gov.uk].

Robertson, R. G., Yaren, S., & Globerman, D. (2004). Assessing risk for violence: A retrospective analysis from a forensic service. *American Journal of Forensic Psychiatry, 25,* 5–12.

Robins, L. N. (1991). Comments on "Supervision in the deinstitutionalized community." Paper given by C. D. Webster and R. J. Menzies at an Advanced Study Institute on Crime and Mental Disorder sponsored by the scientific affairs division of NATO, Barga, Italy.

Rodale, J. I. (1968). *Natural health, sugar and the criminal mind.* New York: Pyramid Books.

Roehl, J., & Guertin, K. (1998). *Current use of dangerousness assessments in sentencing domestic offenders.* Pacific Grove, CA: Justice Research Center.

Rogers, C. R. (1959). A theory of therapy, personality, and interpersonal relationships. In S. Koch (Ed.), *Psychology: A study of a science* (pp. 184–256). New York: McGraw-Hill.

Rogers, R., & Shuman, D. W. (2005). *Fundamentals of forensic practice: Mental health and criminal law.* New York: Springer.

Ross, D. J., Hart, S. D., & Webster, C. D. (1998). *Aggression in psychiatric patients: Using the HCR-20 to assess risk for violence in hospital and in the community.* Printed and distributed by Riverview Hospital, Medicine and Research, British Columbia, Canada.

Ryan, L. (1997). Integrated support: A case approach to the management of impulsive people. In C. D. Webster & M. A. Jackson (Eds.), *Impulsivity: Theory, assessment and treatment* (pp. 424–433). New York: Guilford.

Sales, B. D., & Shuman, D. W. (2005). *Experts in court: Reconciling law, science, and professional knowledge.* Washington, DC: American Psychological Association.

Sammons, M. T., & Schmidt, N. B. (Eds.). (2001). *Combined treatments for mental disorders: A guide to psychological and pharmacological interventions.* Washington, DC: American Psychological Association.

Sartorius, N., & Schulze, H. (2005). *Reducing the stigma of mental illness A report from a global programme of the world psychiatric association.* Cambridge, UK: Cambridge University Press.

Schneider, R. D. (2000). Statistical survey of provincial and territorial review boards (Part XX.1 of the *Criminal Code* of Canada), Report prepared for the Department of Justice, Canada.

Schneider, R. D., Glancy, G. D., Bradford, J. Mc.D., & Seibenmorgen, E. (2000). Canadian landmark case, *Winko v. British Columbia:* Revisiting the conundrum of the mentally disordered offender. *Journal of the American Academy of Psychiatry and Law, 28,* 206–212.

Schumacher, J. A., Feldbau-Kohn, S., Slep, A. M. S., & Heyman, R. E. (2001). Risk factors for male-to-female partner physical abuse. *Aggression and Violent Behavior, 6,* 281–352.

Scott, P. D. (1997). Assessing dangerousness in criminals. *British Journal of Psychiatry, 131,* 127–142.

Seifert, D., Jahn, K., Bolten, S., & Wirtz, M. (2002). Prediction of dangerousness in mentally disordered offenders in Germany. *International Journal of Law and Psychiatry, 25,* 51–66.

Seligman, M. E. P., Steen, T. A., Park, N., & Peterson, C. (2005). Positive psychology progress: Empirical validation of interventions. *American Psychologist, 60,* 410–421.

Sepejak, D. S., Menzies, R. J., Webster, C. D., & Jensen, F. A. S. (1983). Clinical predictions of dangerousness: Two-year follow-up of 408 pre-trial forensic cases. *Bulletin of the American Academy of Psychiatry and the Law, 11,* 171–181.

Seto, M. C., & Barbaree, H. E. (1998). Psychopathy, treatment behavior, and sex offender recidivism. *Journal of Interpersonal Violence, 14,* 1235–1248.

Seto, M. C., Lalumière, M. L., Harris, G. T., Barbaree, H. E., Hilton, N. Z., Rice, M. E., & Schneider, R. D. (2001). *Demands for forensic services in the province of Ontario.* Toronto: Centre for Addiction and Mental Health.

Sjöstedt, G., & Långström, N. (2002). Assessment of risk for criminal recidivism among rapists: A comparison of four different measures. *Psychology, Crime and the Law, 8,* 25–40.

Skeem, J. L., Markos, P., Tiemann, J., & Manchak, S. (2006). Project HOPE for homeless individuals with co-occurring mental and substance abuse disorders: Reducing symptoms, victimization, and violence. *International Journal of Forensic Mental Health, 5,* 1–13.

Skeem, J. L., & Mulvey, E. P. (2001). Psychopathy and community violence among civil psychiatric patients: Results from the MacArthur violence risk assessment study. *Journal of Consulting and Clinical Psychology, 69,* 358–374.

Skinner, B. F. (1953). *The science of human behavior.* New York: Macmillan

Slovic, P., Monahan, J., & MacGregor, D. (2000). Violence risk assessment and risk communication: The effects of using actual cases, providing instruction, and employing probability versus frequency formats. *Law and Human Behavior, 24,* 271–296.

Snow's Annotated Criminal Code. (2002). D. Rose (Ed.). Toronto: Thompson Carswell.

Sonkin, D. G. (1997). *The perpetrator assessment handbook.* Sausalito, CA: Volcano Press.

Spaulding, W. D., Sullivan, M. E., & Poland, J. S. (2003). *Treatment and rehabilitation of severe mental illness.* New York: Guilford.

Spinelli, M. G. (Ed.). (2003). *Infanticide: Psychosocial and legal perspectives on mothers who kill.* Washington, DC: American Psychiatric Publishing.

Starr, R. (2000). *Not Guilty by reason of insanity: One man's recovery.* Chicago: University of Chicago Press.

Starr, R. (2002). A successful reintegration into the community: One NGRI acquittee's story. *Federal Probation, 66,* 59–63.

Steadman, H. J., & Cocozza, J. J. (1974). *Careers of the criminally insane: Excessive social control of deviance.* Lexington, MA: Lexington Books.

Stout, M. (2005). *The sociopath next door.* New York: Broadway Books.

Straus, M. A. (1991). *Factors predicting serious violence towards wives.* Paper presented at the International Conference for Research on Family Violence, University of New Hampshire, Durham.

Sugarman, D. B., & Hotaling, G. T. (1991). Dating violence: A review of contextual and risk factors. In B. Levy (Ed.), *Dating violence: Young women in danger* (pp. 100–118). Seattle: The Seal Press.

Sutton, D. L. (2004). Relapse signatures and might: Implications for CPNs. *Journal of Psychiatric and Mental Health Nursing, 11,* 569–574.

Swanson, J. W. (1994). Mental disorder, substance abuse, and community violence: An epidemiology approach. In J. Monahan & H. J. Steadman (Eds.), *Violence and mental disorder developments in risk assessment* (pp. 99–136). Chicago: University of Chicago Press.

Swanson, J., Holzer, C., Ganju, V., & Jono, R. (1990). Violence and psychiatric disorder in the community: Evidence from the epidemiological catchment area surveys. *Hospital and Community Psychiatry, 41,* 761–770.

Swanson, J. W., Schwartz, M. S., Borum, R., Hiday, V. A., Wagner, H. R., & Burns, B. J. (2000). Involuntary out-patient commitment and reduction of violent behaviour in persons with severe mental illness. *British Journal of Psychiatry, 176,* 324–331.

Taylor, G. (1998). Preparing reports for parole decisions: Making the best use of our information – and time. *Forum on Corrections Research, 10,* 30–34.

Taylor, R. (1999). Predicting reconvictions for sexual and violent offences using the Revised Offender Group Reconviction Scale. Home Office Research Findings No. 104. London: Home Office.

Tengström, A., Hodgins, S., Müller-Isberner, R., Jöckel, D., Freese, R., Özokyay, K., & Sommer, J. (2006). Predicting violent and antisocial behavior in hospital using the HCR-20: The effect of diagnosis on predictive accuracy. *International Journal of Forensic Mental Health, 5,* 39–53.

Tetlock, P. (2006). *Expert Political Judgment.* Princeton: Princeton University Press.

Thornberry, T. P., & Jacoby, J. E. (1979). *The criminally insane: A community follow-up of mentally ill offenders.* Chicago: University of Chicago Press.

Thornton, D. (2002). Constructing and testing a framework for Dynamic Risk Assessment. *Sexual Abuse: Journal of Research and Treatment, 14,* 139–153.

Walsh, E., Buchanan, A., & Fahy, T. (2002). Violence and schizophrenia: Examining the evidence. *British Journal of Psychiatry, 180,* 490–495.

Walsh, E., Gilvarry, C., Samele, C., Harvey, K., Manley, C., Tyrer, P., Creed, F., Murray, R., & Fahy, T. (2001). Reducing violence in severe mental illness: Randomised controlled trial of intensive case management compared with standard care. *British Journal of Psychiatry, 323,* 1–5.

Walters, G. D. (1991). Predicting the disciplinary adjustment of maximum security prison inmates using the Lifestyle Criminality Screening Form. *International Journal of Offender Therapy and Comparative Criminology, 35,* 63–71.

Webster, C. D. (1983–84, Winter). Comment on Barbara Harsch, Power struggles between child care worker and youth. *Child Care Quarterly, 12,* 269–270.

Webster, C. D. (1986). Compulsory treatment of narcotic addiction. *International Journal of Law and Psychiatry, 8,* 133–159.

Webster, C. D., Dickens, B. M., & Addario, S. M. (1985). *Constructing dangerousness: Scientific, legal and policy implications.* Toronto: University of Toronto Centre for Criminology.

Webster, C. D., Douglas, K. S., Belfrage, H., & Link, B. G. (2000). Capturing change: An approach to managing violence and improving mental health. In S. Hodgins (Ed.), *Violence among the mentally ill: Effective treatment and management strategies* (pp. 119–144). Dordrecht, The Netherlands: Kluwer.

Webster, C. D., Douglas, K. S., Eaves, D., & Hart, S. D. (1997). *The HCR-20: Assessing the risk for violence.* Version 2. Burnaby: Mental Health, Law, and Policy Institute, Simon Fraser University, Psychiatric Services Commission of British Columbia.

Webster, C. D., Eaves, D., Douglas, K. S., & Wintrup, A. (1995). *The HCR-20 Scheme: The Assessment of Dangerousness and Risk – Version 1.* Burnaby: Mental Health, Law and Policy Institute, Simon Fraser University.

Webster, C. D., Harris, G., Rice, M., Cormier, C., & Quinsey, V. (1994). *The violence prediction scheme: Assessing dangerousness in high risk men.* Toronto, Ontario: Centre of Criminology, University of Toronto.

Webster, C. D., & Hucker, S. J. (2003). *Release decision making: Assessing violence risk in mental health, forensic, and correctional settings.* Hamilton, Ontario: Forensic Service, St. Joseph's Healthcare Hamilton, Centre for Mountain Health Services.

Webster, C. D., Hucker, S. J., & Bloom, H. (2002). Transcending the actuarial versus clinical polemic in assessing risk for violence. *Criminal Justice and Behavior, 29,* 659–665.

Webster, C. D., Martin, M-L., Brink, J., Nicholls, T. L., & Middleton, C. (2004). *Short-Term Assessment of Risk and Treatability (START): An Evaluation and Planning Guide.* St. Joseph's Healthcare, Hamilton and Forensic Psychiatric Services Commission, British Columbia.

Webster, C. D., Menzies, R. J., & Jackson, M. A. (1982). *Clinical assessment before trial: Legal issues and mental disorder.* Toronto, Ontario: Butterworths.

Webster, C. D., Müller-Isberner, R., & Fransson, G. (2002). Violence risk assessment: Using structured clinical guides professionally. *International Journal of Forensic Mental Health, 1,* 185–193.

Webster, C. D., Nicholls, T. N., Martin, M-L., Desmarais, S. L., & Brink, J. (2006). Short-term Assessment of Risk and Treatability (START): The case for a new violence structured professional judgment scheme. *Behavioral Sciences and the Law, 24,* 1420.

Weisz, A. N., Tolman, R. M., & Saunders, D. G. (2000). Assessing the risk of severe domestic violence: The importance of survivors' predictions. *Journal of Interpersonal Violence, 15,* 75–90.

Whittemore, K. E., & Kropp, P. R. (2002). Spousal assault risk assessment: A guide for clinicians. *Journal of Forensic Psychology Practice, 2,* 53–64.

Williams, K., & Houghton, A. B. (2004). Assessing the risk of domestic violence reoffending: A validation study. *Law and Human Behavior, 24,* 437–455.

Winerman, L. (2005). Intuition. *Monitor on Psychology,* March, 51–53.

Wishnie, H. (1977). *The impulsive personality: Understanding people with destructive character disorders.* New York: Plenum.

Wishnie, H., & Nevis-Olesen, J. (1977). *Working with the impulsive person.* New York: Plenum.

Wong, S., Olver, M., Wilde, S., Nicholaichuk, T. P., & Gordon, A. (2000, July). *Violence Risk Scale (VRS) and Violence Risk Scale-sex offenders version (VRS-SO).* Presented at the 61st Annual Convention of the Canadian Psychological Association, Ottawa, Canada.

Woods, P. (2001). Risk assessment and management. In C. Dale, T. Thompson, & P. Woods (Eds.), *Forensic mental health: Issues in practice* (pp. 85–97). London: Harcourt.

World Health Organization. International Classification of Mental and Behavioural Disorders: Clinical Descriptions and Diagnostic Guidelines (ICD-10, 1992). Geneva, Switzerland: World Health Organization.

Wulach, J. S. (1988). The criminal personality as a DSM-III-R antisocial, narcissistic, borderline, and histrionic personality disorder. *International Journal of Offender Therapy and Comparative Criminology, 32,* 185–199.

Zamble, E., & Quinsey, V. L. (1997). *The criminal recidivism process.* New York: Cambridge University Press.

Ziskin, J. (1986). The future of clinical assessment. In B. S. Plake & J. C. Witt (Eds.), *The future of testing* (pp. 185–201). Hillsdale, NJ: Erlbaum.

INDEX

Note: page numbers in *italics* refer to information contained within tables.